KV-243-105

*MUSIC AND THE BOOK TRADE*

# PUBLISHING PATHWAYS
PREVIOUS TITLES IN THE SERIES

90 0898725 0

Charles Seale-Hayne Library
## University of Plymouth
### (01752) 588 588
LibraryandITenquiries@plymouth.ac.uk

WITHDRAWN
FROM
UNIVERSITY OF PLYMOUTH
LIBRARY SERVICES

# MUSIC AND THE BOOK TRADE
*from the Sixteenth to the Twentieth Century*

*Edited by*
*Robin Myers, Michael Harris*
*and Giles Mandelbrote*

OAK KNOLL PRESS
&
THE BRITISH LIBRARY
2008

UNIVERSITY OF PLYMOUTH

9008987250

© 2008 The Contributors

First published 2008 by
Oak Knoll Press
310 Delaware Street
New Castle
DE 19720
and
The British Library
96 Euston Road
London NW1 2DB

Cataloguing in Publication Data
A CIP Record for this book is available
from both The British Library and
the Library of Congress

ISBN 978-1-58456-245-0 (Oak Knoll)
ISBN 978 0 7123 5030 3 (BL)

Typeset by Ella Whitehead
Jacket design by Lania Herman
Printed in the United States of America by Sheridan Books, Ann Arbor

# Contents

# Introduction

BIBLIOGRAPHERS AND BOOK HISTORIANS have tended to separate out the trade in printed music from the book trade in general, treating it as a self-contained area of research, partly at least because the means of production (reproducing notation rather than letter forms) and of distribution (from an early stage associated with the specialist sellers of musical instruments and equipment) were themselves distinct. On the other hand, musicologists have, until recently, paid less attention to the commercial aspects of printed music, concentrating more on the technicalities of composition and performance. This volume aims to map some of the common ground in the broad area of book history between music and other forms of print, exploring the ways in which the organization of production and the process of publication have developed over time. All the contributors are musicologists who have devoted particular attention to books and manuscripts, while the audience they addressed at the 2007 conference on book trade history came from both sides of the book history/music divide.

The original papers published in this volume, loosely linked thematically, form a chronological sequence spanning more than three and a half centuries of the music trade in London, Spain and Vienna. They show the emergence of an organized publishing and distribution network, while the traditional methods of production, mainly from engraved plates, continued to be used. During the late sixteenth and early seventeenth century, music production and publication was in many places — and particularly at the level of the court and the Catholic church — a pan-European activity, though informed by national traditions. In Iberia, as Iain Fenlon explains, there was substantial foreign influence and many immigrants were employed as printers and in selling their wares on the road. In post-Reformation England, on the other hand, the music trade was more indigenous, and music itself was sometimes closely aligned with national politics and religious controversy. By the end of the seventeenth century, the production and sale of secular music was more firmly established, as exemplified by the activities of the Playfords and the Purcells. An increasingly sophisticated commercial organization, which can be seen in the Walsh-Handel association in the mid-eighteenth century, was reflected in the networks of publication and distribution which extended across Europe. The Artaria ledgers cast much light on the mechanics of music printing, warehousing and selling at the end of the eighteenth century and show clearly how the internal business systems adopted by the major Viennese music publishers were ushering in a new phase in the output of printed music.

In 'Music Printing and the Book Trade in Late-Sixteenth and Early Seventeenth-Century Iberia', Iain Fenlon concludes that the vast majority of liturgical books, largely polyphonic choirbooks, was imported from Italy, France and the Low Countries and that native production, in so far as it existed, was on a small scale and for a local market. Music produced for export went mainly not to Europe, but to the colonies of Latin America. Even choirbooks printed in Spain were often works by foreign composers, particularly Italians, and many of the printers and some of the booksellers were immigrants working in Spain. This, he argues, owed more to lack of technical expertise, under-investment and a general economic recession than (as used to be thought) to ecclesiastical repression.

Jeremy Smith looks at the relationship between William Byrd, Catholic composer, royal patentee and *persona grata* in court circles, and Thomas East, stationer and music publisher. Byrd needed the use of a neutral press as a safe haven for the printing and publishing of his controversial Catholic music, while East needed the protection of Byrd's royal privilege to edge his way into the right to print a version of the Protestant best-selling *Whole Booke of Psalmes*. Smith argues his case in the context of the politico-religious background, building on his recent book on *Thomas East and music publishing in Renaissance England* (Oxford, 2003).

From the time of the Restoration the story of music publishing is increasingly free from religious contention and political danger and becomes a question of fashion, taste, personal relationships and economics. Richard Luckett's paper traces the relationship between the Playfords, father and son, and the Purcells — with John Purcell and his sons, Henry and Daniel, and finally with Henry Purcell's widow, Frances, who became her husband's distributor and posthumous publisher. Luckett moves skilfully through the bibliographical pitfalls of early printed music, with a plethora of variant titlepages, all seemingly first printings. His analysis of the composer-publisher relationships shows the Playfords, particularly Henry Playford (whose importance has been much overlooked), to have been shrewd men of business, with an unfailing grasp of their market and what it would reap, who knew how to publicize their wares and use dedications not only as an advertising technique but also for self-promotion.

The pinnacle of the Playford music publishing years was *Orpheus Britannicus*, which Luckett likens to Shakespeare's First Folio in posthumous and iconic magnificence, although in the case of *Orpheus* what we see is not quite what we seem to see. Booke 1 (1698) was Playford's swan-song as a music publisher: his interest was waning and his remaining few years were given over to more mainstream literary publication. Booke 2 (1702), ostensibly published by Playford, was directed by Purcell's widow, who in gratitude dedicated it to Annabella Howard, who had been one of Purcell's star pupils and, after his death, was the protector and benefactor of his widow.

As we move into the eighteenth century, and to an account of the relations between Handel and his publishers, John Walsh, senior and junior, the personalities of the protagonists become more clearly delineated. By assiduous searching in libraries and repositories in London, Hamburg and elsewhere, Donald Burrows has been able to assemble a formidable mass of evidence about a relationship which seemed to develop falteringly at first and gradually, and which divides into two distinct parts. For the first fifteen years, from about 1720 to 1735, the Walshes seem either to have taken over previously published editions, or to have published without Handel's specific permission, with several clearly unauthorized editions — in one case, with a clumsily forged titlepage. Thereafter the position was regularized and in 1739 Walsh was able to renew Handel's royal privilege of 1730, making it clear that Walsh was his official publisher.

The Walshes began as instrument makers, like so many dealers in printed music of this period, although as 'Musical Instrument Maker in Ordinary to his Majesty' in 1692, John Walsh senior seems to have mended and strung instruments and supplied new ones, rather than actually making them himself. The sale of printed music gradually became more important to him until, after he set up in the newly fashionable West End, music engraving and publishing became his main, and then sole, business. He also acted as agent for concerts and performances, but some aspects of his business remain unknown. Was Handel's own performance copy used to engrave and print from? Did Walsh keep a staff of engravers on his premises at Catherine Street? Rupert Ridgewell's paper, later in this volume, shows the advantage of detailed archival information which we simply do not have in the case of the Walshes — underlining our almost total ignorance of the print runs, number of printings, identity of engravers and printers, capacity of printing houses, cost of paper, and distribution networks of English firms of the period.

The sale catalogue of the possessions of Carl Friedrich Abel (b.1723), who died intestate and a bachelor in 1787, shows that the rich musical life of Handel's London continued long into the eighteenth century. The only known copy of the catalogue, printed here in facsimile for the first time, is in the library of the Frick Collection, New York. It lists printed and manuscript music, musical instruments, paintings and the contents of Abel's house, including china, trinkets, plate and jewels, a snuff box, and much else. Stephen Roe's study of the sale catalogue reveals almost every facet, private and professional, of Abel's career and life-style, from which a detailed picture of the man can be pieced together — not only his musical activities, but also his love of wine, snuff and tobacco.

Abel came of a musical family, long-standing friends of the Bach family — he may have been a pupil of J. S. Bach, and Bach's son Johann Christian (known as 'the London Bach') was Abel's greatest friend from the time he arrived from Milan in 1762. Both men were Freemasons in the same lodge and were dominant in London musical life of the 1760s and 1770s, founding the Bach-Abel concerts from 1765 onwards. Although London was their base, they held concerts in the provinces and each travelled extensively on the Continent. Their cultural interests extended to art circles: Abel, who was an enchanting player of the viola da gamba (an instrument that died with him), may have given lessons to his friend and fellow gamba enthusiast and music lover, the painter Thomas Gainsborough. There are several works by Gainsborough in Abel's sale catalogue.

The Viennese firm of Artaria (1768–1920s) was the leading music publisher in eighteenth-century Vienna, with retail shops in the city's Kohlmarkt and in Mainz, the most important publisher of Mozart during his lifetime and beyond. Rupert Ridgewell's paper extends our knowledge not only of the firm of Artaria, but also of the entire eighteenth-century music trade, making extensive use of the vast archive of ledgers, account books, contracts, catalogues, letter books, press cuttings and incoming letters which survives in Vienna. Above all he has scrutinized the evidence relating to Artaria plate numbers, unique identifiers which were generally engraved in a central position at the base of each plate. One important question was when the plate number was assigned — whether when a work was accepted for publication, when the manuscript was received, when the agreement was finalized, at the point of engraving, or after preliminary work on the plate was done. Was the decision that of the engraver himself? The example of an early Mozart edition first printed without a plate number prompts a reassessment of the role of the numbering system at the heart of Artaria's business administration, from the point of engraving to the storage of engraving plates and unsold copies. After a minute investigation of multiple copies of 48 Artaria editions (1778–84), Ridgewell concludes that the numbers were usually assigned by the publisher on receipt of a manuscript and he discusses the implications of this for our knowledge of working practices and of the dating of editions.

Vienna continued to be an important centre of music publishing in the next century. Unravelling the complexities of Gustav Mahler's publications and copyrights became much more feasible once the *Musikalisch-literarischer Monatsbericht neuer Musikalien, musikalischer Schriften und*

*Abbildungen*, a monthly list of music publications which had begun in 1829, but which survived only in incomplete runs in various libraries, was made available online in a searchable form. Paul Banks has traced the progress of Mahler in print from his first publisher, Theodor Rättig, a bank official turned aspiring publisher, who offered to issue Mahler's Third Symphony (a failure at first performance in 1877) at his own expense. Rättig's business expanded, but when Mahler moved to conduct orchestras in Leipzig, Budapest and Hamburg in 1888, seeking fame and financial security, he moved also to Leipzig publishers. As his reputation grew, Mahler changed allegiance from one publisher to another. He returned to Vienna in 1897 as conductor of the Vienna State Opera. At this time, the business of Joseph Weinberger, who played a leading role in securing performance fees for publishers and composers following the new Austrian copyright law of 1895, was expanding rapidly. For the next five years Mahler was published by Weinberger, but in 1903, when his fame had spread throughout Europe and America, he left Weinberger for the firm of Eberle, which had a wide international music publishing business.

The Foundling Museum, off Brunswick Square in London, provided a perfect setting for this conference, the twenty-ninth in the annual Book Trade History series. Katharine Hogg, Librarian of the Gerald Coke Handel Collection housed in the Museum, put on a special exhibition for the participants and gave a talk on the origin of the Foundling Hospital as London's first home for abandoned children, founded by Thomas Coram in 1739. The close links between G. F. Handel and the Hospital, commemorated in many parts of the Museum, had a particular resonance for the subject of the conference.

The conference was held under the auspices of the Antiquarian Booksellers' Association and we thank warmly John Critchley and Marianne Harwood who shouldered most of the administrative burden. We are also grateful to the Bibliographical Society for a grant that enabled us to offer subsidized student places.

*Robin Myers*
*Michael Harris*
*Giles Mandelbrote*

London
June 2008

# Contributors

PAUL BANKS is Professor of Historical Musicology and head of the Centre for Performance History at the Royal College of Music. The first phase of his *Catalogue of Manuscript and Printed Sources of Mahler's Music* was published online in 2007.

DONALD BURROWS is Professor of Music at the Open University, a member of the editorial board of the Halle Handel Edition and General Editor of the Novello Edition. He has lectured and published widely on Handel and eighteenth-century musical sources.

IAIN FENLON is Professor of Historical Musicology, and Fellow of King's College, Cambridge. His Panizzi Lectures (1994) were published as *Music, Print and Culture in Early Sixteenth Century Italy* (British Library, 1995). *The Ceremonial City: History and Myth in Renaissance Venice* (Yale, 2007) is his most recent book.

KATHARINE HOGG is Librarian of the Gerald Coke Handel Collection at the Foundling Museum. She has published in various library journals and her research interests include music and music publishing in eighteenth-century London.

RICHARD LUCKETT is Pepysian Librarian and a Fellow of Magdalene College, Cambridge. He has published widely on early music, and is an authority on Samuel Pepys, and on the late seventeenth-century St Cecilia's Day festivities.

RUPERT RIDGEWELL is a Curator, British Library Music Collections. His research focuses on music publishing and patronage in late eighteenth and early nineteenth-century Vienna, and the Artaria firm and first editions of Mozart, Haydn and Boccherini. He has published in *Music & Letters*, *Early Music*, *Fontes Artis Musicae* and elsewhere.

STEPHEN ROE is Head of Printed Books and Manuscripts at Sotheby's (Europe) and Head of Music at Sotheby's (worldwide).

JEREMY L. SMITH, Associate Professor of Musicology, University of Colorado at Boulder, has published on the music publisher Thomas East and is editor of a set of William Byrd's songs. He is currently working on a book to be called 'Close to the Flame: Music and Politics in Elizabethan England'.

# List of those attending the Conference

Bob Allder
*Worshipful Company of Stationers & Newspaper Makers*

Susan Bain

Olive Baldwin
*Musicologist and independent scholar*

Jeremy Barlow
*Musicologist and independent scholar*

Simon Beattie
*Bookseller, Bernard Quaritch Ltd*

Karen Brayshaw
*Canterbury Cathedral Library*

John W. Briggs
*Independent scholar*

Chris Calver
*Bookbinder, Newcastle upon Tyne*

Stephen H. Cape
*Cataloguer of Rare Books and Special Collections, Lilly Library, Indiana University*

Professor Kenneth Charlton
*Professor Emeritus, King's College London*

Richard Chesser
*Head, Music Collections, British Library*

James Clements
*Curator, Music Collections, British Library*

Colin Coleman
*Gerald Coke Collection, Foundling Museum*

Blaise Compton
*PhD student, Open University*

Wendy Cruise
*Bookseller, Bernard Quaritch Ltd*

John Cunningham
*University of Leeds*

Carlo Dumontet
*National Art Library, Victoria & Albert Museum*

Judy Edwards
*Independent scholar and conference facilitator*

Colin Franklin
*Antiquarian Bookseller, Oxford*

Paul Gailiunas

Roger Gaskell
*Roger Gaskell Rare Books*

Jane Giscombe
*Conservator, Dr Williams's Library*

Nahoko Gotoh
*PhD Student, Goldsmiths College*

Emma Greenwood
*University College, London*

Julie Gregory
*Researcher (retired conservator)*

Helen Hardy
*Travis & Emery (antiquarian bookseller)*

J. J. van Heel
*Museum Meermanno-Westreenianum, The Hague*

Francis Herbert
*Consultant,*
*Vulnerable Collections Project,*
*British Library*

John Hewish
*British Library (retired)*

Dr John Hinks
*University of Leicester*

Katharine Hogg
*Gerald Coke Collection,*
*Foundling Museum*

Peter Holman
*Professor of Musicology,*
*University of Leeds*

Ashley W. Huish
*Librarian (retired)*

Nancy Ives
*BA researcher,*
*Low Countries Research Group*

Dr Harry Johnstone, FSA
*Emeritus Fellow in Music,*
*St Anne's College, Oxford*

Outi Jokiharju
*University College London*

Rachel Kadel-Garcia
*Book conservation student,*
*West Dean College*

Colin Lee
*Collector*

Christopher Lee
*Independent scholar*

Dr E. S. Leedham-Green
*Darwin College, Cambridge*

Karen Limper
*Curator, British Library*

Kate Loveman
*Lecturer in English,*
*University of Leicester*

Dr Anita McConnell
*Cambridge University*

Christina Mackwell
*Lambeth Palace Library*

Giuseppina Mazzella
*Assistant Librarian,*
*Royal College of Music*

Miriam Miller
*Retired librarian*

Rei Nakamura
*Curator, Printing Museum, Tokyo*

O. W. Neighbour
*Former Head of Music*
*Collections,*
*British Museum Library*

Andra Patterson
*Curator, Music Collections,*
*British Library*

Michael Perkin
*Retired Special Collections*
*Librarian*

Dr Andrew Pink
*University College London*

Ingrid Piperger
*Interested amateur*

Amelie Roper
*Rare Books Reference Team Leader,*
*British Library*

Christopher Rowe
*Collector & PhD Student,*
*School of English,*
*University of Leeds*

Joyce Simett-Moss
*School of Music,*
*University of Liverpool*

Julianne Simpson
*Rare Books Librarian,*
*Wellcome Library*

Lucie Skeaping
*BBC Radio 3*

Christine Thomson
*Book consultant*

Stephanie Tritton
*PhD student,*
*University of Manchester*

Jean Tsushima FSA
*Director & General Editor,*
*HAC Biographical Dictionary*
*(1537–1914) Trust*

Richard Turbet
*Special Collections Cataloguer and*
*Music Librarian,*
*University of Aberdeen*

Geerlinde Van Dÿk
*Research MA student, Musicology,*
*University of Utrecht*

Christel Wallbaum
*Bookseller*

Veronica Watts
*Bookseller to the conference*

Eva Weininger
*Dealer*

Thelma Wilson
*Musicologist and independent*
*scholar*

# Music Printing and the Book Trade in Late-Sixteenth and Early Seventeenth-Century Iberia

## IAIN FENLON

'Now for Spain, his Majesty there, though accounted the greatest Monarch of Christendom, yet if his estate be enquired through, his root will be found a great deal too narrow for his tops.'

Francis Bacon: 'A Short View to be taken of Great Britain and Spain'.

IT IS SOMETIMES SAID that while the Spain of Philip II was both militarily and economically at the centre of the world, in artistic and cultural terms terms it was on the periphery of European developments. As Bacon's words suggest, behind the impressive might of Philip's empire lay a sense of insecurity, perhaps even a contemporary impression of a great enterprise on the verge of decline. There is now little doubt among historians that, by the beginning of the seventeenth century, that process had begun in earnest in Castile, with its extensive bureacratic class, groups of often interlocking élites in charge of both church and state, and what has been described as 'a society of rentiers parasites, clinging to its ancient ways and setting an exaggerated store by outward appearances'.[1] Paradoxically, the late sixteenth and early seventeenth century in Spain is also commonly described as the Golden Age of artistic achievement. These are the years of Cervantes and Quevedo in literature, of Lope de Vega and Calderón in the theatre, of Velázquez and Murillo in painting, and of Guerrero and Victoria in music.[2] Yet while in some areas of cultural activity Spanish developments were distinctive, important, and of wider influence and significance, in others they were not.

This is certainly true of Spanish and Portuguese printing and publishing. Although in both countries there had been centres of activity since the fifteenth century, and the book industry grew in size towards the end of the sixteenth, production remained small in comparison with that of France, Italy, Germany, Switzerland, and the Low Countries. Around the middle of the sixteenth century books in the vernacular, one of the mainstays of the trade since the beginning, began to be produced in considerable numbers abroad; during the subsequent decades the centre of book production in the Spanish language was to shift from Seville, Alcalá, and Salamanca to the Netherlands.[3] By the second half of the sixteenth century,

1

most of what was read in Spain was imported.[4] The same is true of the trade in printed music, whether treatises, liturgical books, or volumes of printed polyphony, all three of which tended to constitute different if overlapping markets served by different printers and publishers.

The second of these sectors was undoubtedly the largest. Among the papers of the powerful Spanish merchant Simón Ruiz of Valladolid is a document, drawn up towards the end of the sixteenth century, which gives an assessment of the market for liturgical books; according to this some 40 presses would have been necessary in order to print the 40,000 breviaries and missals required on an annual basis to supply the 50 bishoprics of the Spanish church.[5] The market for didactic manuals and treatises was the smallest of the three. Between the appearance of Domingo Durán's *Lux Bella*, printed by a consortium of German printers in 1492, and the end of the sixteenth century, only some dozen or so such titles came off the Spanish presses. Juan Bermudo's treatises apart, the only theoretical work of any originality or intellectual standing to be produced in Spain during the period was Francisco Salinas's *De musica libri septem*, printed in Salamanca by Matthias Gast in 1577.[6] Unusual for its emphasis on harmonics and rhythmics, it is also notable for the inclusion of a sequence of Spanish popular melodies as examples in a discussion of metre — in effect a form of early ethnography (Fig. 1). The most popular of all, the *Arte de canto llano* (Valladolid, 1594), a fairly standard treatment of plainsong by Francisco de Montanos, was reprinted some dozen times in Salamanca, Madrid, and Zaragoza up to 1756.

As for the printing of books of polyphony in Spain, the initial phase was evidently stimulated by the demand for domestic music, particularly that for the vihuela.[7] Beginning with Luis Milán's *El maestro* (Fig. 2), printed in Valencia by Francisco Díaz Romano in 1535/36,[8] some seven books of instrumental music were produced by a number of different presses working in different cities in the peninsula including Valladolid and Seville.[9] Indeed, for some twenty years no other repertories of any kind were printed in Spain, and this fashion for music for plucked instruments (some of these titles contain music for guitar), in some cases with voice, continued into the later decades of the century with collections by Tomás de Santa María, Esteban Daza, and Antonio de Cabezón.[10] One of the printers responsible for this first tranche of vihuela books, Martín de Montesdoca, was also the first Spanish printer to produce a set of part-books of vocal music, the *Sacrae cantiones vulgo motecta nuncupata* by Francisco Guerrero, normally considered second only to Victoria as a major Spanish composer of sacred music at work during the second half of the sixteenth century; Montesdoca's book was issued in Seville in 1555.[11]

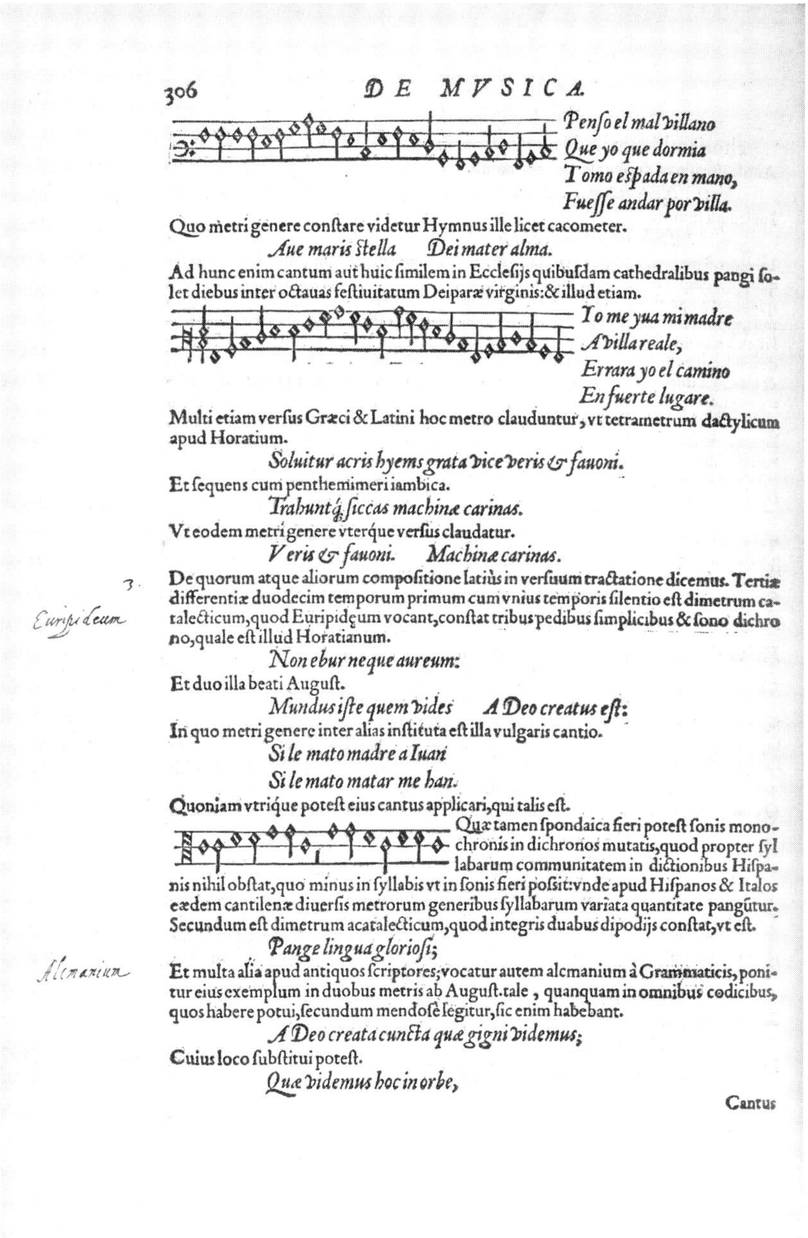

306      *DE MVSICA.*

*Penſo el mal villano*
*Que yo que dormia*
*Tomo eſpada en mano,*
*Fueſſe andar por villa.*

Quo metri genere conſtare videtur Hymnus ille licet cacometer.

      *Aue maris ſtella   Dei mater alma.*

Ad hunc enim cantum aut huic ſimilem in Eccleſijs quibuſdam cathedralibus pangi ſo-
let diebus inter octauas feſtiuitatum Deiparæ virginis:& illud etiam.

*Yo me yua mi madre*
*A villa reale,*
*Errara yo el camino*
*En fuerte lugare.*

Multi etiam verſus Græci & Latini hoc metro clauduntur, vt tetrametrum dactylicum
apud Horatium.

     *Soluitur acris hyems grata vice veris & fauoni.*

Et ſequens cum penthemimeri iambica.

     *Trahuntq́ ſiccas machinæ carinas.*

Vt eodem metri genere vterque verſus claudatur.

    *Veris & fauoni.   Machinæ carinas.*

De quorum atque aliorum compoſitione latiùs in verſuum tractatione dicemus. Tertiæ
differentiæ duodecim temporum primum cum vnius temporis ſilentio eſt dimetrum ca-
talecticum, quod Euripidę̄um vocant, conſtat tribus pedibus ſimplicibus & ſono dichro-
no, quale eſt illud Horatianum.

     *Non ebur neque aureum:*

Et duo illa beati Auguſt.

    *Mundus iſte quem vides   A Deo creatus eſt:*

In quo metri genere inter alias inſtituta eſt illa vulgaris cantio.

     *Si le mato madre a Iuan*

     *Si le mato matar me han.*

Quoniam vtrique poteſt eius cantus applicari, qui talis eſt.

Quæ tamen ſpondaica fieri poteſt ſonis mono-
chronis in dichronos mutatis, quod propter ſyl
labarum communitatem in dictionibus Hiſpa-
nis nihil obſtat, quo minus in ſyllabis vt in ſonis fieri poſsit: vnde apud Hiſpanos & Italos
eædem cantilenæ diuerſis metrorum generibus ſyllabarum variata quantitate pangūtur.
Secundum eſt dimetrum acatalecticum, quod integris duabus dipodijs conſtat, vt eſt.

     *Pange lingua glorioſi;*

Et multa alia apud antiquos ſcriptores; vocatur autem alcmanium à Grammaticis, poni-
tur eius exemplum in duobus metris ab Auguſt. tale , quanquam in omnibus codicibus,
quos habere potui, ſecundum mendoſe legitur, ſic enim habebant.

     *A Deo creata cuncta quæ gigni videmus;*

Cuius loco ſubſtitui poteſt.

     *Quæ videmus hoc in orbe,*

                         Cantus

*Fig. 1.* Francisco Salinas, *De musica libri septem* (Salamanca, M. Gast, 1577)

On 1 June of the previous year the chapter of the local cathedral had successfully applied for a Papal Brief that granted Guerrero both tenure and the right to succeed the ageing Pedro Fernández (whom he had been assisting since 1551) as *maestro de capilla*. The *Sacrae cantiones* effectively inaugurates Guerrero's career in print, and it is indicative of his considerable reputation both inside and outside Spain that all his subsequent collections were printed abroad. Juan de León, having printed one of these early vihuela collections in 1546,[12] went on three years later to produce the first Spanish music treatise, Bermudo's *Comiença el libro primero de la declaracion de instrumentos*, essentially a study of plainsong and polyphony aimed at instrumentalists who needed to master the techniques of intabulation.[13]

Others followed Montesdoca's example. Juan de León entered the field of vocal music with his collection of *Villancicos I canciones*, and in Barcelona Jacobo Cortey issued two books of *odas* by the Catalan composer Pere Alberch i Ferramunt alias Vila, then organist at the cathedral. It would be misleading to describe this short-lived foray into different vocal repertories both sacred and secular by just a handful of printers working in a number of different cities as a trend; the production is tiny by any standards, certainly by comparison with contemporary developments in France, Germany, the Netherlands, and (above all) Italy. Guerrero aside, much of the repertory in these volumes has a distinctly provincial flavour. The most prominent of the composers involved, Juan Vásquez, was a native of Badajoz then (1551) in the service of Don Antonio de Zuniga, a Sevillian aristocrat, and it was to his patron that Vásquez (or his publisher) dedicated the *Villancicos i canciones*. The *Recopilacion de sonetos y villancicos*, the last collection of Vásquez's secular works to be printed (with a dedication to Don Gonzálo de Moscoso y Casceres Penna, an *hidalgo* of the Cáceres family of Badajoz), includes seven songs and three re-worked pieces from the earlier collection.[14] This is the only form of reprinting that takes place with these repertories, and it is perhaps indicative of the limited size of the market that the reprinting of entire books other than treatises does not occur, in contrast to the patterns observable elsewhere in Europe. Nonetheless, Vásquez's music did attract attention; Bermudo, the most influential commentator of his day, recommended it as a model for study, and a number of his courtly villancicos circulated in intabulated form.[15] A final pair of books of vocal music, Joan Brudieu's madrigals and the *Liber primus motectorum* by Nicasio Zorita, were printed in Barcelona by Hubert Gotard.[16] As with a number of early Spanish printers of polyphony, Gotard turned out a broad range of material including a folio broadside printed for the local College of Pharmacists, a three-volume compilation of the

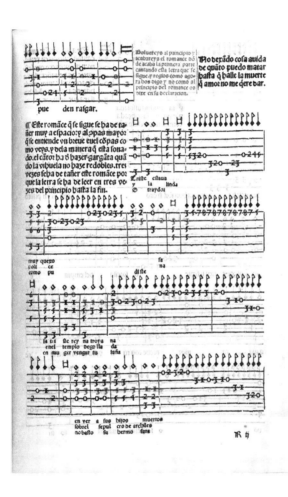

*Fig. 2.* Luis Milán, *El maestro* (Valencia, F. Díaz, 1535/6)

laws of Catalonia, and a commentary on the Book of Jeremiah.[17] In other words, there is a strong local flavour to his list.

The third category of Spanish music printing of the period is that of the choirbook repertory of liturgical music. Here the market had been substantially shaped firstly by Antico's *Liber quindecim missarum* of 1516, which inventories reveal to have been imported into Spain in some numbers, and later by Dorico's choirbook series which is modelled on Antico's volume.[18] Although Martín de Montesdoca was the first Spanish printer to bring out such a collection, Vásquez's *Agenda defunctorum* (1556), it was not until the establishment of the Royal Printing House (Typographia Regia) in Madrid, Philip II's newly established capital city, that any appreciable production of printed polyphonic choirbooks took place in Spain. Following Philippe Rogier's *Missae sex* of 1598, two further substantial choirbooks were printed there: Alfonso Lobo's *Liber primus missarum* (1602), and Victoria's *Officium defunctorum* of 1605.[19] Then there is a gap of more than twenty years until the appearance of the *Libro de missas, motetes, salmos, magnificats y otras cosas tocantes al culto divino* by the Segovian composer Sebastián López de Velasco, who at the time was chaplain and *maestro de capilla* to Doña Juana at the aristocratic convent of the Descalzas Reales in Madrid.

The example of the Typographia Regia was quickly emulated elsewhere in Iberia. Either the type used by Juan de Flandres, who oversaw the operations of the Madrid workshop, or fonts struck from the same matrices, had come into the hands of the Fleming Artus Taberniel, working in Salamanca, by 1607. With these to hand, he began to print a number of ambitious choirbooks alongside his other titles.[20] Beginning with Sebastián de Vivanco's *Liber magnificarum*, Taberniel went on to issue a series of visually imposing folio volumes at a fairly steady rate up to 1610, after which he disappears from view. By this time Vivanco was working as *maestro de capilla* at Salamanca Cathedral, while Juan Esquivel Barahona, the other composer whose sacred music was printed by Taberniel, was then *maestro de capilla* at the cathedral in nearby Ciudad Rodrigo.[21] Some at least of these books were not functioning in the marketplace in the way that was usual according to the system indicated by contemporary commercial contracts. For example, Esquivel's three volumes of Latin church music were paid for by his patron, the Dominican Pedro Ponce de León, Bishop of Ciudad Rodrigo from 1605 to 1609, and seem to have been produced in only small quantities. As such, they are partly propagandistic publications that make powerful statements about the magnanimous and enlightened patronage of Ponce de León, the compositional skills of Esquivel and, most importantly, the religiosity and devotion of both. In common with so much Spanish music printing of the period, the distribution pattern of these choirbook volumes is predominantly local, and certainly not as international as were choirbooks printed in Venice or Rome. That said, a number of exceptions have to be made. One is the presence, in the archives of both the Cappella Giulia and San Giovanni in Laterano in Rome, of copies of Victoria's *Officium defunctorum* and Alfonso Lobo's *Liber primus missarum*, both printed by the Typographia Regia; together with a number of other copies from the same press in other non-Spanish libraries, these may well have been presentation copies. Another departure from the generalization also has to be made in the case of copies in Spanish America;[22] Rogier's *Missae sex* reached Sucre in Bolivia, Puebla in Mexico, and Cuzco in Peru, while Vivanco's *Liber magnificarum* also found its way to Mexico. While the Spanish peninsula may have been on the periphery of the European market for printed music in the sixteenth and seventeenth centuries, it was at the centre of the distribution network to the colonies.

A third printer, Petrus Craesbeeck, working in Lisbon (from 1580 part of the Spanish domains), also issued a series of four choirbooks between 1613 and 1625, conceivably influenced by the examples of Juan de Flandres and Tarberniel. Again the repertory that he chose to print had been composed close to hand; masses and other sacred music by Manuel Cardoso, then *mestre da capela* at the Convento do Carmo in Lisbon, Filipe de Magalhaes's *Cantus ecclesiasticus*, and a book of instrumental music by Manuel Rodrigues Coelho.[23] As befits the official printer to the Portuguese monarch, Craesbeeck put out a number of 'official' publications including an edition of the *Index librorum prohibitorum* and an account of the obsequies for Philip II, as well as a lavish folio edition of the life of St Francis Xavier and a collection of Camoes's poetry.[24]

During the century that stretched from 1535 to 1625, fewer than 50 books of polyphony (including treatises with substantial musical examples and books now lost) were printed in Spain. In these circumstances, most of the printed music that circulated in both Spain and Portugal was imported from the four main centres of music book production: Paris, Lyon, Antwerp, and Venice. Taken together with evidence from booksellers' inventories and similar material, the pattern of surviving copies suggests a strong correlation between trade routes and distribution, as might be expected. Books from Venice, the most important centre of music printing and publication anywhere in Europe, normally travelled overland through the Veneto and Spanish Lombardy to Milan and then on to Genoa. From there they were taken by ship to the major ports on Spain's eastern seaboard: Barcelona and Valencia. Given the importance of Milan in Spanish diplomatic, military and economic affairs, and the commercial importance of the trade route from Milan to the western Mediterranean, it comes as no surprise to discover evidence of a disproportionately high percentage of books (including music) printed in Milan during the second half of the sixteenth century. The second major route, and by far the more hazardous, connected Antwerp to the ports of the Cantabrian coast; the other poles of the trade were Bruges in Flanders and Antwerp in Brabant, the two most important entrepôts before the growth of Amsterdam and London. The route, which was a highly important one, carried goods including food, iron manufactures and, above all, wool; at the height of its prosperity it is said to have been surpassed only by the trade to the Indies. Intermediate stops were sometimes made at Nantes and, more importantly, at Le Havre close to the major city of Rouen (Fig. 3).

In order to illustrate the general character of the book trade in late sixteenth-century Iberia, and of the place of printed music within it, I shall consider the case of Salamanca where, from fragile beginnings, the press followed the familiar trajectory of medium-sized Castilian towns; from two or three titles *per annum* in the 1520s, production steadily grew to the two or three dozen editions that became the annual norm by the second half of the sixteenth century.[25] This expansion, which shadows population increases in the same period, is reflected in an increase in the number of printing houses operating in the city. In 1570 the names of no fewer than seven printers appear on the titlepages and in the colophons of books produced in Salamanca; between them they issued 46 editions in that year, a number that was not to be equalled, or even approached, during the rest of the century. This increased activity is partly to be explained by two factors. Firstly, the local response to a general phenomenon — the reaction of the press in Catholic Europe to the post-Tridentine world. Religious literature both doctrinal and devotional, traditionally one of the largest fields of interest that the press had always sought to satisfy, was produced in greater quantity from 1564 onwards as the arguments of the reformers, crystallized in the publications of the Council of Trent and in the stream of decrees and legislation that followed its conclusion, touched the reading habits of the average clerical or lay believer.[26] Second, educational expansion. As in other parts of Europe, universities in Castile grew rapidly during the sixteenth century to reach a peak in the 1590s, after which decline set in. This was in response to demographic and economic expansion, the requirements of the counter-reformation church, a growing royal bureaucracy, and the demands for education from the nobility, and particularly from the *hidalgo* class. During the course of the century the University of Salamanca acquired 28 new colleges; matriculations, which at mid-century had

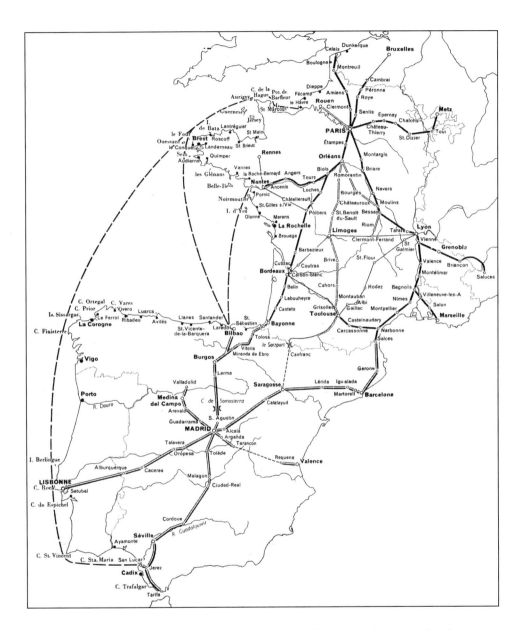

*Fig. 3.* Trade routes in western Europe at the end of the sixteenth century, based on H. Lepeyre, *Une famille de marchands: les Ruiz* (Paris, 1955)

stood at just over 5,000, rose to almost 7,000 in 1595.[27] In these circumstances it is hardly surprising that academic texts, whether learned treatises or student manuals, lay at the heart of local book production, together with the missals and breviaries directed at the substantial population of regular and secular clergy in the city.

After 1570 the manufacture of books in Salamanca stabilized at just under 30 new titles annually for twenty years, after which the figure then fell by almost 30 percent during the 1590s. The collapse is no surprise in view of the severe economic recession that took hold in Spain, as well as in a number of other European countries, in the final decade of the sixteenth century.[28] This amounts to a yearly average output of some 25,000 books in the last 30 years of the century, in a city whose population then stood at between 15,000 and 20,000, of whom some thousands would have been students. As such Salamanca was one of an unusually high number of lower-to-middle ranking towns in Castile with a population of 10,000 or more. During the course of the sixteenth century the number of such urban centres in the region more than tripled from about 25 to almost 80, and their inhabitants grew in number to a total of about half a million.[29] While it is clear that the Salamancan press had worked from the start for an outside market as well as an internal one, it may be that much of its output was absorbed by the immediate catchment area which was, in terms of the general European pattern, unusually dense in medium-sized urban centres.[30] Books printed there were substantially directed at the local ecclesiastical, academic, and merchant class, but were also produced to be sold to 'foreigners', through shops in the city or the book fairs in Medina del Campo and elsewhere. Here they mingled with imported volumes which were readily available in bookshops, which served a large university population, of which many came from abroad, as well as a locally educated élite.[31]

The contents of a number of institutional libraries indicate the extent to which books, including music, printed in most of the major European centres of production, circulated in sixteenth-century Salamanca. An eighteenth-century catalogue of the library of the monastery of San Esteban contains a sixteenth-century core which is largely ecclesiastical in tone, but which also includes a decent number of classical authors and a smattering of vernacular texts. Here the *Acta ecclesiae mediolensis,* and the canons and decrees of the Council of Trent, rub shoulders with Alberti's *De architectura* and Garzoni's *Piazza universale.* Polyphonic music does not appear, but the library owned a copy of Boethius *De música* and, less predictably, an edition of Gaffurius.[32] The mixture (the collection also includes a copy of Erasmus) is not untypical of the institutional ecclesiastical libraries of the city, of which the most important was that of the Jesuit

College, first established in the city in 1548. An eighteenth-century catalogue of its books, drawn up when the Jesuits were expelled and its library
transferred to the University, contains a bedrock of sixteenth-century
editions which represents almost one half of the total number of books
inventoried. The majority of them were printed outside Spain — principally in Basle, Paris, Lyons, and Venice — suggesting a considerable
reliance on imports for the formation of a collection of texts necessary to
pursue the Jesuits' educational and devotional objectives. The rapid rise in
lay enrolments at the Jesuit Colleges in Spain in the second half of the
sixteenth century coincided with the decline in the teaching of grammar in
the universities, and it has been calculated that by the middle of the seventeenth century the Society was responsible for almost half of all organized
teaching in the kingdom.[33] In the Jesuit Colleges this was offered at university level, principally in the arts, grammar, and theology, a fact reflected in
both the size and character of libraries such as that in Salamanca. Among
the books from the collection are a number of sets of music partbooks, all
of which were printed in Antwerp by the Plantin firm. Their presence in
the Jesuit library may be related to the order's well-known encouragement
of music and theatre as part of its didactic activities, but they are also a
clear indication of the effectiveness of Plantin's distribution network
within Spain.[34]

Plantin's contemporary reputation was undoubtedly high. The general
perception was confirmed by Philip II's decision to award the printer generous
commissions for the printing and distribution in Spain and its dominions
of missals and breviaries revised in accordance with the edicts of the
Council of Trent.[35] During the years 1570–6, Plantin printed more than
50,000 service books, mostly for the Spanish market, and when Philip II
unexpectedly withdrew his promised subsidy of a sumptuous antiphonal
(planned as a companion to the polyglot Bible) after only seven sheets had
been pulled, Plantin turned to printing polyphony.[36] For his first venture
into the field of music printing he chose to produce a large-format choirbook containing eight masses by the Flemish composer George de La Hèle.
In part this was a pragmatic decision, designed to make use of the 1,800
reams of royal-format paper that had been ordered for the abandoned antiphonal, but it was also an astute entry into the Antwerp music-printing
business at a moment when local production had eased off.[37] At an average
price of eighteen florins per copy, La Hèle's *Octo missae* was an expensive
book, but the 375 copies printed sold well.[38] Of these some, together with
Plantin's other music books, found their way to Spain,[39] travelling along
the same commercial routes that Plantin had already established for his
other books, and profiting from the business contacts outside the Low

Countries that the Antwerp printer had already made to facilitate the distribution of his liturgical publications. Plantin's Spanish operation apart, the other important foreign firm that had fairly direct contacts with Salamanca was that of the Giunta family. Florentine in origin, it also had presses in Venice and Lyons, as well as bookshops in major cities throughout Europe. In Burgos two generations of the dynasty, Felipe Junta and Juan de Junta, were between them productive printers for much of the sixteenth century. Although they printed other kinds of texts liturgical books were, much in the tradition of the Venetian branch of the family, something of the firm's speciality.

Among the new printers who set up business in Salamanca during the 1580s, a number were foreigners, as were so many of the men who worked the Spanish presses in the last decades of the sixteenth century, evidently attracted from France and Flanders by the high wages to be earned in the Spanish trade, and in some cases driven into refuge by the growing wave of religious repression in northern Europe.[40] It was this small community that Artus Tavernier,[41] a printer and type-caster from Antwerp, joined on his arrival from Flanders.[42] He is first encountered in the city acting as godfather to the child of a fellow printer, in the spring of 1588.[43] The registers of the cathedral, where the baptism took place, describe him as a type-caster, and by then he was evidently well established in the small local printing community. Thereafter the trail goes cold, but beginning in 1603 Taberniel ran a modest printing operation capable of producing on average about three books per year. He began, rather curiously it might seem, with a single folio broadsheet in English, which lays out the opinions of eighteen Spanish theologians and professors of divinity at the two universities about the right of Catholics in Ireland to support Hugh O'Neill, who had taken up arms against Elizabeth I nine years earlier, and who had been waging civil war ever since.[44] Thereafter he followed a cautious policy in his choice of material, focusing on González Dávila's *Historia de las antiquedades de la ciudad de Salamanca*, which would have had a virtually guaranteed sale among the university and clerical élite of the city, a number of devotional texts, and the *Constituciones* of the church synod held in the cathedral in September 1604.[45] The latter must have been something of a coup, since it was an official publication issued on the instructions of Fernández de Córdoba, Bishop of Salamanca, and Taberniel must have beaten the local competition in order to secure the commission. For his printing of Martino Rio's edition of Saint Orientius, Taberniel introduced an elegant allegorical printer's mark, based on Italian practice.[46] All these titles show him working for the local ecclesiastical and university élite: González Dávila, later official historiographer to Philip III, was then a deacon and treasurer of Salamanca Cathedral; Solórzano Pereira, later a prominent jurist at Salamanca Cathedral, was then at the start of his career; and Antonio Pérez, the author of what is arguably Taberniel's most elegant book apart from his choirbooks, was the Rector of the College of San Vicente in the city. The first of Pérez's two related volumes, which are normally found bound together, is dedicated to Philip III, the second to the Duke of Lerma, and both are prominently advertised on their titlepages as being 'Cum Privilegio Regio'. Thereafter Taberniel seems to have changed tack, and apart from a couple of exceptions does not seem to have been concerned with purely literary texts, presumably because he was more or less fully occupied with printing the five Esquivel and Vivanco choirbooks which were his main concern in the years 1607–10.

Taberniel began his own series of choirbooks with a volume of magnificats composed by Sebastián de Vivanco, appointed *maestro de capilla* at Salamanca Cathedral in 1602, and the successful competitor in the following year for a chair in the university. His achievement in obtaining these prestigious professional posts is prominently advertised on the titlepage, which also includes an engraving showing the composer kneeling in front of a simple altar, whose only decoration is a standing crucifix, and offering a closed book, lettered on its cover with the words 'DONVM DE DONIS TVIS' (Fig. 4). This ties the titlepage to the dedication on the verso, which is a prose continuation and amplification of the iconography of the titlepage engraving. Of earthly patrons there is no sign.[47]

That is not true of the two choirbooks, one containing masses, the other motets, that Taberniel devoted to the music of Juan Esquivel Barahona. Both were paid for by Pedro Ponce de León, Bishop of Ciudad Rodrigo, Esquivel's native city, from 1605 until 1609. Esquivel had been a pupil of Juan Navarro during the latter's brief period as *maestro de capilla* at the cathedral there in the 1570s. After holding posts at the cathedrals of Oviedo and Calahorra, Esquivel returned to Ciudad Rodrigo as *maestro*, where he was already in post by the time that the first of Taberniel's two choirbooks containing his music were published, and it may well be that he had been there since his departure from Calahorra in 1595.[48] Artus began with a book of masses in 1608, of which only one incomplete copy is known to have survived,[49] but the titlepage engraving from a complete example, offered for sale by the Munich antiquarian bookseller Ludwig Rosenthal at the beginning of the twentieth century, has been partially reproduced; it shows the composer kneeling in front of an altar, on which stands a retable of the virgin and child,[50] an iconographical arrangement that is very similar to that of Vivanco's *Liber magnificarum*. In the same year Taberniel also published a collection of Esquivel's motets.[51] No doubt

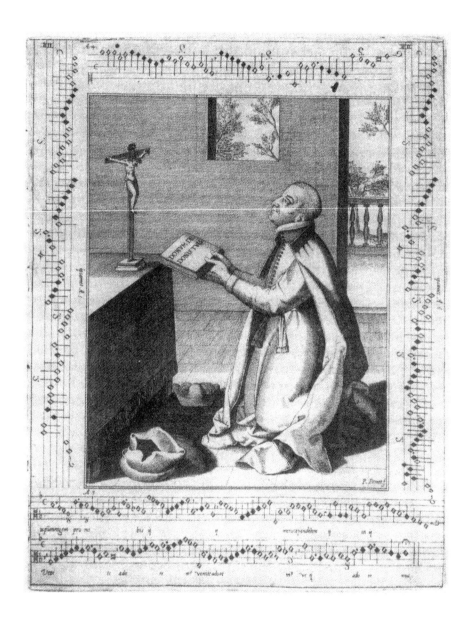

*Fig. 4.* Sebastián de Vivanco, *Liber magnificarum* (Salamanca, A. Taberniel, 1607)

he intended to follow these two with a third book devoted to psalms, hymns, and magnificats, but in the end the work was printed by Francisco de Cea Tesa, who brought it out some three years after Taberniel's death.[52] Nothing is known to have been printed by Artus in the course of 1609, but at some juncture he printed a further volume of music by Vivanco, this time containing a sequence of motets. Only two copies survive, but unfortunately both lack titlepage and colophon. The next books known to have come from Taberniel's press in 1610 were printed by his widow.[53]

Evidently Taberniel began to plan his choirbook series without any previous experience of music printing, and without suitable fonts immediately to hand. These he obtained from Madrid, or at least from the same matrices from which Juan de Flandres had cast the type that he used to print a number of monumental choirbooks, beginning with Philippe Rogier's *Missae sex*. Following Rogier's death in 1596, his testamentary instructions that a volume containing five of his masses be printed, a project for which Philip II had promised his support, were brought to completion by his pupil and *vicemaestro de capilla*, Géry de Ghersem, who in the process added a mass of his own.[54] With its opening mass (which makes use of the traditional and authoritative device of the *soggetto cavato*), and a dedication to Philip III (who had recently acceded to the throne), the *Missae sex* is an ambitious attempt to produce a Spanish equal to the Italian and Flemish choirbooks which had been circulating in the country for decades, while at the same time honouring the monarch. Rogier's volume was followed by two volumes containing sacred music by Victoria and Alfonso Lobo respectively, and then by Victoria's *Officium defunctorum*, brought out in 1605. Thereafter he stopped. As so often in the history of early Spanish music printing, the career of Juan de Flandres was short-lived; his entry into the market was a brief if initially ambitious enterprise, in this case apparently designed to advertise and make available the repertorial riches of the Spanish Royal Chapel to a wider audience. The pattern is typical of the early history of both Spanish and Portuguese music printing.

Taberniel's dependence upon Juan de Flandres's examples extended beyond type to layout, design, and the whole *mise en page*, in short to the very concept of how a choirbook should look. Apart from the choirbooks printed by Moderne and Dorico, which were disseminated in some numbers in Spain, the *ur* model for the whole tradition of the printed choirbook was Andrea Antico's *Liber quindecim missarum*, printed in Rome in 1516 by the woodcut method. Although only one exemplar still survives in Spain[55] from a print run of 1,001 copies, it is clear from inventories that it circulated quite widely in the kingdom.[56] It is evident from the design of Taberniel's titlepage to Vivanco's *Liber magnificarum*, and to a lesser extent

*Fig. 5.  Liber quindecim missarum* (Rome, A. Antico, 1516)

that of Esquivel's *Missarum liber primus*, that Taberniel had seen a copy either of Antico's volume, or perhaps one of the Dorico choirbooks that are so clearly based on the design of Antico's titlepage.[57] Following a convention established by fifteenth-century manuscripts copied for the papacy, this shows Leo X receiving a music book from a kneeling figure, presumably Antico himself. Open and legible, this volume, perhaps intended to be a stylized representation of the *Liber quindecim missarum* itself, presents a simple canon to the words 'Vivat Leo Decimus, Pontifex Maximus' (Fig. 5). This, or one of Dorico's titlepages based upon it, is clearly the direct ancestor of Taberniel's design. It seems likely that printers such as Gardano in Rome or Plantin in Antwerp produced these books with a specifically Spanish market in mind. It was this market requirement that Artus Taberniel, if only in a local and limited way, was also attempting to satisfy.

From the example of Salamanca can be extracted a more general conclusion. It used to be argued that the underdeveloped character of the press in Iberia was attributable to the repressive effects of Catholicism. According to this interpretation the religious debates promoted by northern Protestantism encouraged reading, particularly at the lower levels of society, whereas Catholicism had the opposite effect. This view is no longer tenable. At the statistical level it is now clear that production in Italy, for example, grew consistently throughout the century to reach a peak during the 1570s; the subsequent falling off was due to a complex of factors including the impact of the plague of 1575–7. In Spain itself literacy was evidently high, both among the rural population as well as town dwellers.[58] It seems much more likely that the undernourished condition of the Iberian presses was due to technical factors such as poor investment and an inadequate supply of good paper.[59] In these circumstances the trade was heavily reliant upon imports. The same holds true for the market in printed music, where both the surviving books themselves and the information provided by inventories reveal that most music titles were imported from abroad, particularly from Flanders and Italy. In consequence, the repertories to be heard in the cathedrals and collegiate churches of the peninsula, as well as in private residences, were substantially shaped by the works of foreign composers as well as being bolstered by those of Spaniards.[60]

## References

*Note:* Much of the material on which this article is based was gathered during the course of a project, *Music, Print, and Culture in Portugal and Spain during the Renaissance*, based in the Faculty of Music in Cambridge and funded by the Leverhulme Trust, during the years 2000–3. Tess Knighton worked as a full-time research assistant on the project, and valuable contributions were also made by Emilio Ros-Fabregas and Yfat Fellner-Simpson, thanks to financial support from the Banco

Bilbao Vizcaya Argentaria and the Faculty of Music, University of Cambridge, respectively.

1.  J. H. Elliot, *Spain and its World 1550–1700* (New Haven and London, 1989), p. 266. For some of the more prominent general accounts of the period as a whole see A. Domínguez Ortiz, *The Golden Age of Spain, 1516–1659* (London, 1971); J. H. Elliott, *Imperial Spain, 1469–1716* (London, 1963); H. Kamen, *Spain in the Later Seventeenth Century, 1665–1700* (London, 1980); John Lynch, *Spain under the Hapsburgs*, 2nd edn (Oxford, 1981).
2.  On these cultural aspects there is a considerable literature. Good starting points include F. Bouza, *Imagen y propaganda: capitulos de historia cultural del reinado de Felipe II* (Madrid, 1998); F. Checa Cremades, *Felipe II, mecenas de las artes* (Madrid, 1992), and the exhibition catalogues published by the Sociedad estatal para la conmemoracion de los centenarios de Felipe II y de Carlos V in 1998.
3.  T. S. Beardsley, 'The Classics and their Spanish Translators in the Sixteenth Century', *Renaissance and Reformation* VIII (Toronto, 1971), p. 5.
4.  C. Griffin, 'Itinerant Booksellers, Printers and Pedlars in Sixteenth-Century Spain and Portugal', in R. Myers, M. Harris, and G. Mandelbrote (eds.), *Fairs, Markets and the Itinerant Book Trade* (London, 2007), pp. 43–59, particularly pp. 43–5.
5.  H. Lepeyre, *Une famille de marchands: les Ruiz. Contribution à l'étude du commerce entre la France et l'Espagne au temps de Philippe II* (Paris, 1955), pp. 571–3; Ian Maclean, 'Murder, Debt and Retribution in the Italico-Franco-Spanish Book Trade: The Beraud-Michel-Ruiz Affair, 1586–91', in Myers, Harris, and Mandelbrote (eds.), *Fairs, Markets and the Itinerant Book Trade*, pp. 61–84, at p. 75.
6.  There is a considerable literature on Salinas. On his importance as a student of Greek musical theory see C. Palisca, *Humanism in Italian Musical Thought* (New Haven and London, 1985), and for his contribution to modal theory P. Otaola, 'Francisco Salinas y la teoría modal en el siglo XVI', *Revista aragonesa de musicología* XI (1995), pp. 367–85.
7.  For a list of books of polyphony printed in Iberia see the appendix to this article. A more detailed listing, including all known surviving copies, appears in I. Fenlon and T. Knighton (eds.), *Early Music Printing and Publishing in the Iberian World* (Kassel, 2006), pp. 181–214.
8.  The titlepage is dated 1535, the colophon 1536.
9.  See J. Griffiths, 'Printing the Art of Orpheus: Vihuelas Tablatures in Sixteenth-Century Spain', in Fenlon and Knighton (eds.), *Early Music Printing and Publishing*, pp. 181–214. For the typographical processes involved see A. Corona Alcade, 'The Fernández de Córdoba Printers and the Vihuela Books from Valladolid', *Lute Society of America Quarterly* 40 (2005), pp. 20–30.
10. Appendix, nos 19 and 20.
11. See Appendix, no. 11. For Martín de Montesdoca see K. Wagner, *Martín de Montesdoca y su prensa: contribucion al estudio de la imprenta y de la bibliografía sevillanas del siglo XVI* (Seville, 1982).
12. Namely Alfonso Mudarra, *Tres libros de música en cifras para vihuela* (Seville, 1546).
13. Appendix, no. 6. It was followed in the following year by Bermudo's second treatise, the *Comienca el arte tripharia*; see A. Domínguez Gusman, *El libro sevillano durante la primera mitad del siglo XVI* (Seville, 1955). The contents of the 1549 edition of the *Comienca el libro primero de la declaracion* mostly re-appear in a new edition of 1555, also printed by Juan de León in Osuna.
14. Appendix, nos 12 and 16.

15. See E. Russell, *Villancicos and Other Secular Polyphonic Music of Juan Vásquez: A Courtly Tradition in Spain's Siglo del Oro* (Ph.D. diss., University of Southern California, 1970), and the same author's article 'The Patrons of Juan Vásquez: A Biographical Contribution', *Analecta musicologica* XXVI (1973), pp. 495–502.

16. See Appendix, nos 21 and 22.

17. Namely, the *Concordia Pharmacopolarum Barcinonensium* (1587), the *Constitutiones y altres drets de Cathalunya* (1588; 1589), and Andrea Capella's *Commentaria in Ieremiam* (1586).

18. For which, see pp. 15–17.

19. Appendix, nos 23–6.

20. Taberniel's production of music books is discussed in detail in I. Fenlon, 'Artus Taberniel: Music Printing and the Book Trade in Renaissance Salamanca', in Fenlon and Knighton (eds.), *Early Music Printing*, pp. 117–46, with a provisional listing of the books that Taberniel printed on pp. 143–4 (Appendix I).

21. For Esquivel Barahona see A. Geiger, 'Juan Esquivel: ein unbekannter spanischer Meister des 16. Jahrhunderts', in F. Zierfuss (ed.); *Festschrift zum 50. Geburtstag Adolf Sandberger* (Munich, 1918), pp. 138–69; R. J. Snow, *The 1613 Print of Juan Esquivel Barahona* (Detroit, 1978), pp. 10–17, describing the unique copy in Ronda, and R. Stevenson, 'Spanish Polyphonists in the Age of the Armada', *Inter-American Music Review* XII (1992), pp. 17–114, at pp. 103–12.

22. There is an extensive literature on Spanish sources of polyphony in the New World; for the most recent contribution, which makes reference to the most important ones, see María Gembero Ustárroz, 'Circulacíon de libros de música entre España y America (1492–1650): notas para su estudio', in Fenlon and Knighton (eds.), *Early Music Printing and Publishing*, pp. 147–79.

23. For Craesbeeck see J. J. Alves Dias, *Uma dinastia de impressores em Portugal* (Lisbon, 1996), and H. Bernstein, *Pedro Craesbeeck & Sons: 17ᵗʰ-Century Publishers to Portugal and Brazil* (Amsterdam, 1987).

24. *Index librorum prohibitorum* (1597); L. de Camoes, *Rimas* (1598); J. de Lucena, *Historia da vida do padre Francisco de Xauier* (1600); *Relacao das exequias d'el rey dom Filippe, com algus sermoes* (1600).

25. For the repertory of books printed in Salamanca in the sixteenth century see F. J. Norton, *A Descriptive Catalogue of Printing in Spain and Portugal 1501–1520* (Cambridge, 1978), pp. 165–219, and L. Ruiz Fidalgo, *La imprenta en Salamanca (1501–1600)*, 2 vols. (Madrid, 1996).

26. See Griffin, 'Itinerant Booksellers', p. 43.

27. R. L. Kagan, 'Universities in Castile 1500–1810', in L. Stone (ed.), *The University in Society*, 2 vols. (Princeton, 1974), pp. 355–405, especially pp. 356–9, Graph 1, and Table 4.

28. For the general phenomenon see the introduction to P. Clark (ed.), *The European Crisis of the 1590s. Essays in Comparative History* (London, 1985).

29. P. Sánchez León, 'Town and Country in Castile, 1400–1650', in S. R. Epstein (ed.), *Town and Country in Europe* (Cambridge, 2001), pp. 272–91, at pp. 281–3.

30. For the phenomenon see the introduction to P. Clark (ed.), *Small Towns in Early Modern Europe* (Cambridge, 1995).

31. For one recorded example see G. Antolín, 'La librería de Felipe II', *Boletín de la Real Academia de la Historia* 90 (1927), p. 341, recording purchases made for Philip's library in both these places by Calvet de Estrella in 1545.

32. The catalogue is in Salamanca, University Library, MS 565.

33. Kagan, 'Universities in Castile', pp. 374–6; 387–8.

34. See Fenlon, 'Artus Taberniel', Appendix II.

35. Plantin did not have, as is sometimes stated, a monopoly from Philip II for the supply of Tridentine service books; see V. B. Botas, *Arias Montano y Plantino: el libro flamenco en la España de Felipe II* (León, 1999), pp. 98–112.

36. For a general account of his career see L. Voet, *The Golden Compasses: A History and Evaluation of the Printing and Publishing Activities of the Officina Plantiniana at Antwerp*, 2 vols. (Amsterdam, 1969).

37. J. A. Stellfeld, *Bibliographie des éditions musicales plantiniennes* (Brussels, 1949), pp. 12–16; S. E. Bain, *Music Printing in the Low Countries in the Sixteenth Century* (Ph.D., University of Cambridge, 1973), p. 128. See also the same author's article 'Plantin, Christoffel' in S. Sadie (ed.), *The New Grove Dictionary of Music and Musicians*, 29 vols (London, 2001), 19, pp. 894–6.

38. For the figures see Stellfeld, *Bibliographie des éditions plantiniennes*, pp. 32–41; L. J. Wagner, 'Some Considerations on Plantin's Printing of De La Hèle's *Octo Missae*', *Die Gulden Passer* 64 (1986), pp. 49–59, at pp. 56–7.

39. Stellfeld, *Bibliographie des editions musicales plantiniennes*, frequently records the dispatch of bales of books to his Spanish agent Jan Poelman, for whom see below. See, *inter alia*, p. 50 ('En une balle envoyée à Pulmanno'); p. 69 ('Inventario de los libros qui quedan en Sal.[amanca]. En la tienda de Juan Pulman inventoriado en Junio 1586'). All the music books from the library of the Jesuit College in Salamanca are named somewhere in these extracts; see, for example (p. 66), 'Fact.[ure] de 8 balles envoyées à Jan Pulman 2 Cantiones Severini Corneti 4o'.

40. C. Griffin, 'Heretical Printing-Workers in Sixteenth-Century Spain', in P. A. Escapa (ed.), *El libro antiguo español VI. De libros, librerías, imprentas y lectores* (Salamanca, 2002), pp. 135–52, at p. 140.

41. Hereafter Taberniel, the form in which his surname appears on all his publications.

42. V. B. Botas, *Avance para una guía del mundo del libro salmantino del siglo XVI* (Zamora, 2002), p. 130, and J. Delgado Casado, *Diccionario de impresores españoles, siglos XV–XVII*, 2 vols (Madrid, 1996), II, 'T', for what little is known of his biography.

43. Robben, *Jan Poelman*, pp. 40–50.

44. See A. W. Pollard, and G. R. Redgrave, *A Short-Title Catalogue of Books Printed in England, Scotland, & Ireland and of English Books Printed Abroad 1475–1640*, 2nd rev. edn, 3 vols (London, 1976–91), p. 187, no. 21595; A. F. Allison and D. M. Rogers, *A Catalogue of Catholic Books in English Printed Abroad or Secretly in England 1558–1640* (London, 1968), p. 187, no. 298; A. F. Allison and D. M. Rogers, *The Contemporary Printed Literature of the English Counter Reformation between 1558 and 1640*, 2 vols (Aldershot, 1994), pp. 137–8, no. 690.5.

45. A provisional list of Taberniel's output is given in Fenlon, 'Artus Taberniel', Appendix I.

46. See F. Vindel, *Escudos y marcas de impresores y libreros en España durante los siglos XV a XIX (1485–1850)* (Barcelona, 1942), p. 323.

47. S. Vivanco, *Liber magnificarum* (Salamanca, 1607). Only five copies are known to have survived.

48. For the details see A. Geiger, 'Juan Esquivel', (n. 21 above); 'Esquivel, Juan Barahona, Juan (de)' in *The New Grove Dictionary*, 8, pp. 325–6.

49. J. Esquivel Barahona, *Missarum...liber primus* (Salamanca, 1608). Only one copy is known.

50. F. Blume (ed.), *Die Musik in Geschichte und Gegenwart*, 17 vols (Kassel and Basel, 1949–86), 3, cols. 1538–42 (Anglés), at cols. 1539–40. This copy, whose present whereabout is unknown, appears as item 807 in Rosenthal's catalogue.

51. J. Esquivel Barahona, *Motecta festorum* (Salamanca, 1608), of which two copies are recorded.

52. J. Esquivel Barahona, *Liber secundus psalmorum, hymnorum, magnificarum* (Salamanca, Francisco de Cea, 1613). The only known extant copy is in the church of Santa María la Mayor in Ronda; see R. J. Snow, *The 1613 Print of Juan Esquivel Barahona*.

53. Namely D. Jubero, *Post Pentecosten*, and A. de Salazar, *Fiestas que hizo el insigne Collegio de la Compañía de Iesus*.

54. Wagner, 'Some Considerations on Plantin's Printing', pp. 58–9.

55. Pastrana, Museo parroquial, no shelfmark. This copy, whose binding is decorated with the coat-of-arms of the Duke of Pastrana, is unrecorded in the secondary literature.

56. Information about the size of the edition comes from the contract of 20 August 1516 between the bookseller Ottaviano Scotto and Antico; see C. W. Chapman, *Andrea Antico* (Ph.D., Harvard University, 1964), App. III, no. 5a.

57. For a detailed account of the influence of Antico's choirbook on Dorico's mass volumes (the first of which was devoted to the music of Morales) see S. G. Cusick, *Valerio Dorico: Music Printer in Sixteenth-Century Rome* (Ann Arbor, 1981), pp. 66–73. The connections extend beyond the design of the titlepages to Dorico's direct copying of Antico's initial letters; see also I. Fenlon, *Music, Print and Culture in Early Sixteenth-Century Italy* (London, 1994), pp. 54–9.

58. S. Nalle, 'Literacy and Culture in Early Modern Castile', *Past and Present* 125 (1989), pp. 65–95; T. J. Dadson, 'Literacy and Education in Early Rural Spain:The Case of Villarrubia de los Ojos', in N. Griffin, C. Griffin, and E. Southworth (eds.), *The Iberian Book Trade and its Readers: Essays for Ian Michael, Bulletin of Spanish Studies* 81 (2004), pp. 1011–37.

59. C. Griffin, *Journeymen-Printers, Heresy, and the Inquisition in Sixteenth-Century Spain* (Oxford, 2005), pp. 78–9, 160–1.

60. For some inventories from the second half of the sixteenth century and the first decades of the seventeenth, see in particular T. J. Dadson, 'Private Libraries in the Spanish Golden Age: Sources, Formation and Function', *Journal of the Institute of Romance Studies* 4 (1996), pp. 51–91; T. J. Dadson, *Libros, lectores y lecturas: Estudios sobre bibliotecas particulares españolas del Siglo de Oro* (Madrid, 1998). For the stocklist of one bookseller see V. Becares and A. L. Iglesias, *La librería de Benito Boyer Medina del Campo, 1592* (Salamanca, 1992). Music books are treated as a category in E. Ros-Fabregas, 'Libros de música en bibliotecas españolas del siglo XVI', *Pliegos de bibliofilia* 15 (2001), pp. 37–62, 16 (2001), pp. 33–46, and 17 (2002), pp. 17–54. See also T. J. Dadson, 'Music Books and Instruments in Spanish Golden-Age Inventories. The Case of Don Juan de Borja (1607)', in Fenlon and Knighton (eds.), *Early Music Printing*, pp. 95–116, and, for the music books of a single major ecclesiastical establishment, M. Noone, 'Printed Polyphony Acquired by Toledo Cathedral, 1532–1669', in Fenlon and Knighton (eds.), *Early Music Printing*, pp. 242–72.

# *Appendix*

## Short-Title Catalogue of Polyphony
## Printed in Spain and Portugal, 1535–1628

1.  Luis Milán, *Libro de musica de vihuela de mano. Intitulado El maestro* (Valencia, Francisco Díaz Romano, 1535/1536)

2.  Luis Narváez, *Los seys libros del Delphin de musica de cifras para tañer Vihuela* (Valladolid, Diego Fernández de Córdoba, 1538)

3.  Gonzalo de Baena, *Arte nouamente inuentada pera tañer* (Lisbon, Germão Galharde, 1540)

4.  Alonso Mudarra, *Tres libros de musica en cifras para vihuela* (Seville, Juan de León, 1546)

5.  Enríquez de Valderrábano, *Libro de musica de vihuela, intitulado silva de sirenas* (Valladolid, Francisco Fernández de Córdoba, 1547)

6.  Juan Bermudo, *Comiença el libro primero de la declaracion de* instrumentos (Osuna, Juan de León, 1549)

7.  Juan Bermudo, *Comiença el arte Tripharia* (Osuna, Juan de León, 1550)

8.  Diego Pisador, *Libro de musica de vihuela* (Salamanca, Guillermo de Millis, 1552)

9.  Miguel de Fuenllana, *Libro de musica para vihuela, intitulado Orphenica lyra* (Seville, Martín de Montesdoca, 1554) (two editions)

10. Juan Bermudo, *Comiença el libro llamado declaracion de instrumentos musicales* (Osuna, Juan de León, 1555)

11. Francisco Guerrero, *Sacrae cantiones, vulgo moteta nuncupata* (Seville, Martín de Montesdoca, 1555)

12. Juan Vásquez, *Villancicos i canciones* (Osuna, Juan de León, 1555)

13. Juan Vásquez, *Agenda defunctorum* (Seville, Martín de Montesdoca, 1556)

14. Luis Venegas de Henestrosa, *Libro de cifra nueva para tecla, harpa y vihuela* (Alcalá de Henares, Juan Brocar, 1557)

15. Pere Alberch i Ferramunt alias Vila, *Odarum spiritualium ... liber secundus* (Barcelona, Jacobo Cortey, 1560)

16. Juan Vásquez, *Recopilacion de sonetos y villancicos* (Seville, Juan Gutierrez de Genova, 1560)

17. Pere Alberch i Ferramunt alias Vila, *Odarum* (*quas vulgo madrigales appellamus*) ... *liber primus* (Barcelona, Jacobo Cortey, 1561)

18. Tomás de Santa María, *Libro llamado Arte de tañer fantasia* (Valladolid, Francisco Fernández de Córdoba, 1565)

19. Esteban Daza, *Libro de musica en cifras para vihuela, intitulado el Parnasso* (Valladolid, Diego Fernández de Córdoba, 1576)

20. Antonio de Cabezón, *Obras de musica para tecla arpa y vihuela* (Madrid, Francisco Sánchez, 1578)

21. Nicasio Zorita, *Liber primus ... motectorum* (Barcelona, Hubert Gotard, 1584)

22. Joan Brudieu, *De los madrigales* (Barcelona, Hubert Gotard, 1585)

23. Philippe Rogier, *Missae sex* (Madrid, Juan de Flandres, 1598)

24. Tomás Luis de Victoria, *Missae, magnificat, motecta, psalmi & alia quam plurima* (Madrid, Ex typographia regia [Juan de Flandres], 1600)

25. Alfonso Lobo, *Liber primus missarum* (Madrid, Ex typographia regia [Juan de Flandres], 1602)

26. Tomás Luis de Victoria, *Officium defunctorum: in obitu et obsequiis sacrae imperatricis* (Madrid, Ex typographia regia [Juan de Flandres], 1605)

27. Sebastián de Vivanco, *Liber magnificarum* (Salamanca, Artus Taberniel, 1607)

28. Juan Esquivel Barahona, *Missarum liber primus* (Salamanca, Artus Taberniel, 1608)

29. Sebastián de Vivanco, [*Libro de Misas*] (Salamanca, Artus Taberniel, 1608)

30. Juan Esquivel Barahona, *Motecta festorum et domenicarum* (Salamanca, Artus Taberniel, 1608)

31. Francisco Garro, *Missae quatuor defunctorum lectiones* (Lisbon, Petrus Craesbeck, 1609)

32. Francisco Garro, *Opera aliquot* (Lisbon, Petrus Craesbeeck, 1609)

33. Sebastián de Vivanco, [*Liber motectorum*] (Salamanca, Artus Taberniel, [1610])

34. Juan Esquivel Barahona, *Liber secundus psalmorum, hymnorum, Magnificarum* (Salamanca, Francisco de Cea Tesa, 1613)

35. Manuel Cardoso, *Cantica beatae Mariae virginis* (Lisbon, Petrus Craesbeeck, 1613)

36. Miguel Navarro, *Liber Magnificarum* (Pamplona, Carolus Labayen, 1614)

37. Filipe de Magalhaes, *Cantus ecclesiasticus commendandi animas corporaque* (Lisbon, Petrus Craesbeeck, 1614)

38. Sebastián Aguilera de Heredia, *Canticum beatissimae Virginis deiparae Mariae* (Zaragoza: Petrus Cabarte, 1618)

39. Manuel Rodrigues Coelho, *Flores de musica pera o instrumento de tecla & harpa* (Lisbon, Petrus Craesbeeck, 1620)

40. Stefano Limido, *Armonia espiritual* (Madrid, Tomás Junta, 1623)

41. Manuel Cardoso, *Missae … Liber primus* (Lisbon, Petrus Craesbeeck, 1625)

42. Francisco Correa de Arauxo, *Libro de tientos y discursos de música práctica, y theórica de órgano intitulado Facultad Orgánica* (Alcalá de Henares, Antonio Arnao, 1626)

43. Juan Carles Amat, *Guitarra española de cinco ordenes* (Leida, Viuda Anglada & Andrés Lorenço, 1627)

44. Sebastián López de Velasco, *Libro de missas, motetes, salmos Magnificats, y otras cosas tocantes al culto divino* (Madrid, Ex typographia regia, 1628)


## LOST BOOKS

45. Pere Alberch i Ferramunt alias Vila, [*Tentos de organo*] (s.l., s.d.)

46. Juan Carles Amat, *Guitarra espanola, y vandola en dos maneras de guitarra* (Barcelona, 1586)

47. Diego de Brucenas, [*Libro de misas y vísperas*] (Salamanca, Susana Muñoz, 1620)

48. Sebastián Aguilera de Heredia, [*Liber missarum*] (s.l., 1622)

49. Juan Esquivel Barahona, [*Libro … de canciones para ministriles y favordone himnos y motetes*] (Salamanca, 1623)

# Turning a New Leaf: William Byrd, the East Music-Publishing Firm and the Jacobean Succession

JEREMY L. SMITH

IN THE MUSIC BOOK TRADE there are three sets that stand out for the ambitious scope of their content. One of them — Heinrich Isaac's *Choralis Constantinus* (1550–5) — was judged to represent 'one of the most grandiose tasks ever attempted by a composer'.[1] One would have to look back over three centuries to Leonin and Perotin and their *Magnus Liber* of Notre Dame to find anything like it in the past; and in searching forward, only William Byrd of the English Chapel Royal, with his two compendious books of published *Gradualia* of 1605 and 1607, seems ever to have actually matched Isaac's achievement. All of these constitute nearly single-handed attempts to provide polyphonic settings for a whole year of celebrations of the mass and, without exception, they are recognized to this day to contain compositions of the highest aesthetic order, while the composers involved have been duly ranked among the finest of their respective times. Only Byrd's nearly unsurpassed compositional project seems not to have received its due. It would be as if Richard Wagner were recognized only as a great composer of opera overtures and arias, but not as the composer of the *Ring* cycle as a whole. Some scholars have even suggested that Byrd himself wished to keep this achievement in the shadows. One, for example, has claimed that Byrd worked 'anonymously' in order to 'avoid direct association with [his own] books'.[2] A quick glance at the titlepages, where Byrd's name appears prominently, however, reveals this is hardly a tenable assertion (Fig. 1).[3] Although one looks far for another such ill-founded opinion, it is fair to say that it reflects basic problems that face the student of English music publishing. This paper will address some of the current confusion through a look at the contentious underlying politics, noting in particular the role played by the Citizen and Stationer Thomas East, who had printed Byrd's set and who seems to have been drawn rather deeply into the fray.

As far as the *Gradualia* confusion is concerned, one might try to point the finger of blame at Byrd, pleading — as many have done — that he had adopted such a complex system for putting pieces of the set together that he had obscured from view the full scope of his accomplishment.[4] But in a prefatory address to a group of 'true devotees of music', Byrd explained just how 'easily' works could 'be found and grouped together' to provide music for 'the whole year' of Sundays and for many of the chief feasts as well.[5] No, the problem more likely had to do with the audience that Byrd was speaking to. For if he really meant to address a well-disposed group of true music lovers among his contemporaries, many of them might have wondered why he should have gone to so much trouble as to put together a whole series of Catholic masses and offices when they lived in a Protestant state. Perhaps we might surmise that centuries of scholarly neglect could be traced to a similar impatience with Byrd's peculiar assumption that his volume had some legitimate purpose, when quite apparently it did not. Ultimately, this seems to have undercut the achievement.[6] We can all agree that Isaac's effort was 'grandiose' and no doubt was intended to make that impression, but in the words of Walther Lipphardt, 'when the Catholic William Byrd published a Latin Gradual comprising the whole liturgy of the principal and Marian Feasts of the Church year, it was not to make a grand public appearance'.[7]

In the same preface where Byrd described the scope of his work he also exclaimed: 'public indeed and clearly worthy are those things, which are communicated not only by these Songs of mine, such as they are, but also by the voices and pens of all men, as much to our descendants as to foreign nations'.[8] Under the standard cloak of prefatory self-deprecation, Byrd thus stated something precisely at odds with Lipphardt's contention that there was no public aspect involved here. Then, after moving through more false humility — expressing facetiously the hope that he had not produced something altogether 'valueless' — Byrd also conveyed his rather grand purpose for the whole musical endeavour, namely to represent his king, James I, whose 'honour' he 'wished to increase'.[9] Even if this was a preface, at the very least we must conclude, *pace* Lipphardt, that Byrd was trying to make a 'grand public appearance' and we ought to take that purpose seriously. But this brings us, finally, to yet another point of current confusion about this whole project, one having to do with Byrd's message to James.

In the preface to the first volume Byrd communicated all the respect and subservience one would expect from a dutiful subject addressing a king. The composer indirectly but graciously thanked James for increasing the wages for the Chapel Royal musicians and he exuded a healthy optimism about England's future, along with a sense of his confidence in its leader.[10] In the body of the work itself, however, Byrd went off in a rather different direction. Although most of the contents were pre-determined by the liturgy, there were a few non-liturgical items in the book and these, according to the late Philip Brett, contained highlighted

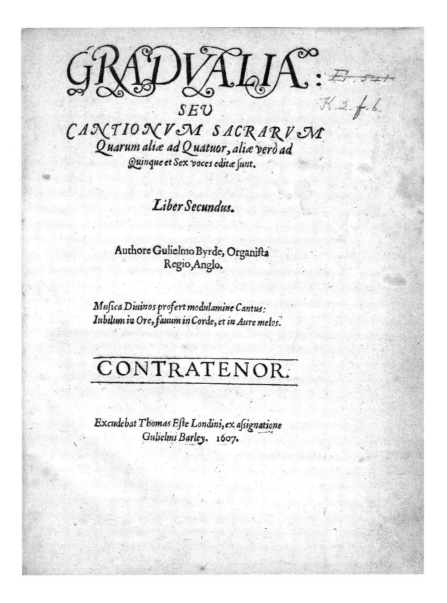

*Fig. 1.* Titlepage of Byrd's *Gradualia* (London, Thomas East, 1607
(British Library, K.2.f.6)

messages of a political nature. In one of them, *Plorans plorabit*, the City is in ruins and the Lord's flock has been taken captive thanks to a disobedient ruler. At this point Jeremiah tearfully sets out to fulfil his task as God's messenger and 'tell the King and Queen, "be humbled, sit down, for the crown of your glory has fallen from your head"' (Jeremiah 13:17–18).

Brett claimed this freely chosen text was 'surely directed towards a Stuart king and his wife' and Richard Turbet characterized the gesture itself as 'fairly spitting … contempt at [them]'.[11] However much this would seem obviously to contradict the flattering message of the preface, the work is so forward-looking in its musical style that it is wholly reasonable to assume that Byrd wrote it, as with the preface, with publication in mind. Thus it may be just as difficult to disassociate Byrd the message-bearing prophet from the self-described 'author' who speaks about 'this epistle of mine' in the preface.[12] As Renaissance literary historians would quickly point out, both of these authorial positions were inevitably socially constructed. Byrd's personal life experiences, as a persecuted but occasionally relieved and tolerated recusant Catholic, give credence to the idea that he might present himself as a messenger with a solemn warning for his king and queen.[13] Further evidence for this supposition stems from a tradition in music publishing that Byrd himself did much to establish. Byrd, as I will argue, had fashioned himself through his publications into something of a royal counsellor. In doing so he took a position similar to that of Edmund Spenser and other poets who had been promulgating their art through the medium of print in the interests of high politics.[14] But by maintaining his Catholic voice, Byrd also put himself and others at risk, and perhaps none more so than the Stationer Thomas East, who by 1605 had been long associated with Byrd as an assigned printer and sometime publisher of his music.

Significantly, it was not a composer but another Stationer, Thomas Vautrollier, who set the political tone for the English enterprise in music publishing. In 1570 Vautrollier printed and published the first work of a recognized international composer to have been produced in London, a mixed collection of the works of Orlando di Lasso.[15] Just to copy the French edition would have constituted something of a breakthrough effort, but Vautrollier had not simply reproduced the material. He had also edited the poems Lasso set to music, taking the liberty, as he explained, of blocking out their 'impurities'.[16] Because he set a trend for appropriating and 'purifying' the texts, Vautrollier's work has been seen as 'the first systematic attempt by a Protestant printer to assimilate … [the Catholic composer's music] … to the ideals of Huguenot musical devotion'.[17] Joseph Kerman, however, revealed that Vautrollier did as much to skirt as to emphasize sectarian divisions.[18] In this light it is significant that Vautrollier did not choose a Protestant grandee as the book's dedicatee, but picked instead his English patron Henry Fitzalan, the Roman Catholic twelfth earl of Arundel.

Although a firm Catholic, in musical circles Arundel is mostly remembered now for maintaining a well-stocked music library at None-such Castle as he quietly lived out his life, keeping his religion to himself.[19] But in the late 1560s and early 1570s Arundel was quite busy with a plan to unite the Catholic Mary Queen of Scots in marriage to his widower son-in-law, Thomas Howard, the fourth duke of Norfolk.[20] Mary was standing trial in England for the capital crime of adultery and regicide. She was also next in line for the English crown. Her marriage to Arundel's son-in-law, England's highest peer, would only shore up a Catholic base of power, as the other side was well aware. But because Norfolk was a nominal Protestant, the plan had at least the patina of religious compromise that might have appealed to Elizabeth as well as to the country at large. Had it succeeded, we might have better appreciated all along how well Vautrollier had met the political demands of his patron.[21]

Following Plato's view of music and social order, Vautrollier cast Lasso's music as 'political harmony' in a preface that went to some lengths to extol a brand of harmonious moderation in governmental policy.[22] As any royal counsellor would instinctively know to do, Vautrollier allowed himself ample space for royal flattery. Thus it was already in 'this Christian and flourishing realm (under the dominion of a wise and virtuous queen)' where 'the variety of estates [were] joined in a union admired by all neighboring realms'.[23] Parenthesis aside, this was of course a rather clear reference to Elizabeth and her accomplishments. But perhaps Vautrollier was purposely ambiguous when he discussed the 'admirable beauty of the harmony with which wisely administered republics temper the unified diversity of their various parts'.[24] Did this refer to Lasso's 'beaut[iful] … harmony', Elizabeth's 'wisely administered republic' or Arundel's plan to 'unif[y religious] diversity' with the Norfolk match? If it might have occurred to Elizabeth that it could have been all three, then Vautrollier had surely done as much as he could to make his patron's point to the English queen in this preface to a musical edition.

Given the moderate tone and the Elizabethan flattery, an innocent reader might be forgiven for failing to note that this edition would also have appealed greatly to Mary. Lasso was closely connected to her family and many of the poems the composer set in the collection were those of Pierre de Ronsard, who was still functioning as Mary's greatest and firmest champion in letters.[25] If it ever came into her hands, Mary would probably have taken comfort in the collection and if Arundel hoped it might have been seen as a gesture of his loyalty, it would likely have been construed as considerate of her interests. We can only guess what Vautrollier knew about Mary. He seems in any case to have set the pattern whereby a preface and body of work in a musical edition seem to run at cross-purposes. With Arundel's activities in mind, it seems possible to read into it an appeal for moderation from the Catholic minority, asking the Queen to take 'her middle way' in the matter of religious tolerance.

The same political reading could be applied to the next book of music that Vautrollier printed, the *Cantiones quae ab argumento sacrae vocantur* of 1575 by Byrd and Thomas Tallis. Here the preface did more than simply elaborate on a Platonic theory linking music to politics and statecraft. A whole cadre of 'Philosophers, Mathematicians and Statesmen' were figuratively 'summoned' to provide 'arguments and proofs [that] would wring from even the most hostile enemies of music an admission that music is indispensable to the state'.[26] It introduced 'political harmony', if anything, and English harmony at that. Thus the idea Vautrollier had promulgated that there would be international admiration for English music, along with its government, was understandably emphasized significantly more than before. As before, though, the preface suggested throughout a dutiful respect for England's ruler and a determined aloofness from religious positioning. Yet again, however, it was in the body of the work that another viewpoint was voiced.

Some of the works of the *Cantiones* did speak to the 'unity in diversity' that Vautrollier had also celebrated, such as the charmingly choreographed *Diliges Dominum* by Byrd. In this work the composer had contrived things so that the music was running forwards and backwards simultaneously on the page. In performance the singers soon realize they must face one another and share a book as they sing the 'golden rule', to 'love thy neighbor as thyself' (Fig. 2). If this neighbourly musical gesture was viewed as an apt analogy for idealized ecumenical relations, it would fit in neatly with the moderate message of the preface.[27] Yet other works evoked the greatest tensions of the confessional divide to the point where, in Byrd's *Emendemus in melius*, the idea of death and an uncertain afterlife was placed almost mockingly before those who had strayed from the true religion.[28]

The emphasis on music as a political force, the obsequious preface and the potentially disturbing contents are traits of the *Cantiones* that link this work to its predecessor. In this case, however, Byrd and Tallis published the set rather than Vautrollier. The composers assembled an extensive preface that reflected their interests and had even dedicated their volume to Elizabeth, from whom they had just received a patent of monopoly over

Fig. 2. Byrd, *Diliges Dominum*, in Byrd and Tallis, *Cantiones ... sacrae*
(London, Thomas Vautrollier, 1575), fols. F2v–F3r (British Library, K.3.f.9)

printed music, printed music paper and music importation. The whole endeavour might seem to reflect their interest in celebrating the patent, which they printed in the volume.[29] In any case, they were right to perceive it as a distinct honour. Elizabeth's personally selected patentees were meant ostensibly to serve her, but all knew it was a reciprocal arrangement. As James I would later put it, 'for as no sovereign can be without service, nor service without some reward'.[30]

Tallis and Byrd used the patent as an instrument through which they might achieve what — according to the historian Simon Adams — 'mattered supremely to everybody: influence over the Queen, and, through that influence, control'.[31] In political terms, the composers gained the means to control the message they might send out regarding the Catholic faith. They also enjoyed a powerful control over their craft, with the royal backing to act as gatekeepers, directing the nation's musical output. And, finally, of course, there was the economic control, or what James described as the 'revenue' that was wholly fitting 'to reward the merits of our servants'.[32] Since revenue from printed books of music would only come to the composers through the Company-run book trade, this is where East enters into the story. But before he does it is important to note that whereas Vautrollier's actions can best be explained with an eye to the politics of his patron Arundel, from 1575 onwards musical composers, as royal patentees, took on something of this patronage role themselves. It was not until 1587, however, that *anyone* sought to print music again under the privilege — as the *Cantiones* was so unmarketable.[33] By this time Tallis had died and Byrd was left as the sole patentee.

In their policy of inaction, Tallis and Byrd were the exception to the rule. Other royal monopolists in the book trade were busy at the time producing edition after edition of profitable works that were out of reach to those without patents.[34] At some point during this period, East had set his sights on the *Whole Booke of Psalmes*, one of the era's protected bestsellers which also happened to be a music book. To use Byrd's monopoly to gain access to this market might have been easy to conceive in theory. It presented some rather formidable obstacles in practice. The *Whole Booke* featured metrical psalm texts with simple music and was directed at a vast Protestant audience. Given Byrd's musical and political inclinations it seems improbable that the composer would have been immediately open to an arrangement that would help East's endeavour. It is noteworthy that he even approached the composer, as his fellow Stationers had openly condemned Byrd's monopoly from an economic standpoint, casting it as the most trivial of all the patents affecting their trade.[35] It is thus to their credit that the printer and composer found a way to work this seemingly untenable situation to their mutual advantage.

At the heart of the relationship was a simple equation: East needed Byrd's protection as much as Byrd needed a press. It was probably at the point of realizing this that they found a way to strike a religious compromise. On the one hand, Byrd demonstrated he would not only allow East to use his patent on the titlepages of music editions that were not to his taste, he would also even bend to the point of composing works on texts favoured by the Protestants, albeit elaborate ones, in order to help serve as East's effective protector.[36] On the other side, East offered Byrd the rare opportunity to have at his full disposal a Company-authorized press for the sake of serving a select market for an elaborate brand of music with a rather dangerous political agenda.

Over the next four years, while East slowly and effectively moved into the *Whole Booke* market, Byrd used East's firm to promulgate a whole series of highly controversial works of a Catholic nature. These ranged in tone from the general cry for freedom to the rather specific and searing tribute in music to such dangerous foes of the state as the Jesuit missionary Edmund Campion and Mary Queen of Scots, both of whom were being

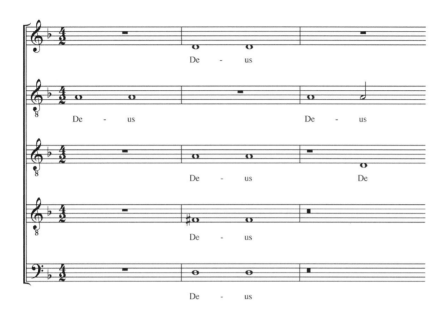

*Fig. 3.* Byrd, *Deus venerunt*, mm. 1–3

viewed as martyrs for their faith after their execution on the orders of Elizabeth's ministers.[37] These were very sensitive issues to portray in sound. The government had discovered and destroyed a secret Catholic press and punished severely the 'spreader' involved in the publishing of 'Why do I use my paper ink and pen', a poem on Campion's death.[38] It was the same poem that Byrd set before East to print again, if only in part.

Equally disturbing for East, a group of musicians had been arrested and imprisoned in the Fleet for the peculiar crime, it seems, of singing dirges to Campion.[39] This occurred on 24 September 1586, just one year before Byrd gave East the printing copy of a series of musical memorials of the same figure. Since the singers served a political activist who was one of Byrd's Catholic patrons (Lord Thomas Paget), it is almost certain that what they had sung were the actual pieces that East would soon set in type. The most evocative of these was *Deus venerunt*, which East had probably never seen laid out in score (Fig. 3). If he had, the printer would probably have thought twice about putting this musical rendition of a cross through his presses, as the image of martyrdom here was all too obvious and pro-vocative.

Works that were dangerous to sing would surely also be rather risky to print or compose. But perhaps the royal monopoly offered some protection to all the parties involved, as the interrogation of the singers suggests. Pressed about these dirges for Campion, one prisoner confessed that he had sung some 'songes of Mr Byrdes and mr Tallys [but, as he claimed] no other unlawfull songes'.[40] This seems to be a clear reference to the 1575 set and also seems to indicate that the pieces therein were countenanced, at least in the eyes of the singer, because of their published status. East was probably further protected by Byrd's careful tactics. Published along with his Catholic-inspired works were the exquisite funeral songs Byrd composed for Sir Philip Sidney, a popular poet and soldier who had died for the Protestant cause. Even here, however, those who studied the set carefully might note that Byrd, through East, had made a provocative gesture, placing his tribute to Sidney precisely alongside his equally moving — if less obviously advertised — homage to Campion (Fig. 4).

In 1592, when Byrd had apparently exhausted his stock of 'political motets' and songs that he wished to send through the press, East finally realized a goal he seemed to have had in mind from the time he began working with the composer. In that year, under the auspices of Byrd's monopoly, East printed and published his own version of the otherwise restricted *Whole Booke of Psalmes*. In his preface East chose to present himself as someone who worked altruistically for the 'publique benefit', but it was a marketing coup all the same.[41] Thanks to Byrd's patent, which was advertised on the titlepage, East had successfully overtaken his competitors by defeating the effect of their monopolistic privilege. It seems to have stretched the Byrd/East compromise nearly to its limit. To reach a wide audience, East cast his book as simple material for the Puritan 'godly' and made it quite clear that the kind of musical 'curiousity' Byrd specialized in was to be 'shunned'.[42] Not surprisingly, no music by Byrd appears in this set. If East had even bothered to ask him for any, which seems unlikely, the composer would surely have responded that his scruples would not permit it.

Yet within a year of printing his triumphal *Whole Booke*, East produced Byrd's settings of mass ordinaries for the benefit of another market altogether. At this time Byrd had moved away from London to a Catholic enclave in Essex where he probably hoped to disseminate the masses among his new co-religionist neighbours for their private devotions. And now it was East who demurred. We can see from the extant copies of these masses that East must have produced them, owing to some tell-tale music type and initials.[43] But East provided no titlepages and thus no obvious evidence that he had actually printed these works. Incidentally, Byrd's covert use of East's press at this time has caused much of the confusion surrounding his

*Fig. 4.* Byrd, *Psalmes, Sonets and songs* (London, Thomas East, 1588), fols. F4v–G1r
(British Library, K.2.f.1)

publishing strategies, for although some have thought that these works
were traded openly, the omission of East's imprint suggests they may not
have been intended for legitimate sale.[44] Byrd's move to Essex marked the
end of the composer's mainstream publishing efforts, and, in any case, his
monopoly expired soon thereafter. It was at this juncture that East
discovered that in order to stay in the music trade, he would have to
contend with Byrd's successor as royal monopolist, the great madrigalist
Thomas Morley.

If similarly drawn to matters of state, Morley was in many ways a different kind of politician from his predecessor. On the economic front,
Morley competed with East as much as he worked with him, exacerbating
some of the internal Stationers' Company issues and pushing East out on
his own in the music trade.[45] On the larger political front, along with
religious matters, Morley, like many others, was rather swept up in the
factional struggle at Court concerning the era's two most powerful court-
iers, Robert Cecil and Robert Devereux, the second Earl of Essex.[46] Both of
these leaders were Protestant, but each was wise enough not to exclude
Catholics from their faction. For a while, Morley's dedications suggest he

was trying to work both sides of the fence. By the turn of the seventeenth century, however, he, along with many other English Catholic activists, was drawn deeply into the wave of popular support for Essex, later executed as a traitor.

In an effort to secure his place as the nation's primary counsellor after the Scottish King James succeeded to the English throne, Essex mounted a *coup d'état* against the reigning queen.[47] It was poorly carried out and was effectively stopped by the City pikemen. But many were caught up in this ill-fated plan as it developed. East's residence, for example, became a site of governmental interest when spies caught some Catholic activists who were residing there, reading aloud a letter about the succession. The activists were subsequently imprisoned and tortured. The letter in question was a statement of support for James by a prominent Jesuit who was known as the author of an illegal book on the succession which was dedicated to Essex.[48] At the time East was also probably working on a new edition of Byrd's masses and Morley's collection entitled *Triumphes of Oriana*. The *Triumphes* has traditionally been seen as a paean of praise to Elizabeth. A closer look suggests it was originally intended to promote Essex's *coup* by celebrating, if prematurely, the triumphal arrival in London of his champion James with his consort Anne of Denmark. That Anne had converted to Catholicism at this time was probably why the musicians had become involved in the project.[49] Her new religious affiliation might also explain why she was celebrated more conspicuously than Essex or James in the set (as *Ori*ANNA).

The Catholics at East's house were surely of more pressing interest to the government than the much more veiled threat represented by whatever musical tributes East was preparing at the press. Nonetheless, after the Essex *coup* failed, the evidence suggests that East decided (or it was decided for him) that he should cover his tracks as best he could on all counts. Thus, in a reprinted edition of the *Triumphes*, East altered one of the madrigal poems in order to suggest that Elizabeth had been the subject all along. More obviously, with his adopted son Thomas Snodham, East printed and sold some books on topical political matters, such as: an attack on the book of succession which had been attributed to the Jesuit whose letter was read at East's premises; a book that exposed an earlier Catholic plot against James which had been organized in Scotland, in part by the person to whom the Jesuit had addressed his letter; a pamphlet that supported James's views on tobacco; and, perhaps most pointedly, an elaborate description of James's visit to Cecil's residence at Theobalds at the time of his coronation (Fig. 5).[50] In political terms, this was a complete

# KING IAMES
## his entertainment
## at Theobalds:

With his welcome to London,
*together with a salutatorie*
*Poeme.*

By *John Sauile.*

*Dicito Iŏ paan,& Iŏ bis dicito paan.*

*LONDON*
Printed by *Thomas Snodham,* and are to be fould
at the houfe of T. Efte. *1603.*

Fig. 5.  Titlepage of John Savile, *King Iames his entertainment at Theobalds*
(London, Thomas Snodham, 'and are to be sould at the house of T. Este', 1603)
(British Library, C.33.g.28)

about-face. However much East's press had served Essex's faction before his *coup* failed, it would serve Cecil's in the aftermath.

Thus as James came to occupy the English throne, East had prudently veered to the Protestant cause. But his former partner, Byrd, must have noticed that, in the larger scheme of things, his country overall had veered rather towards the right. For now, with Anne on the throne as Queen Consort, there was a Catholic again in the English royal household. Nor was she the only adherent of the 'Old Religion' close to the King. At the ceremony at Theobalds James had appointed another Catholic, Henry Howard, earl of Northampton, to his privy council. Northampton was perhaps the most powerful and most trusted member of Cecil's faction at court during the Essex revolt. He was acting in a key role as intermediary in a secret correspondence with James that Cecil had engaged in during the last years of the Elizabethan era.[51] As Essex was clumsily and noisily promoting his doomed enterprise, Northampton and Cecil had quietly but deftly secured their future position of extraordinary power.

One likes to imagine that Byrd knew all along that Cecil rather than Essex would win the day. Perhaps this kind of foreknowledge might explain why Byrd did not join the twenty-odd other composers whom Morley had commissioned to contribute madrigals to his collection celebrating Oriana.[52] In any case, that two powerful Catholics were so close to the king after his accession probably encouraged Byrd to approach East again for the use of his press. It is less obvious why the Stationer would have agreed to work again for the composer, however. They had enjoyed a mutually productive partnership before, as we have seen, but East now faced a different situation. Byrd was no longer the owner of a monopoly, and so he had nothing to offer East in terms of Stationers' Company protection. Furthermore, East by now had experienced the kind of political troubles that could be generated by running a music press for purposes such as Byrd's.

Revealingly, when East took on Byrd's latest musical project, the two struck a very different kind of business deal from their previous one. This time East would turn towards rather than away from his Company. Rather than seeing the Company's register in terms of establishing copyright or evading it, East used it to ensure that Byrd's work would come before the Bishop of London, Richard Bancroft, for licensing and political protection.[53] As far as East was concerned, this was probably done simply for the sake of safety. Yet there is a somewhat sinister aspect to Bancroft's role in this matter. By this time the Bishop had been secretly sponsoring a number of Catholic authors as a means of exposing some of their factional disputes.[54] Bancroft may have licensed the *Gradualia* for an anti-Catholic purpose, perhaps to entrap its customers. Indeed, one Catholic activist was apparently arrested for possessing a copy of the set.[55] But this was in the aftermath of the Gunpowder Plot, when anti-Catholic sentiments were running at such a high pitch that almost anything might have aroused governmental suspicion. Over a year earlier, in late 1604 when Byrd's *Gradualia* was on Bancroft's desk, the Bishop may simply have regarded the set in the way many have seen it ever since, as an oddly extensive and misguided, but utterly harmless musical conceit. Bancroft, however, may have been wise enough to suspect that even this kind of project might have enjoyed the support of some powerful Catholics at court.

Not surprisingly, Byrd dedicated his first volume of the *Gradualia* to Northampton. Perhaps it was no coincidence that both king and *queen* were named in Byrd's provocative setting of *Plorans plorabit*. Did Byrd compose works expressly for these two prominent Catholics at court? It is not wholly unreasonable to suggest that he did. Anne kept her own chapel, which had been set up with an altar for Catholic worship.[56] Northampton, as Byrd noted, was responsible for persuading the king to raise the wages of the Chapel Royal musicians. Would it be so surprising if these musicians, led by Byrd, were not also called upon to sing pieces that served Northampton's particular religious needs as they lobbied for his favour? At some level, Byrd was probably inspired by the exhilarating prospect of filling a Chapel at the new court with the exquisite sound of his Catholic music.

In any case, when he published this set, Byrd returned with new vigour, it seems, to a public form of communication with his rulers that he had earlier established with the help of the Vautrollier and East presses. In this light it seems likely that James was the primary target of Byrd's panegyric address in the preface, as well as the one who received word of warning in the *Plorans* motet. But perhaps Byrd perceived that Anne and Northampton could also be instructed in their faith. East, it seems, had prudently decided it was time to secure now as much political protection as he possibly could for these endeavours. Byrd, however, continued to walk a tightrope of flattery intertwined with pointed remarks in his messages to king, queen and country. Musically, Byrd went as far as he possibly could, it seems, in composing such a monumental work in support of his cause. It shows that in the end he chose consistently to follow the risky path of a royal panegyrist and counsellor, one that Erasmus of Rotterdam had well described when noting:

Those who believe panegyrics are nothing but flattery seem to be unaware of the purpose and aim of the extremely far-sighted men who invented this kind of composition, which consists in presenting princes with a pattern of goodness, in such a way as to reform bad rulers, improve the good, educate the boorish, reprove the erring, arouse the indolent, and cause even the hopelessly vicious to feel some inward stirrings of shame.[57]

## References

1.   T. D., Review of *Heinrich Isaac's Choralis Constantinus Book III* by Louise Cuyler, *Music & Letters*, 32 (1951), p. 82.

2.   David Flanahan, 'The Music of Royal Appendix Mss 12–16: A Reconsideration', *Music Review*, 52 (1991), pp. 161–70, at p. 163. It must be noted that Flanahan was probably referring in this case to Byrd's Mass ordinaries, not, apparently, to the two books of *Gradualia*; and that he had drawn the material from the following statement by Charles W. Warren: 'It is not likely that such a large, carefully composed, exquisitely copied work [of Lamentations] would have failed to include the author's name unless it was expedient to do so. Probably, the name was omitted for the same reason that Byrd's Masses were not labeled as such and were not registered in the books of the Stationers' Company — to avoid association with an overtly popish book', 'The Music of Royal Appendix 12–16', *Music & Letters*, 51 (1970), pp. 357–72, at p. 370. Flanahan had obviously read Warren's ambiguous comment to mean that Byrd had attempted to remain anonymous in publishing the Masses. But it was only the printer, Thomas East, who took any steps to distance himself from the project.

3.   Facsimiles of the 1605 and 1607 titlepages appear, respectively, in Philip Brett (ed.), *Gradualia I (1605): The Marian Masses, Byrd Edition* 5 (London: Stainer & Bell, 1989), p. xxix; and idem, *Gradualia II (1607), Christmas to Easter, Byrd Edition* 7a (London, Stainer & Bell, 1997), p. xxii.

4.   See James L. Jackman, 'Liturgical Aspects of Byrd's *Gradualia*', *Musical Quarterly*, 49 (1963), pp. 17–37. Philip Brett has shown that Byrd's plan was based on that of contemporary Graduals, see *Gradualia I (1605), The Marian Masses*, p. viii.

5.   Ibid., p. xxxvii. See also John Irving, 'Penetrating the Preface to *Gradualia*', *Music Review*, 51 (1990), pp. 157–66.

6.   On religion and its effect on English music historiography see Benjamin Davies, 'The Historiography of the Reformation, or the Reformation of History', *Early Music*, 29 (2001), pp. 263–73. The trend to emphasize the importance of Byrd's Catholicism in his music was set some time ago by Joseph Kerman in his classic article, 'The Elizabethan Motet: A Study of Texts for Music', *Studies in the Renaissance*, 9 (1962), pp. 285–305. On Byrd's music for the *Gradualia*, see Kerman's *Masses and Motets of William Byrd* (Berkeley and Los Angeles: University of California Press, 1981). Only lately has the set generated similarly sustained treatments. Philip Brett's *William Byrd and his Contemporaries: Essays and a Monograph*, ed. Davitt Maroney and Joseph Kerman (Berkeley and Los Angeles: University of California Press, 2006) includes all of Brett's revised prefaces from the *Gradualia* volumes of the *Byrd Edition*. Kerry McCarthy's *Liturgy and Contemplation in Byrd's Gradualia* (New York and London: Routledge, 2007) stands as the first monograph devoted to the topic.

7.   *Die Geschichte des mehrstimmigen Proprium Missae* (Heidelberg: F. H. Kerle, 1950), p. 67, as quoted and translated in Jackman, 'Liturgical Aspects', p. 18.

8.   Brett, *Gradualia I (1605), The Marian Masses*, p. xxxvi.

9.   Ibid., xxxvii.

10.  Byrd extols the 'majesty of this whole Realm happily joined together under James the First', ibid., p. xxxvi.

11. Brett, *Gradualia I (1605), All Saints and Corpus Christi, Byrd Edition* 6a (London: Stainer & Bell, 1991), viii; Richard Turbet, 'Review: Well Played', *Musical Times,* 133, no. 1787 (January, 1992), p. 24.

12. Brett, Gradualia I (1605), *The Marian Masses,* p. xxxvi.

13. David Mateer, 'William Byrd's Middlesex Recusancy', *Music & Letters,* 78 (1997), pp. 1–14.

14. See, for example, Robin Headlam Wells, *Spenser's Faerie Queen and the Cult of Elizabeth* (London and Canberra: Croom Helm, Totowa, New Jersey: Barnes & Noble, 1983), pp. 1–5 and Hugh Craig, 'Jonson, the Antimasque and the "Rules of Flattery"', in *The Politics of the Stuart Court Masque,* ed. David Bevington and Peter Holbrook (Cambridge: Cambridge University Press, 1998), pp. 176–96.

15. Joseph Kerman, 'An Elizabethan Edition of Lassus', *Acta Musicologica,* 27 (1955), pp. 71–6; Frederick Sternfeld, 'Vautrollier's Printing of Lasso's *Recueil du Mellange',* *Annales Musicologiques,* 5 (1957), pp. 199–227.

16. Richard Freedman, *The Chansons of Orlando di Lasso and Their Protestant Listeners* (Rochester, NY: University of Rochester Press, 2001), p. 190.

17. Ibid., p. 169.

18. Kerman, 'Elizabethan Edition', p. 73. Freedman suggests that Vautrollier's readership is 'difficult to measure' as the music was intended to 'transcend ... the seemingly wide gulf that separated Protestants and Catholics' and 'avoid ... overtly Protestant positions', pp. 5–8.

19. Charles W. Warren, 'Music at Nonsuch', *Musical Quarterly,* 54 (1968), pp. 47–57.

20. See Neville Williams, *Thomas Howard, Fourth Duke of Norfolk* (London: Barrie and Rockliff, 1964), p. 126ff.

21. On Arundel's patronage of Vautrollier as part of a long tradition of politique positioning, see A. Boyle, 'Hans Eworth's Portrait of the Earl of Arundel and the Politics of 1549–50', *English Historical Review,* 117, no. 470 (February, 2002), pp. 25–47, at p. 37.

22. Freedman, *Chansons of Orlando di Lasso,* pp. 188–90.

23. Ibid., p. 189.

24. Ibid.

25. The publisher of Lasso's first book of four-voiced madrigals dedicated the volume to Louis, Cardinal of Guise, Mary's uncle, see Donna G. Cardamone, 'The Salon as Marketplace in the 1550s: Patrons and Collectors of Lasso's Secular Music', in *Orlando di Lasso Studies,* ed. Peter Berquist (Cambridge: Cambridge University Press, 1999), pp. 64–90, at pp. 76–8. Lasso was further drawn into the Guise family sphere of interest when early in 1568 Wilhelm V of Bavaria married Renate of Lorraine, Mary's second cousin. Wilhelm, who was a close friend of Lasso's and was later to become his benefactor, was the son of Lasso's patron, the Wittelsbach Duke Albrecht V. Lasso was to contribute his musical as well as his acting talents as a commedia dell'arte player to this lavish wedding at Trausnitz Castle, where Lasso soon transferred his choir: see Susan Maxwell, 'A Marriage Commemorated in the Stairway of Fools', *Sixteenth Century Journal,* 36 (2005), pp. 717–41. Ronsard's role as a Marian defender is discussed in James Emerson Phillips, *Images of a Queen; Mary Stuart in Sixteenth-Century Literature* (Berkeley and Los Angeles: University of California Press, 1964), pp. 11–22.

26. Craig Monson (ed.), *Cantiones sacrae, Byrd Edition,* 1 (London: Stainer & Bell, 1977), p. xxv.

27.  On a likely continental model for Byrd's extraordinary compositional conceit, see Davitt Maroney, 'Byrd's New Commandment: *Diliges Dominum*', paper read at the William Byrd Symposium, King's College London, 23 July 2007.

28.  Joseph Kerman, 'On William Byrd's *Emendemus in melius*', *Musical Quarterly*, 49 (1962), pp. 431–49; David Trendell, 'Aspects of William Byrd's Musical Recusancy', *Musical Times*, 148, no. 1900 (Autumn, 2007), pp. 27–50.

29.  Monson, *Cantiones sacrae*, p. xxiv.

30.  Quoted in Simon Adams, 'The Patronage of the Crown in Elizabethan Politics: The 1590s in Perspective', in *The Reign of Elizabeth I: Court and Culture in the Last Decade*, ed. John Guy (Cambridge: Cambridge University Press, 1995), pp. 20–45, at p. 24.

31.  Ibid., p. 21.

32.  Ibid., pp. 24–5.

33.  Mark Eccles, 'Bynneman's Books', *The Library*, 5th ser., 22 (1957), pp. 81–92, at p. 88.

34.  W. W. Greg, *Companion to Arber* (Oxford: Clarendon Press, 1967), pp. 117–23; John Feather, *Publishing, Piracy and Politics: An Historical Study of Copyright in Britain* (London: Mansell, 1994), p. 21ff.

35.  Edward Arber (ed.), *A Transcript of the Registers of the Company of Stationers of London, 1554–1640 AD* (Birmingham: The editor, 1875–94), I, p. 144.

36.  Jeremy L. Smith, *Thomas East and Music Publishing in Renaissance England* (New York: Oxford University Press, 2003), pp. 69–75.

37.  Craig Monson, 'Byrd, the Catholics and the Motet: The Hearing Reopened', in *Hearing the Motet: Essays on the Motet of the Middle Ages and Renaissance*, ed. Dolores Pesce (Oxford: Oxford University Press, 1997), pp. 348–74.

38.  Anthony Petti, 'Stephen Vallenger, 1541–1591', *Recusant History*, 6 (1962), pp. 256–61.

39.  London, The National Archives (Public Record Office), State Papers, SP/12/193, ff. 166–71.

40.  Ibid., f. 170r.

41.  *The Whole Booke of Psalmes: With Their Wonted Tunes* (London, Thomas East, 1592), A1r–v.

42.  Ibid., A1v.

43.  Peter Clulow, 'Publication Dates for Byrd's Latin Masses', *Music & Letters*, 47 (1966), pp. 1–9.

44.  On the supposition that these Masses were produced for an 'open market', see Eric Van Tassel, 'Byrd's Masses', *Early Music America*, 6 (1999), pp. 37–41.

45.  Smith, *Thomas East*, pp. 76–87.

46.  Lillian M. Ruff and D. Arthur Wilson, 'The Madrigal, the Lute Song and Elizabethan Politics', *Past and Present*, 44 (1969), pp. 3–51.

47.  On the Essex revolt see Mervyn James, *Society, Politics and Culture: Studies in Early Modern England* (Cambridge: Cambridge University Press, 1986), pp. 416–65; Paul E. J. Hammer, 'Devereux, Robert, Second Earl of Essex (1565–1601)', *Oxford Dictionary of National Biography* (Oxford University Press, 2004) [http://www.oxforddnb.com/view/article/7565, accessed 24 Nov. 2007].

48.  Smith, *Thomas East*, pp. 49–53.

49.  Jeremy L. Smith, 'Music and Politics in Late Elizabethan England: The Identities of Oriana and Diana', *Journal of the American Musicological Society*, 58 (2005), pp. 507–58.

50. John Hayward, *An Answer to the First Part of a Certaine Conference* (London: [Thomas East and Thomas Snodham] for S. Waterson and C. Burbie, 1603); George Ker, *A Discouery of the … Conspiracie of Scottish Papists* (London: Thomas Snodham [for] Thomas East, 1603); J. H., *Work for Chimny-sweepers: Or A warning for Tabacconists* (London: Thomas East for Thomas Bushell, 1602) and John Savile, *King Iames his entertainment at Theobalds* (London: Thomas Snodham [for] Thomas East, 1603).

51. Pauline Croft, 'Howard, Henry, earl of Northampton (1540–1614)', *Oxford Dictionary of National Biography* [http://www.oxforddnb.com/view/article/13906, accessed 25 Nov. 2007].

52. On the 'conspicuous absence' of Byrd in the *Triumphes* collection, see Joseph Kerman, *The Elizabethan Madrigal: A Comparative Study* (New York: American Musicological Society, 1962), p. 199.

53. Teruhiko Nasu, 'The Publication of Byrd's *Gradualia* Reconsidered', *Brio*, 32 (1995), pp. 109–20.

54. Gladys Jenkins, 'The Archpriest Controversy and the Printers, 1601–1603', *The Library*, 5th ser., vol. 2 (1948), pp. 180–6.

55. *Gradualia I (1605), The Marian Masses*, p. xiv.

56. Molly Murray, 'Performing Devotion in the *Masque of Blackeness*', *Studies in English Literature*, 47 (2007), pp. 427–49, at p. 434.

57. Quoted in Wells, *Spenser's Faerie Queen*, p. 3.

# The Playfords and the Purcells

## RICHARD LUCKETT

IN THE CHURCH OF BREMHILL, Wiltshire, stands a large wall-monument commemorating Edward, eldest son of Sir George Hungerford of Caden-ham, who died in 1698, aged 24. As a piece of sculpture it is chiefly remarkable for having evoked a joke from Nikolaus Pevsner; what is likely to attract a musician is the presence, amongst the trophies that flank the bust, of a violin, though it may be disconcerting to find this balanced, on the other side, by a pair of pistols: 'the arts of peace, the arts of war'.

Few visitors are likely to persevere with the dauntingly long and sadly abraded inscription beneath. Yet it is as surprising as the rest of the ensemble. Hungerford, in so short a span, was educated at Salisbury and Oxford, studied the law in London, spent time, presumably on campaign, in the Low Countries, and was returned to parliament for Calne. He was a young man of many accomplishments, but foremost — as a pastime — music; indeed, 'Clarissimi *Purcelli* Fautor Æmulus'. Information of all kinds finds its way into seventeenth- and eighteenth-century English epitaphs, but it is difficult to think of any allusion to a contemporary artist, whether writer, painter, or musician, with which this can be compared. There it stands, emphatic in an elaborated script, the name not of a safely classical exemp-lar, but of an Englishman who, himself dying young, had predeceased the subject of the eulogy by a mere three years.[1]

Monuments are not erected overnight, and some post-date by decades the interments they mark, so it should be pointed out that we know Hungerford's was in place by 1712 at the latest and may perfectly well have been put up in the year of his death. As it is the dates could not be more convenient, since Henry Playford's great posthumous anthology of Henry Purcell's songs, *Orpheus Britannicus*, was first published in 1698; 'The Second Book, which renders the First Compleat' (but buyers of the 1698 volume had had no indication that it did not stand alone) in 1702; a revised edition of the original volume in 1706; and a revised edition of Book II in 1711. Since the 'Third Edition' of both books in 1721 merely consists of the sheets of the second with new titlepages, this constitutes the entire printing history of *Orpheus Britannicus*, and without *Orpheus Britan-nicus* the allusion to Purcell on the Hungerford monument would make little sense.

45

Or would it? The question is worth raising because the epitaph might be used to suggest a personal link between Edward Hungerford and Purcell, in that it asserts that Hungerford's mother was a close, if annoyingly indeterminate connection of Charles, Duke of Somerset, to whom Purcell had dedicated *Dioclesian* in 1690. But the terms of the dedication are circumspect; indications of a close association are lacking and the connection with Hungerford appears fortuitous. Had Purcell taught Edward, as he taught Rhoda Cartwright (Cavendish) or Annabella Dyves (Howard) we could reasonably expect that to be made explicit. As it is we are confronted with a proposition which — however hyperbolic as regards the musical skills of the heir of a locally celebrated family then in terminal decline — demands assent as to its basic proposition, which has nothing to do with the Duke or the Hungerfords: 'Clarissimi *Purcelli*', where, in Virgilian language, 'Clarissimi' conveys both 'bright splendour' and 'greatness in renown'.

It was *Orpheus Britannicus* that set the seal on that renown, being at once a commemoration and an anthology, in print, of the work of a single composer on a scale never attempted in England before. It was, as Michael Burden has said, 'a posthumous anthology of monumental proportions';[2] yet it has many curious, even disconcerting features, less discussed than might be expected, because it so successfully imposes its air of authority. One aspect of this, the association between publisher and composer, has been intensified by the subsequent development of the music trade and our awareness of the special relationships that have existed between, say, Beethoven and Gahn, Verdi and the Casa Ricordi, Britten and Boosey & Hawkes. That such relationships have often been sentimentalized and seldom without their problems is another matter. The music trade has always been more conservative than the book trade in its topographical parochialism, the relative scarcity of its retail outlets, and this sense of identification between particular publishers and particular composers. It is not that this has not also existed in the book trade — Byron and Murray, Eliot and Faber are sufficient examples — but that it has been less of a promotional point. *Orpheus Britannicus*, in England, established that point. The eulogies that preface the original volume end with a poem by Henry Playford which concludes:

> Touch but thy *Lyre* the stones will come,
> And dance themselves into a Tomb —

This is precisely what, editorially, Playford has achieved. Three poems preface the Second Book, the first on the death of 'the late Famous Mr.

Henry Purcell', but the other two celebrating Playford as his publisher, the last, by 'Henry Hall, Organist of Hereford', ending:

> By this my Friend, you'll get immortal Fame,
> When still with *Purcell* we read *Playford's* name.

It could scarcely be more explicit. But what of Playford's name? That of John Playford, Henry's father, born in Norwich in 1622/3, has been recognized as crucially important by historians of English music from Hawkins and Burney onwards, Henry himself generally coming in as something of an afterthought.[3] Yet there is no unanimity of opinion about John except for acknowledgement of his priority as the first publisher of English music — in the sense that, despite his being liveried to the Company of Stationers, he apparently never touched print, rather as Al Capone never touched a gun. The earlier students of his work tended to approach it from specialized points of view: national song in the case of Frank Kidson, folk-song and dance in that of Margaret Dean-Smith (though her researches took her considerably beyond this), and the music of the English parish church in that of Professor Nicholas Temperley, who in his article for the *New Grove Dictionary* suggests that the contribution made by John (and continued by Henry) to the development of congregational singing was more significant than the publication of music 'addressed to the proficient performer'.[4]

What is generally agreed is that John Playford's publishing practices make him an elusive subject for investigation. A frank and sometimes comic statement of this position appears in D. W. Krummel's *English Music Printing, 1553–1700*, which helpfully formulates the principles on which Krummel assumes Playford worked: that he saw music publishing as 'democratic and patriotic', that he unabashedly addressed himself to a lowest common denominator, that he always bore in mind novelty, or at least the appearance of novelty, and that though he favoured certain printers and certain music types he was never afraid of experiment when a special need seemed to demand it. Krummel goes on to urge that, despite the usual experience of bibliographers, 'Playford should be taken as meaning exactly what he says in his imprints, and that, those works "sold by" him, and those which he listed for sale in his catalogues but which in their imprints do not specifically name him as publisher, were not actually published by him.'[5] Whilst this may not invariably be the case it is certainly generally true and I believe can be extended to cover all Playford's statements in dedications, introductions and advertisements. It has been doubted that 'Honest John Playford' was a contemporary sobriquet, but he was precisely that to Roger North, although he was 'poor old Playford' as well.[6] We should not read sharp practice into his retitlings and expansions of existing material. Both as parish clerk of the Temple church and as a businessman with a shop built into the angle of its porch and, latterly, a house in Aldgate, Playford was a public and accountable figure and the last person to risk antagonizing his customers. He was a person to whom John Aubrey could turn for serious historical information.[7] When Pepys called at his shop on 23 November 1666, 'and there find that his new impression of his Ketches are not yet out, the fire having hindered it; but his man tells me that it will be a very fine piece — many things new being added to it', he was being told the truth and would have no hesitation in discarding an earlier edition when he gained the 44 'new fooleries' that he was eventually to acquire on 15 April 1667. Amongst those 44 was 'Sweet Tyraness, I now resign my heart', by 'Mr. Hen. Purcell', the first documented contact between the Playfords and the Purcells.

Before considering this, I want to look at an earlier episode in John Playford's career. He first emerges as the publisher of a royalist tract in 1648, and served a prison sentence, possibly on that account. At around the same time, it seems, he was carefully monitoring the fate of the organ and music-books from the Chapel Royal and after the Restoration played a part in their restitution. In 1651 by licensing *The English Dancing Master* he commenced his career as music publisher, the collapse of the regime he supported having apparently resolved the problems of monopolies and permissions. But the disappearance or nullity of legal inhibitions did not obviate the moral problems, as is apparent from his *Select Musicall Ayres and Dialogues* of 1652.[8] The contributors (if that is the word) to this anthology were the brothers Henry and William Lawes, John Wilson and Charles Coleman, both Doctors of Music, and William Webbe — Henry Lawes being the best represented, with 20 songs out of a total of 65. The dedication was to the four composers who were still alive, William Lawes having been killed at the siege of Chester in 1646. It is generous to a fault, but whether the dedicatees had been consulted before their compositions were included is unclear. In the case of Henry Lawes it seems he was not consulted until the anthology was actually going through the press.

In the next year Playford published *Ayres and Dialogues by Henry Lawes, Servant to his late Ma[tie] in his public and private Musick. The First Booke*. There is an engraved portrait of Lawes by Faithorne on the title-page, and a *Second* and a *Third Booke* were to follow in 1655 and 1658. It is in the address 'To all Understanders or Lovers of Musick', which prefaces the first book, that Lawes claims that the previous year's publication had been without his prior consent. 'Therefore now the Question is not, whether or no my Compositions shall be Publick, but whether they shall come from me, or from some other hand; and which of the two is likeliest to afford the true correct Copies, I leave others to judge.' None of those in this present volume, he goes on, has been published before and, if they please, further volumes will follow — but in fact Playford had pre-empted their promise on the titlepage, and in due course he fulfilled it.

It might be thought that the three volumes together give us an embryonic collected Lawes, although the effect is rather spoiled since Playford reproduces the engraving of the composer on each separate titlepage. It might also be thought that Lawes's survival into the Restoration, his reappointment to his old places in the Chapel Royal and the King's Musick, his election as Clerk of the Cheque in the Chapel, and the commission to set *Zadock the Priest* for the coronation might have made an omnibus publication timely. But he was old and, by December 1660 as Pepys reports, 'very sick'; on 21 October 1662 he died. He was buried in the cloisters of Westminster Abbey; no slab or tablet marks the place and, far from creating the commemorative volume that was lying ready-made and to hand, Playford effectively unpicked it by publishing a *Select Ayres and Dialogues*. This does not survive but evidently harked back, via a publication of 1659, to the original 1652 volume, and looks forward to *The Treasury of Musick* of 1669, when Playford, by ingenious (because minimal) juggling, involving the re-use of a frontispiece, new titlepages and a new introduction and contents page, has transformed those earlier publications into a satisfactory and rather imposing anthology of what might be called the Lawes era. The purchaser had to put up with considerable confusion. The first Book itself was divided into three 'Books'; the contents page, however, described those books as 'parts', as well as suggesting both that the printer had been incompetent and that errors are inevitable and so it is up to the 'Judicious to mend with their pen'. In the Preface to the Second Book (proper) of *The Treasury*, Playford with devastating candour explains the whole thing: 'This second book doth chiefly consist of Mr. Henry Lawes Composition, being Transcribed from his Originals, a short time before his Death, and with his free consent for me to Publish them, if occasion offer'd.' This gives Playford to wonder whether it is worth his reprinting the first two of his original early Lawes collections: surely, from the buyers' point of view a selection would answer their needs best, and would allow for the insertion of other ayres by English composers, undeservedly unprinted, and a few of the Italian masters, unknown in England. Take the three volumes together and you have 'an intire Volume of the most choice Songs that have been Composed for Forty Years past, and I doubt not but will maintain their Fame for many years to come.'

This is an elegant and optimistic way of saying that an era had passed and that the future did not lie in republishing Lawes. When Lawes's brother William died, eight musical elegies mourning his death were printed at the end of his and Henry's *Choice Psalmes* (1648); but Henry, in contrast, was commemorated by just one, 'Farewell brave *Lawes*, sweet peace possesse thy Soul'. This appeared in the final section, '*Canons* and *Hymnes*', of Playford's new edition of John Hilton's *Catch that Catch can* in 1663. Since no composer is named it may well have been by Playford himself. But when the next edition emerged with the alternative title of *The Musical Companion*, that last serious section was dropped (surely a sign of the times), and with it the elegy.[9] In fact the only compositions of Henry's which proved to have historical durability were atypical: metrical psalm tunes which became hymn tunes and a handful of catches and dance-like songs. The main body of his work, the courtly ayres in which his professed aim was 'to shape *Notes* to the *Words* and *Sense*', was left embalmed in the perfection of an aesthetic theory, summed up in Milton's sonnet addressed to him, which meant that whilst poets had once proudly recorded on their titlepages the fact that Lawes had set these words, Playford found the actual settings (and he published almost half of Lawes's 400 and more songs) a rapidly wasting asset.

As is in the nature of publishing he moved on to other things, of which *Catch that Catch can, or the Musical Companion* was one. It has been generally assumed, since Charles Burney drew attention to the piece, that *Sweet Temptress*, a posthumous publication, is by Henry Purcell the elder, the composer's father who died in 1664 (when his son, Henry, was only eight). Stylistically it is wholly typical of the Lawes generation, and I think the conventional attribution rests, even though Alphonso Marsh father and son are carefully distinguished in a publication with which Playford was involved in 1673. The publication of *Sweet Temptress* does not in the least suggest any special relation between Playford and Purcell senior: the latter ranks as the least published among those Gentlemen of the Chapel who composed. His work is often indistinguishable from that of his brother Thomas and we do not know with which of them Pepys sang on 21 February 1660. Both were most notable for their chants, which were well known through extensive manuscript circulation; but Playford did not choose examples by either of them when he began to publish the first Anglican chants from 1674 onwards.

The problem of identity recurs in Playford's *Choice Ayres, Songs & Dialogues* of 1675, where the song 'When *Thirsis* did the Splendid Eye' is attributed to 'Mr. Purcell'. Mainly to annoy those who have not thought of the possibility I suggest that this could be the one published song by

Thomas Purcell, on the grounds that, at that date, 'Mr. Purcell' was more likely to indicate the socially well-established uncle than the sixteen-year-old youth; if it did not, it is more likely to be Henry jun. than his long-deceased father. This would be disputed by the editor of the New Purcell Society edition, who is also disinclined to accept as Henry junior's the songs attributed to 'Henry Purcell' in the *New Ayres, Dialogues, and Trialogues* by 'sundry Authors' of 1678.[10] Since this was published by Henry Brome, not Playford, it does not strictly concern us; the songs are printed along with an arrangement of 'Sweet Tyraness' as an air, so that it might either be supposed that they are all by Henry sen., or that an adaptation of his father's work was a natural starting point for Henry jun. as a song-writer. In any case the doubts do enable us to say that *Choice Ayres & Songs to Sing to the Theorbo-Lute or Bass-Viol* ... 'The Second Book ... Printed by Anne Godbid, and sold by John Playford, at his shop near the Temple Church' in 1679, contains, amongst the 79 songs printed, the first five published works that can, without dispute, be attributed to 'our' Henry Purcell, with his authorship unequivocally asserted. In 1681 the third book followed, and here, in a collection of 59 songs by fourteen composers, Purcell wins pride of place as the author of nine.

In the interim year a publication had appeared which had a significant, though indirect, bearing on the course of the Playford/Purcell association although it did not involve Playford. This was *Theodosius: or, the Force of Love. A Tragedy*, by Nat. Lee, an heroic extravaganza which had proved a major success in the autumn of 1680. According to John Downes, the prompter at the Dorset Garden Theatre: 'All the parts in't being perfectly perform'd with several Entertainments of Singing; Compos'd by the Famous Master Mr. Henry *Purcell*, (being the first he ever Compos'd for the Stage) made it a living and Gainful Play to the Company.' When Bentley and Magnes published the play they tried to capitalize on the success of the music by appending it to the play-text, but did so without any allusion to the composer, and in a very imperfect form. As it was, purchasers of the third book of *Choice Ayres* would find three of the songs there, properly ascribed and better presented. It is an illustration of one of the besetting problems of a period in which all theatre music aspired to the condition of opera, but every practical consideration prevented this, leaving adrift a flotsam of powerful but homeless music. Although as a music publisher Playford was prepared to innovate, he must have seen the theatre as a trap except in so far as songs could be contained within song books, and tunes, however they first appeared, within his anthologies for solo instruments — which is what happened to two of the items from *Theodosius* in *Musick's Recreation on the Viol Lyra-way*, 1682.

We find the same principle at work, although in a quite different context, in 1683, in many ways an *annus mirabilis* for Purcell as a composer. There are two very particular demonstrations of his closeness to John Playford but, superficially, they point in different directions. *Choice Ayres and Songs* reached a fourth book, printed by Anne Godbid and John Playford jun., the publisher's nephew. In his preface to the third book Playford had taken up the Lawesian trope of the necessity of an inwardness with the language if English is to be effectively set, and emphasized along with this (it had always been part of the equation) the fears of English musicians who felt their reputation or even livelihood threatened by the incursions of foreigners. He seems to have compounded this with a professional jealousy when he makes the matter specific: he has 'seen lately published a large Volum of English Songs, composed by an Italian Master, who has lived here in England many years … a very able Master but not being perfect in the true Idiom of our Language, you will find the Air of his Musick so much after his Country-mode, that it would sute far better with Italian than English Words'. This can only apply to Pietro Reggio, whose sumptuous *Songs* had been issued by subscription in 1680, the engraved frontispiece showing a harping Amphion making a menacing landfall on a splendidly aggressive dolphin.

The first song, 'She loves and she confesses too', yokes a celebrated poem from Cowley's *The Mistresse* to a well-known ciaccona bass. In *Choice Ayres … The Fourth Booke*, Purcell takes the same words and same bass, and with them makes an entirely different song. Peter Holman cogently suggests it is 'a response and rebuke to Reggio, probably at Playford's instigation'.[11] Even if Playford was not the instigator it shows Purcell responding in a spirited way to a hint he had been offered; and what is indisputable is that Playford chose to publish it. Playford did not, by contrast, choose to publish the work by which, in that same year, Purcell staked his claims and the claims of English music by confrontation rather than implication, the *Sonnata's of III Parts*, which, although sold by Playford in partnership with John Carr, is unequivocally 'Printed for the Author'.

The *Sonnata's* is the assertion of Purcell's fully fledged artistic maturity. To what extent the stylistic debate adumbrated in the preface really signified seems irrelevant now. All that need be said is that when Roger North described them as Purcell's 'noble set of sonnatas, which however clog'd with somewhat of an English vein, for which they are unworthily despised, are very artificiall and good musick', the carefulness and precision of his writing worked against him; indeed it was an opinion he was at pains to rephrase.[12] 'Clog'd' is ironical, and 'unworthily despised' in any case negates it; this is defensive praise, but not for a moment qualified praise. As for Purcell's professed aim, 'he has faithfully endeavour'd a just imitation of the most fam'd Italian Masters; principally, to bring the seriousness and gravity of that sort of musick into vogue, and reputation amongst our Country-men'; and *pour épater* the French. The presentation of the work is part of this aim: its frontispiece portrait of the author, the assertion of his offices, 'Composer in Ordinary to his most Sacred Majesty and Organist of his Chappell Royall', the dedication to the King. But it was not a work on which Playford was prepared to take a risk: 'Printed for the Author: And Sold by I. Playford and I. Carr at the Temple, Fleet street'. Yet, as Robert Thompson pointed out in 1995, the engraver, Thomas Cross, junior, 'was almost certainly working from, and closely imitating, an exemplar in [John] Playford's hand'.[13]

I believe we can remove Thompson's 'almost', but understand why it is there. Assertion has bedevilled Purcell biography and caution is the natural reaction now. For the same reason I have not, in this account, touched on those spheres of musical activity in which it must be assumed there was frequent contact between the families, whether when delivering materials to the Abbey or copy to Playford's house or shop. The intimacy becomes particularly apparent when we read the advertisement for the *Sonnata's* in the *London Gazette* for 28 May 1683: the price to subscribers is 10s. for a set, proposal forms are available at Mr William Hall's house in Norfolk Street, and at Playford's and Carr's shops; publication is to be on 11 June. On that day the *Gazette* advised subscribers that they could collect their copies from Purcell's house in St Anne's Lane, beyond Westminster Abbey. There, should Mr Purcell not be at home — and the demands of services, rehearsing, teaching and tuning made it very likely he would not be — Mrs Purcell (whose mother, after all, had kept a tavern) would presumably have conducted a transaction involving more money than it would have been usual to allow a maid to handle. To that it might be added — but this is certainly speculation — that from what we know of the comparative wealth of her family (Peters), and his, she might well have been the source of the capital required, given that Playford, although prepared to sell the publication and to give necessary help in its preparation (there are fewer mistakes in the *Sonnata's* than we should anticipate in a Purcell autograph), was not willing to commit himself to financial risk.

By this time John Playford was 60 and had been in business for over 30 years. His publications had played a crucial part in making possible the boom in musical activity evident from 1683, though of course many other factors were involved, including James II's retrenchments in the Court establishment, intensified under William & Mary, which made it essential for musicians to exploit every possibility of the commercial market. Among obvious evidence of this, from 1683 onwards, are the London Cecilian celebrations, the opening of the York Buildings Concert Room, the increased use of music in the theatres, *The Gentleman's Journal* with its monthly supplement of songs (1692–4) and, of course, the proliferating activities of rivals in the field. Playford's swan-song was the fifth book of *Choice Ayres* in 1684. Then 'Age, and the Infirmities of Nature' enforced his retirement and brought about the succession of Henry, on whom the verdict of history, according to Krummel, has been that he was 'the weak son of a strong father'. The only notable dissenting voice has been that of Arthur Bedford, who in *The Great Abuse of Musick* (1711) attempted a castigation of that art to rival Jeremy Collier's 1696 assault on the contemporary stage. Bedford took particular exception to John Playford's *The Musical Companion* (or *Catch that Catch can*), but regarded Henry's *Pills to Purge Melancholy* as an even greater enormity: 'In the *Preface* he informs us that as his father before had spar'd no Cost or Pains to oblige the World with *Smut and Profaneness*; so he would make it his Endeavour to come up to such an Example; and indeed he hath done it effectually.'[14]

As it happens *Pills* contains a significant amount of Purcell, some rather out of place because of its gravity, but Henry had ended his connection with the anthology by 1706 and the third volume; it was to run to three more and end up in the hands of the supposedly respectable Tonson. It has been held against Henry that he diversified into print-dealing, but it is often forgotten that music was never John's exclusive line in the book-trade either. It is certainly the case that Henry failed seriously to engage with engraved music (which is odd, considering the venture into prints), that he became involved in litigation with colleagues, though this seems to have been resolved without lasting acrimony, and that he had ambitious schemes for provincial music clubs — but this was simply an extension of an idea of his father's.[15] None of this prevented his successful publication of the four books of the *Theater of Music* (1685–7), the six books of *The Banquet of Musick* (1688–92), the extremely significant two volumes of *Harmonia Sacra* (1688 and 1693) with their seventeen major songs by Purcell, the four books of *Deliciae Musicae* (1695–6) with 23 songs by Purcell, and much else besides, including the monthly *Mercurius Musicus*, *The Second Part of Musick's Handmaid* (1689) for keyboard (the 'first part' was published by John 27 years earlier), and the *Three Elegies upon Queen Mary*, two of which are by Purcell, the other by Blow.

Whilst it is not clear whether Purcell's hand in that steady best-seller, John Playford's *An Introduction to the Skill of Musick* (1694) was quite as far-reaching as the titlepage implies ('Corrected and amended'; but the thirteenth edition of 1697 limits this to the third book, *The Art of Descant*), it can still stand for the extensive editorial work for which Henry credits Purcell in *The Theater of Musick*, *The Second Part of Musick's Handmaid* and *Harmonia Sacra*. In *The Theater of Music*, Book I, he elegantly contrives to turn his acknowledgement of editorial help, from John Blow as well as Purcell, into a joint dedication. Since Henry was not himself a composer, as John had been, this assistance was particularly necessary. As a collection *The Theater* has much to recommend it, including an impressive titlepage engraving, and is innovatory in that several songs come complete with ritornelli for violins or flutes, rather than their silent omission or the lame 'you have all which is to be sung to the Theorbo, and is suitable to the rest in this book'. But in other respects it is as chaotic as anything John produced, although considerably more elegant. There is a misprint on the titlepage, 'theorbo-bass' for 'thorow-bass', which is corrected at the bottom of the last page of the book; the advertisements contain an advance notice, a year late, of the pre-première publication of Blow's Cecilian Ode for 1684, and despite an obvious attempt to achieve a more generous layout than usual there are some extreme impracticalities, such as a 'singing bass' on the verso of the treble it is intended to accompany.

John Playford died in the autumn of 1686, apparently a poor man. In his will he provided, not legacies, as is sometimes said, but for mourning rings for Blow and Purcell; these were tokens of esteem and valued as such. The next year Henry published Purcell's 'Gentle Shepherds, you that know the charms of Tunefull Breath', 'A Pastoral elegy on the Death of Mr. John Playford', to words by Nahum Tate, who was not only a Playford author but seems to have worked for him editorially as well, acting in a literary capacity much as Blow and Purcell did musically. The elegy is quietly impressive, a reminder of the significance of the type in English song, and of elegies on musicians in particular: a tradition that, in its insular form, begins with Byrd on Tallis, to which Purcell contributed with his early lament for Locke and later elegy on Thomas Farmer; and which played a vital part in the concept of *Orpheus Britannicus*, the anthology as memorial.[16]

When John Playford died, much was changing. Publication by subscription was becoming more general and there were rivals in the field whose business was primarily, if not exclusively, music. John Carr and John Hudgebut produced folio song-books in direct competition with Henry Playford, and Purcell's songs — with or without his approval — appeared in all of them. The only indication of loyalty that can be discerned is that from 1687 his brother Daniel often appears alongside him, and this most frequently occurs in Playford's publications. But after 1690 Daniel ceased to publish for five years, presumably because taken up with his duties at Magdalen College, Oxford, reappearing in print when he returned to London — as it has generally been assumed, to help an overburdened Henry.

Henry Playford, however, was by no means entirely a slave to the market, though it is surprising that his most innovatory publishing venture has not received more acclaim. Perhaps that is because it self-consciously looked backwards as well as forwards. The first book of *Harmonia Sacra* was published in 1688; the second in 1693. Between them they contained seventeen songs by Henry Purcell (and one by Daniel), including several of his greatest, and Purcell himself had a more than usually important hand in the editing. This was a consequence of the collection's studied disregard for the mode, its express aim not 'to gratify a delicate Ear and a wanton Curiosity' but to address those who are 'no less *Musical* though they are more *Devout*'. Hence the inclusion of songs by composers 'who are now dead', Locke and Pelham Humphrey, whose 'Composures have been reviewed by Mr. *Henry Purcell*, whose tender Regard for the Reputation of those great Men made him careful that nothing should be published, which, through the negligence of Transcribers, might reflect upon their Memory'. In the case of the words, the promise of the titlepage ('*Composed by the Best Masters of the Last and Present Age*') was brilliantly reinterpreted, so that we find Purcell and Blow setting George Herbert, which doubles the anachronism of Pelham Humfrey's setting of Donne. In the face of the sacred, time and fashion stand still. Moreover, the first book is dedicated to 'The Right Reverend Father in God, Thomas Lord Bishop of Bath and Wells': that is Thomas Ken, as a poet the inheritor of Herbert, as a musician a player of the theorbo into the eighteenth century, in 1688 one of the seven bishops imprisoned for his resistance to James's extension of toleration to Roman Catholics, but shortly afterwards — though Playford had no way of knowing this — to be ejected from his see for his refusal to take the oath to William and Mary. That all this, except for Ken's abjuration, conforms with Playford's own religious and political convictions is confirmed by the non-musical books he was publishing at the same time. That Purcell, whenever he had a choice, was conservative in the matter of texts and concurred, seems beyond doubt — settled in his 'constant observation' (to quote Roger North), 'that what took least was really best'.[17] It is this that gives us, amongst others, The Evening Hymn, 'Awake and with attention hear', 'With sick and famish'd eyes', and in Book II, 'The Blessed Virgin's Expostulation' and 'Saul and the Witch of Endor'. Book II had a safer dedication to Henry Aldrich, Dean of Christ

Church; when both books went into second editions that did not need to be changed, but in 1703 Book I was re-dedicated to Queen Anne. Nevertheless the poem prefacing the second book, 'To Dr. John Blow and Mr. Henry Purcell', which in 1693 must have been a comparatively innocuous effusion by a member of Daniel Purcell's college, had become by 1714 — since its author was Henry Sacheverell — a highly charged assertion of Tory and high church allegiances. If Purcell's settings in *Harmonia Sacra* have never been given their due it is a back-handed testimony to the fact that the gap in the market Henry Playford had identified is still a gap in criticism; it is also because, since *Harmonia Sacra* remained very much a going concern, they did not appear in *Orpheus Britannicus*.

In 1691, between the two volumes of *Harmonia Sacra*, came *Dioclesian*. I shall not attempt here to describe the tangled skein of its publication except to note that, as originally announced in *The London Gazette* for 7 July 1690, Henry Playford and John Carr were both involved, at least to the extent of taking subscriptions. But by the time, after many vicissitudes, publication was eventually achieved, in March 1691, Playford had dropped out. As with the *Sonnata's*, Purcell was his own publisher, though I cannot accept Shay and Thompson's proposal that 'self-advertisement' was the motive for publication.[18] Would they say that of the *Clavier-Übung* or the *Musical Offering*? But *Dioclesian* was what I should call a dramatick opera — what Tonson, the original publisher of the word-book described as being 'with Alterations and Additions, After the Manner of an Opera', and what Purcell was scrupulously careful never to refer to as an 'opera' at all. Whatever its category this new form simply did not fit the existing pattern of publishing. We have seen how a problem existed for the play with only a modest amount of music: the formula that had failed for Bentley with *Theodosius* in 1680 was repeated again by Knight and Saunders for *A Fool's Preferment or the Three Dukes of Dunstable* in 1688 and, most prestigiously, by Tonson for Dryden's *Amphitryon*, one of his greatest plays, in 1690. Neither of these, despite (this time) the prominent display of Purcell's name, seems to have succeeded. In 1683 and 1684 John Playford had published Purcell's and Blow's Cecilian Odes in full score, subsequently selling both stitched together; there were copies on Henry's hands fifteen years later, and no one subsequently felt impelled to attempt publication of later Cecilian Odes, Court Odes, or orchestral odes of any description whatsoever. Cathedral music was the copyists' preserve. Attempts were made to pirate the songs from the dramatick operas, but as Purcell maintained in his 'Advertisement' to *Dioclesian*, the songs often were not the point. As it was, he had to struggle with two printers, one of whom 'fell into some trouble'; he had in any case promised personally to examine each sheet. The evidence of missing copies and of advertisements suggests that sales were slow; uncorrected copies show little signs of use; corrected copies, which are overwhelmingly in the hand of Francis Piggott (not, as was once believed, of Purcell or, failing that, Frances Purcell), are in a minority.

*Dioclesian* in score was not a success. Indeed in 1702 John Walsh, in a note which appears in some, but not all, copies of his publication of Daniel Purcell's *The Judgment of Paris*, claimed that it 'found so small encouragement in Print, as serv'd to stifle many other intire Opera's, no less excellent'. *Dioclesian* on stage was another matter, and *King Arthur*, *The Fairy Queen* and *The Indian Queen*, all with music by Purcell, were the consequences of its popularity. In 1692 the composer, apparently chastened by his experiences with *Dioclesian*, abandoned his professed principles and published *Some select songs As they are Sung in the Fairy Queen*, which was sold by the familiar team of John Carr and Henry Playford, and also at Dorset Garden theatre itself. But there are indications that this too failed to be profitable, and that Playford's reluctance to act as a principal was prudent, although at some point, probably after Purcell's death, he took a chance with the songs from the play *Bonduca*.

Henry Purcell died, with exquisite timing, on the eve of St Cecilia's Day, 1695. By then Playford was entirely re-engaged with music publishing, having embarked on *Deliciae Musicae*, probably his most successful collection, and had gone to very considerable trouble, for obvious reasons, over the *Three Elegies upon the Much Lamented Loss of Our late most Gracious Queen Mary*. Perhaps he subsequently rather spoiled the effect of this by binding unsold copies up with the four books which constituted the 'First Volume' of *Deliciae Musicae*. But he certainly learned from producing it, since some of its features, such as the printing of the words of the text of the first poem before the setting, were echoed in the presentation of 'An Ode on the Death of Mr Henry Purcell ... The Words by Mr. Dryden, and sett to Musick by Dr. Blow'. He had succeeded in bringing together the greatest poet of the day, who of course had been Purcell's recent collaborator, with the musician who had both taught Purcell and had become, by his death, incontestably the greatest composer of the age. John Heptinstall printed it in his 'new-ty'd note' and with the simplest means — the black-bordered titlepage, the spacious layout of the text of the Ode, the considered disposition of the music — made of it a noble production, marred only by the surrender, as also in the *Elegies* for the Queen, to the Playfordian itch to fill up any spare space at the end with advertisements. But perhaps one should not allow aesthetic preferences to rule here, because the advertisements do, importantly, invite subscriptions for 'the more Compleat Printing of Mr. Henry Purcell's Vocal Musick in 2 and 3 Parts'. There had evidently been an earlier proposal, which had met with 'small Incouragement', but Playford reacted by promising a more substantial publication and an extension of the time before subscriptions closed — an optimistic approach which, against the odds, was ultimately to pay off, though it took a long time to do so.

When *Orpheus Britannicus* eventually appeared in 1698, it was with apologies for the delay and the placatory reflection that the fruit of wise delay had been 30 extra pieces. It also profited from the fact that public response to Purcell's death had been cumulative: from the moment when the Dean and Chapter of Westminster waived the burial fees and offered Frances Purcell her choice as to where Henry should be buried, through to the cumulative tide of elegies, whether printed, or, when musical, per- formed, and even in one instance staged, there was no abatement of the sense of loss. There was, of course, a tradition of such public mourning — improbable as the conjunction seems, it embraced Sir Philip Sidney and the Earl of Rochester, and all the literary echoes are in place in the preliminaries to *Orpheus Britannicus*. Playford had grumbled that the delay was costing him money, but if he had not been sure of his market he would surely have priced it at more than 16s. bound; the frontispiece sold on its own as a print for 6d. By the time of the publication of the second book in 1702, the price of the first volume had risen to £1 (Henry was never afraid of putting up his prices). The second book cost 12s., and the two volumes 'Bound both together' cost £1.10s., including the Dryden/ Blow Ode which was also sold on its own for 2s. Many purchasers, it seems, chose the inclusive option.

This leads to what must be the nub of an assessment of the association between the Playfords and the Purcells. Just how significant is *Orpheus Britannicus*? If it was intended to be taken as a musical equivalent of the stately procession of literary folios from Jonson and Shakespeare through to Tonson's Dryden — as presumably Playford hoped — it proves to be nothing of the kind. It is of course the appropriate size, but that is where the problems begin. Not only does music convey less in more space than words, but if your choice of type is Heptinstall's new-ty'd note you require a heavier gauge paper than with conventional print, while the more ritornelli you conscientiously include, the less far the paper goes.[19] To compound the problem, the more your musical folio resembles a literary folio the less readily will it sit on the music desk of a harpsichord or spinet (insofar as such desks existed in the late seventeenth century), or on a music stand (with the same proviso). The two books of *Orpheus Britannicus* bound together are very substantial indeed.

Playford seems not to have regarded this as a problem. In due course he encouraged the assumption that owners would want to bind the two volumes together, and it is evident from the preface to the fourth book of *The Theater of Musick* that he expected that 'this excellent Book may be joyn'd and bound with the three former [and] will make a compleat Volume'. This would be at least as big as *Orpheus* Book I, and surviving examples show that the suggestion was often acted on. It is likely that we overestimate the use of harpsichord or spinet as an accompanying instrument before 1700, that the theorbo or bass viol were more common (as indeed the titlepages of the song collections indicate) and that in those circumstances a large volume propped on a table would pose no problem. Certainly Samuel Pepys, who very practically had vocal and instrumental parts bound in marbled paper, encased his song-books in calf, presumably because they were only used by himself accompanying himself or being accompanied by just one other person, his domestic musician, Cesare Morelli.

Underlying this doubt is, of course, the question: was *Orpheus Britannicus* for use or ostentation? It cannot claim to be anywhere near completion, or even to be representative. Book I adopts the procrustean device of ordering its hugely diverse contents according to the gamut;[20] Book II, because most of the materials came from Frances Purcell, does at least preserve an element of its contents' original context within an ode, or play, or dramatick opera. In almost no instance does an *Orpheus Britannicus* printing represent the best text or anything like it; 'From Rosy Bowers', the mad song in *Don Quixote* Part III, may be the unique case. Nor should it be forgotten that, assuming that the inclusion of 'Ah! Belinda' means that Playford had sight of a manuscript of *Dido and Aeneas*, he momentously overlooked 'When I am laid in Earth'. If there is a consistency in editorial practice to be observed, it is the lavish provision of figurations in the bass for which there is no evidence in the surviving originals. This may be an informed reflection of Purcell's practice, or it may be a half-way house to 'additional accompaniments'.

For the original purchasers of *Orpheus Britannicus*, the lack of textual authority would not have been an immediate matter of concern. It gave them a great deal of material in a usable form. But (to revert to the question) did they use it? What, if anything, can surviving copies tell us about the extent to which *Orpheus Britannicus* was a trophy, part of the furniture of a library? To what extent was it alive as a working score?

Long ago I must have fallen for Henry Playford's pitch. If we have anything approaching a Purcellian first folio then *Orpheus Britannicus* must be it, wildly incomplete, selective, and arbitrarily edited as it is. It has become a rare book, for better or worse, and — at the very least — as near to an original Purcellian volume as, given the fragility of other materials, people are likely in the twenty-first century to get. For that reason surviving copies are less liable to answer the kind of questions I want to ask than might be expected. Copies have been sophisticated in almost every imaginable way, a process that it can reasonably be claimed started in Playford's shop, just as deficiencies obviously also began there. It is clear, for instance, from offsets, that the portrait was added only when the sheets were bound, and the eventual existence of the two books, sold together or separately, involved a juggling process that could easily become confused. It is not merely a matter of the portrait; it is common to find second editions of Book I bound with first editions of Book II, evidently as sold, and as some copies are in later bindings anything might have happened, and often has.

It is not my purpose to inveigh against sophistication, especially in the case of music, which is so exposed to wear and tear. A sedulous search for unsophisticated copies, the worse the better, suggests that there is less to be learned than might be imagined, for the simple reason that marking up copies for performance seems to be very largely a post-eighteenth-century practice. Students of accompaniment know that to find workings-out of figured basses in contemporary notation is extremely unusual indeed, though emendations to figuring are more common. Indeed, markings in early printed music are more likely to be illiterate scribblings and scrawls, even vandalism, than informative marks with evident purpose. Perhaps the simple fact is that less marking was required when a particular standard of attainment could be taken for granted — which may seem heretical but is not necessarily untrue. A particular instance will illustrate this point. A second edition of Book I, lacking the portrait, titlepage and most of the prelims, but in a very grubby and torn but tough wrapper in which it might always have lived, looked extremely promising — dog-eared, stained and used. Needless to say it had some inexplicable obliterations, this time of inoffensive words. Yet in fact it contained a carefully annotated sequence, the setting of Ismeron's 'from thy Sleeping Mansion rise' in *The Indian Queen*, memorably singled out by Constant Lambert in *Music Ho!* as an exceptional evocation by a pre-Romantic composer of strangeness and awe: an 'amazing passage'. It evidently struck a contemporary in just the same way, since he added a direction, 'Slow', and a meticulous set of figures which accurately represent the progression of the string parts and presumably clarified for the annotator an effect which must have impressed him as much as, over 200 years later, it did Lambert.[21]

Several copies of the first edition of Book II, which on the whole is less fully figured than Book I, have added figuration; this is not sufficiently consistent to indicate an in-house origin, but is of interest in that it apparently reflects a need felt by early owners. Copies of the first editions of both books often contain corrections, in the bass line, of the many places where figuring and accidentals have become confused. On the whole verbal modifications, sometimes for Bedfordian reasons, are more common than musical. The numerous ink-stains and pen-trials, in 'used' copies, which serve no apparent purpose might be explained by the use of these as masters from which transcripts were made, in the form of single sheets, for performance. The evidence for such a practice is thin, but the survival of the masters itself provides a reason why such abstracts have seldom been preserved.

Comparison of the two editions of both books has proved equally perplexing — though Playford's purposes cannot be impenetrable. To omit from the original *Orpheus* 'Sighs for our late Sovereign *King Charles the Second*' was to lose a work written in circumstances which had become politically confusing — it could be read as an argument for abjuring when the terms of that debate had shifted entirely — and the austerity of its musical language unpleasing. It would make room for, amongst other things, the accompaniments to 'You twice Ten Hundred Deities', the analysis of which would so fascinate our anonymous annotator (and the absence of which must have deeply puzzled anyone who had been fortunate enough to hear *The Indian Queen* and was then left to depend on the 1698 *Orpheus*).

Some of these decisions seem principled; others look merely opportunist. We can follow the composer of the 1706 *Orpheus* at work, correcting rather acutely from 1698 but usually stumbling a few bars after a correction; we cannot tell to what extent Playford looked over his shoulder, or why he should have decided what was in and what was out. But two things about the 1698 *Orpheus Britannicus* deserve emphasis, for all its deficiencies.

The first of these is the effectiveness of its design, and particularly its title.[22] In *Harmonia Sacra* (1688) Playford put together, apparently for the first time in a musical publication, a full-page frontispiece and a rubricated titlepage. His father had previously used both devices, the frontispiece for *The Treasury of Musick*, rubrication for liturgical publications. Here they came together, although the frontispiece stood rather cumbrously against the titlepage.

The well-printed book was not a Restoration novelty; the sophistication of Sir Robert Stapylton's *Juvenal* of 1660, printed by Richard Hodgkinson, and the opulent vulgarity of John Ogilby's ventures, notably his *Aesop* of 1665, show what was possible. They were both expensive. With *Orpheus Britannicus* and *Harmonia Sacra*, Playford contrived something substantial, effective, and cheap. The Robert White engraving of the Closterman portrait is a brilliant approximation of what mezzotint might have done had the cost and the print-run permitted the medium. There can be little doubt that with the publication of the Dryden and Blow *Ode on the Death of Mr. Henry Purcell*, Playford had learnt a great deal about what could be achieved by simple typographical means, seriously deployed. His catchy title must derive from Dryden's apotheosis of Purcell as the English Orpheus. (For a complementary failure, ironically involving a poem that haunts the *Orpheus* elegies, compare Tonson's treatment of John Oldham's *Bion*, prefixed to his edition of Rochester's *Poems ... with Valentinian* (1691), with its hint of a mourning border.) For all that, the ultimate success of the anthology depended on an extension of the necrological beyond the typological into the editorial, and this is my second and final point, the crucial involvement of Frances Purcell.

This involvement may be in detail unknowable, although the scantest awareness of Frances's activities makes nonsense of, for instance, Heinz Gärtner's claim for Constanze Mozart, that she was the first composer's widow to manage her husband's estate and reputation.[23] The difference of a hundred years aside, Frances Purcell was apparently a capable businesswoman before her husband's death obliged her to be so. But with the exception of one recent writer the achievements of Mrs Purcell have been not so much ignored as taken for granted.[24] In summary, it appears that Henry Playford had presumed that he could assemble a sufficient commemoration of Purcell from whatever he and John, senior, had published or had in hand. When it came to it, it was evident he could not. Book I of *Orpheus* takes in the available material, but moves beyond into what, from manuscript, only Frances could provide. Hence its long gestation, and hence, perhaps most importantly, its dedication by Frances to 'the Honourable the Lady Howard'.

This is a small masterpiece, and though there is no particular reason to doubt its authorship, it must have been requested and approved by Playford, whose dedication of *Harmonia Sacra* to Thomas Ken had demonstrated a remarkable command of the form. It was typographically bold rather than elegant, and almost shockingly laconic, which was, of course, the point. In 1688 no prospective buyer of a 'Collection of *Divine Musick*' needed to have it explained that the 'Lord Bishop of Bath and Wells', known for his sanctity, his writings and his love of music, was fearless in the face of monarchical abuse of power and in defence of the Church of England, but that this could not be said. The empty spaces on the page spoke for themselves.

The dedication of *Orpheus Britannicus* admitted of no such reticence. The typography remained bold and the text, by contemporary standards, brief. Annabella Howard was the fourth wife of Sir Robert Howard, poet, playwright, and Auditor of the Exchequer, who had married her in 1693 when she was 18 and he 70. His literary reputation had had something of a revival at the same time, culminating in the production in 1695 of the operatic version of his *The Indian Queen*, written as long ago as 1674. It had been Henry Purcell's last work for the stage, and since his death restaged with an additional masque by Daniel. Its history in the playhouse is contentious, but it was undoubtedly a popular success, and it would have been easy to have accorded Howard a higher place in the dedication, but he was simply 'among' the poets whom Purcell admired.[25]

Lady Howard was a renowned beauty, the subject of two popular mezzotints by John Smith after paintings by Kneller. What was less well known was that she had unusual musical abilities and had been one of Purcell's most esteemed pupils, for whose entertainment, as both listener and performer, he had written several of his compositions. She had been responsible for the monument commemorating him in Westminster Abbey and, since his death, had assisted his children. All of this information, conveyed with a minimum of hyperbole in the dedication, can be confirmed from independent sources. But its real force, for its original public, must have come from its being inscribed by a grieving but courageous widow — and many of its readers must have reflected that Lady Howard herself was, in the way of things, likely to become a widow soon, as she did later in the year, adding to the poignancy. However vulnerable such generalizations may be, it is inescapable that during the 1690s the cynicism of the Restoration was increasingly giving way to sentiment. It could be perceived as early as Nahum Tate's 'Alteration' of *King Lear* in 1681 and was beginning to predominate when Congreve's *The Mourning Bride* was produced a year before the publication of *Orpheus Britannicus*. The plight of widows was no longer being expressed primarily as posing a threat to the unwary unmarried male. It is interesting that Purcell's *Te Deum*, although Cecilian in origin, should become associated with the Society for the Sons of the Clergy, which was as much as anything a society for the relief of clergy widows.

That Frances Purcell was facing her widowhood with courage would have been obvious to any reader of the list of 'Books Printed for and Sold by Henry Playford' presented, with far more elegance and generosity of layout than usual, on the verso of the *Table of the Songs* in *Orpheus Britannicus*. This leads off with 'All the Excellent Compositions of Mr. *Henry Purcell*, both Vocal and Instrumental, that have been publish'd ... These Six [Compositions] printed for Madam *Purcell*, and sold for her by *Henry Playford*'. This was not really the case: the *Sonnata's* of 1683 and *Dioclesian* had been printed for the composer in his lifetime. But the remaining four, the *Choice Collection of Lessons for the Harpsichord or Spinnet* (1696), the *Collection of Ayres, Compos'd for the Theatre*, the *Te Deum and Jubilate ... made for St. Cecilia's Day*, 1694 and the *Ten Sonata's in Four Parts*, which all appeared in 1697, were indeed her responsibility. Even though Daniel Purcell is the most likely candidate as an editor, the manuscript corrections which frequently occur in copies of the *Ayres* and *Ten Sonata's* are almost certainly hers. After 6 November 1699 the business of selling them certainly was, since she formally withdrew all copies from the booksellers, and sold them from her house in Dean's Yard, Westminster.[26] (When she later moved to Richmond, they were handled by John Cullen in Fleet Street, and on her death acquired by Walsh.) All this is symptomatic of Playford's declining interest.

It seems that he regarded *Orpheus Britannicus* both as his *magnum opus* as a publisher and as a discharge of his responsibilities to serious secular music, there being quicker returns in *Pills* and Psalms. The dedication of the second book, to the second Marquess of Halifax, is perfunctory: the mawkishly self-seeking address from 'The Bookseller to the Reader' does not fail to mention the 'Dearness of Paper'. Of the three prefatory poems one is about Purcell and two about Playford as his publisher.[27] It is the material acquired from Frances Purcell which makes the content of the two volumes seamless. The epigraph in the second volume, taken from the *Aeneid*, describing the Golden Bough cut from Proserpina's grove, made clear to contemporaries that this volume would equal the first volume in excellence (as it does). Playford appears to have undertaken to publish John Blow's *Amphion Anglicus*, often regarded as the consort of *Orpheus*, replicating its layout and design; but he must have withdrawn from *Amphion*, which was printed 'for the Author', and (needless to say) better planned and edited, when it eventually appeared in 1700.[28]

Yet for all its faults *Orpheus Britannicus* survived, and if it would not sit on the desk of a spinet, it stood conveniently on a grand piano; it is striking that so many copies bear evidence of nineteenth-century use, showing how much it was venerated. *Orpheus* came to be the authoritative source for republication in anthologies and songsheets, starting with John Johnson's *A Collection of Songs taken from Orpheus Britannicus* (c.1765).

The tradition culminated in Benjamin Britten's 'realizations' (though they are more 'transcriptions' in the Busoni sense) of the 1940s and 1950s.[29] Purcell would not have approved of Playford's apparent preference for the songs, even though justified with the marvellous phrase that it was his 'peculiar Genius to express the Energy of *English* Words'. Nevertheless, despite the long relationship with the Playfords, it is not unreasonable to claim that Henry Purcell found his best and most devoted publisher in his wife Frances.

*References*

1. John Aubrey, *Wiltshire: The Topographical Collections*, corrected and enlarged by Canon J. E. Jackson (Devizes, 1862), p. 62, reports the Purcell allusion.

2. Michael Burden, *Purcell Remembered* (London, 1995), p. 116; Burden's anthology provides a convenient synoptic view of Purcell's reputation.

3. Robert Thompson, 'John Playford', *Oxford Dictionary of National Biography* (Oxford, 2004), establishes the essential biographical facts for all the members of the family, and subsumes the previous literature, of which D. R. Harvey's University of Wellington dissertation, *Henry Playford: A Bibliographical Study* (1985), remains particularly significant.

4. *The New Grove Dictionary of Music and* Musicians, 2nd edn., ed. Stanley Sadie (London, 2001).

5. D. W. Krummel, *English Music Printing, 1553–1700* (London: The Bibliographical Society, 1975), pp. 115–24.

6. Krummel (p. 124) wrote before the publication of Mary Chan and Jamie C. Kassler (ed.), *Roger North's Cursory Notes of Musick* (Kensington, N.S.W., 1986), where North refers to 'honest John Playford' (p. 208). 'Poor old Playford' is from John Wilson (ed.), *Roger North on Music* (London, 1959), p. 137.

7. Andrew Clark (ed.), '*Brief Lives' set down by John Aubrey*, 2 vols (Oxford, 1898), II, p. 62.

8. Titlepage transcription of Playford editions of Purcell is fraught with bibliographical pitfalls. There are often several variants of the same date; it is impossible to know which is the true first and listing all is impractical. I have followed the practice of Cyrus Lawrence Day and Eleanore Boswell Murrie, *English Song-Books, 1651–1702* (London: The Bibliographical Society, 1940) in my choice of title, whenever possible.

9. *Catch that Catch can or A New Collection of Catches, Rounds, and Canons* (London, 1663), unsigned section at end, p. 19. The title to the canon reports 'Who dyed *Oct.* 23 1662'; the accepted date is recorded in the Cheque Book of the Chapel Royal. Charles Burney, *A General History of Music*, 4 vols (London, 1776–89), III, p. 477, notes the change in the character of the 1667 edition with apparent approval.

10. *The Works of Henry Purcell*, vol. 25, ed. Margaret Laurie (Sevenoaks, 1985), p. viii and Appendix D.

11. Peter Holman, *Henry Purcell* (Oxford, 1994), pp. 38, 41.

12. cf. Wilson, *Roger North*, p. 310, n. 65, and Chan and Kassler, p. 229.

13. Robert Thompson, 'Manuscript music in Purcell's London', *Early Music*, vol. XXIII/4 (November 1995), p. 616.

14. Krummel, p. 126; Arthur Bedford, *The Great Abuse of Musick ... containing ... An Account of the Immorality and Profaneness, which is occasioned by the Corruption of that most Noble Science in the Present Age* (London, 1711), p. 67. Seldom can *Pills to Purge Melancholy* have been read with such attention.

15. Ian Spink, 'The Old Jewry "Music-Society": A 17th-Century Catch Club', *Musicology* II (1967), pp. 35–41.

16. For the background see Vincent H. Duckles, 'The English Musical Elegy of the Late Renaissance', *Aspects of Medieval and Renaissance Music* (New York, 1966), pp. 134 ff.

17. Chan and Kassler, p. 229.

18. Robert Shay and Robert Thompson, *Purcell's Manuscripts: The Principal Musical Sources* (Cambridge, 2000), p. 17.

19. Playford complains about the cost of paper in 'The Bookseller to the Reader' in both books of *Orpheus Britannicus*.

20. Andrew Parrott, 'Performing Purcell', in Michael Burden (ed.), *The Purcell Companion* (London, 1995), p. 305, remarks of the arrangement by the gamut, 'surely a convenience for performers rather than a theoretical scheme', an observation about which I was sceptical until I encountered a copy of *Harmonia Sacra* which an early owner had indexed by gamut.

21. Defective copy of *Orpheus Britannicus* I/II in the writer's possession; Constant Lambert, *Music Ho! A Study of Music in Decline* (London, 1934), 3rd edn., 1966, p. 62.

22. It would be pleasing to think that Playford derived the title from Horatio Moore's characterization of Henry Lawes as 'our Orpheus' in the prefatory poem to *Select Ayres and Dialogues ... The Third Book*. But it seems more likely that he simply derived it from the brilliant trope in Purcell's *Ode*; it seems very likely, however, that Dryden knew Moore's poem.

23. Heinz Gärtner, *Constanze Mozart: After the Requiem*, trans. Reinhard G. Pauly (Portland, Oregon, 1991).

24. Maureen Duffy, *Henry Purcell* (London, 1994), p. 213, describes *Orpheus Britannicus* as 'Frances's posthumous collection'. This is hyperbolic, although Frances was, by inference, an important contributor to the second book, and, by Playford's direct admission, to the 2nd edition of the first book.

25. The account by Julia K. Woods in Michael Burden (ed.), *Henry Purcell's Operas: The Complete Texts* (Oxford, 2000), does all that can be done to revive the record.

26. *The Works of Henry Purcell*, vol. 7, ed. Michael Tilmouth (Borough Green, 1981), p. x.

27. It seems scarcely avoidable that Henry Playford is playing with the equivalence of his initials to those of Henry Purcell.

28. The undertaking to publish *Amphion Anglicus* is implied by the advertisement in *Orpheus Britannicus* (1698) for Dr Blow's 'Choice Songs'.

29. Benjamin Britten, 'On realizing the continuo in Purcell's songs', *Henry Purcell, 1659–1695: Essays on his Music*, ed. Imogen Holst (London, 1959), pp. 7–13. The Britten/Pears series of Purcell transcriptions emerged directly from *Orpheus Britannicus* and *Harmonia Sacra*.

# John Walsh and his Handel Editions

DONALD BURROWS

THE EDITIONS OF MUSIC by George Frideric Handel that were published
by the London firm of John Walsh were the fruit of an authoritative,
though not continuous, relationship with the composer who made London's music-making special in the first half of the eighteenth century.
However, we have scant knowledge of the business practices and working
methods of the firm during Handel's lifetime, beyond what can be gleaned
from the music itself, the advertisements in the London newspapers that
announced current publication programmes, and the occasional printed
catalogues. Advertisements appeared under the formula 'This day is publish'd', introducing titles of publications that were currently available: the
first appearance of a work in one of these lists is usually our best evidence
for the launch of a new edition. Most of the 'catalogues' consisted of
similar lists that were printed on otherwise unused spaces in the music
editions themselves.

On the titlepages the publisher's name appears variously as 'I', 'J', or
'John' Walsh. These forms refer to two individuals, father and son, who
were successively responsible for, and indeed owners of, the publishing
house. John senior began publishing in the 1690s, and gradually expanded
his activities to achieve the premier position in London's music trade that
had formerly been occupied by the Playfords. He died in 1736, having
made special provision in his will for his eldest surviving son Samuel, who
'seems not to have an Inclination to follow business but to live retired'.[1]
Things were otherwise with his younger son John, who apparently took up
his father's career without hesitation. In the 1730s he was almost certainly
responsible for a number of technical innovations that attempted to bring
some order into what had become a rather unwieldy range of musical publications, and also for developing a permanent formal arrangement with
Handel: it is John Walsh junior who can most appropriately be described
as 'Handel's publisher'. However, the professional succession between
father and son seems to have been effected smoothly, and it is only in the
transitional period from 1731 to 1736 that there is any ambiguity about
the 'John Walsh' concerned: they were never distinguished on the titlepages. In the absence of evidence that would have established their individual responsibilities during the overlapping period, I shall use 'Walsh' as a

continuous description, on the understanding that earlier and later references are to John senior and John junior, respectively.

The documentary materials relating to the publishing house up to the time of Walsh junior's death in 1766 are few, in contrast to the more fortunate situation with some other London printer-publishers such as the Tonsons. There are no surviving records of sales, payments to staff and contractors, print runs, stock, or site costs. Correspondence is represented by just one letter, written by Walsh junior to James Harris in 1744, and now in the collection of Harris's descendant, the Earl of Malmesbury (Fig. 1).[2] The only contemporary business record does not survive in the original, but is known from a later transcription. It is a list of payments to Handel for music copy that was printed in George Macfarren's *A Sketch of the Life of Handel*, published in 1859.[3] Macfarren claimed that this was a faithful transcript from a single leaf that had been sent to him in 1844, as Secretary of the Handel Society, by a Mr Nottingham. It is unlikely that the leaf was an original item from Walsh's records, but rather a selective transcript of items extracted from the accounts. The content is thus only available from a third-generation copy, and may have lost something in the translation, but I am inclined to trust it in general substance. What we cannot know, of course, is the basis on which the hypothetical extractor collected the items in the list, and the nature of the original sources from which they were derived. Although the list is not chronological, the entries are in date-groups, which perhaps suggests that they were taken from a series of account ledgers that were not shelved in chronological order. To these two documents may be added a few others that refer to the Walshes and I will employ them in due course, in attempting to reconstruct something of the history of their working relationship with Handel.

First, however, it is necessary to have some sense of the scope of their business, for music printing and publishing was not initially — and probably not ever — their sole activity. The story begins, indeed, with something entirely different, the appointment of Walsh senior on 24 June 1692 as 'Musical Instrument Maker in Ordinary to his Majesty, in place of John Shaw, surrendered'.[4] Some form of institutional succession is suggested by the circumstance that Walsh apparently took over Shaw's trade sign, 'The Golden Harp and Hoboy'. Unlike the court's Musical Instrument Keeper, the Instrument Maker did not receive a regular salary or pension, and the nature of his income from the post during William III's reign is uncertain, but from Anne's reign onwards Walsh was paid regularly for mending and stringing instruments, and for supplying new instruments to the royal band of 24 Musicians (an ensemble of stringed instruments) and to the Chapel Royal. The payments for new instruments refer mainly to tenor or bass

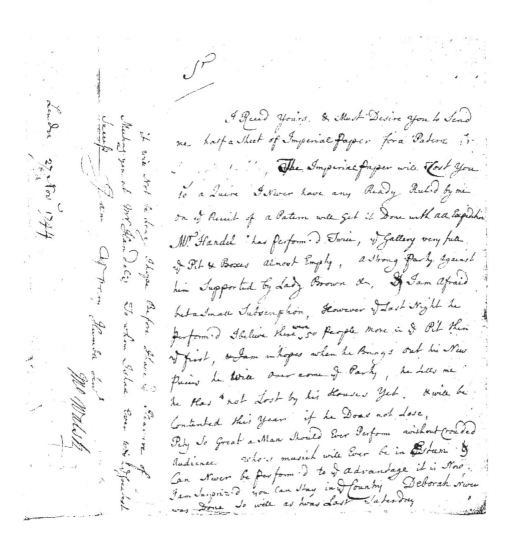

*Fig. 1.* Letter from John Walsh the younger to James Harris, 27 November 1744 (Hampshire Record Office 9M73/G610, reproduced by courtesy of the Earl of Malmesbury)

violins, or bass viols: while it is not possible to be certain of the exact nature of the instruments covered by these descriptions, it is curious that they needed replacing more often than violins. From the beginning of George II's reign, flutes also suddenly appear in the payments for new instruments. It seems fairly certain that the Walshes did not make the instruments themselves, since not a single instrument attributed to them is or has been known. The court appointment featured regularly in the imprint of the firm's publications. Walsh senior usually confined the description to 'Servant to her [or his] Majesty', but Walsh junior hit on the formula 'Musick Printer and Instrument Maker to his Majesty' that, by omitting the comma, suggested that he was also Music Printer to the King, which no doubt served to increase the perceived status of his publications among those who were not aware that the office was non-existent. However, the payments to Walsh in the Lord Chamberlain's records sometimes include references to music as well as instruments: the earliest one that I have been able to trace mentions 'Books of Musick and Dances for the Birthday Ball' in the last years of Queen Anne's reign.[5] Annual collections of 'Minuets, Rigadoons and French Dances' as performed at court became one of Walsh's regular publication series.

Two events from 1695, no doubt related, mark the start of the new direction in the activity of Walsh senior: he took a house in Catherine Street, Strand, and produced his first musical publication. Catherine Street lay in that ambiguous region between the City of London and the fast-expanding smart area of Westminster's 'West End', in the Bedford-Estate swathe of London that included the theatres at Drury Lane, Lincoln's Inn Fields and (from 1732) Covent Garden (but not the West-End opera house in the Haymarket). The music shop in Catherine Street was therefore accessible to customers from both the City and Westminster; Playford's premises had been in the same area. Walsh's rivals as music publishers were either close by or were located in the City. John Hare also started publishing in 1695, and the houses of Walsh and Hare seem to have collaborated closely for about 35 years, with John and Joseph Hare named successively as partners on Walsh's imprints. It is very likely that the Hares made many of the instruments that Walsh supplied to the court, and the collaboration provided Walsh with a City outlet for his music from Hare's shop at Cornhill, near the Royal Exchange. Walsh himself moved briefly to Dutchy Lane, but by Easter 1697 he was back in Catherine Street, and that address, covering a succession of different houses, became the permanent home for the firm.

What would we have found at the Harp and Hoboy? The Catherine Street property served two functions as well as providing a family dwelling:

a showroom that was described as the 'music shop', probably modest in size and with a public counter, and a warehouse facility that may also have housed printing presses. The shop presumably sold instrument accessories such as violin strings, and acted as an agency for the purchase of new instruments in addition to selling musical publications. Subscription lists for publications were released through, and probably administered from, the shop, and for Handel's ambitious oratorio season of 1744–5 Walsh acted as one of the agents for performance subscriptions.[6]

The 'music shop' business and the retail sale of printed music is mentioned in the course of letters now in the Malmesbury archive, written to James Harris by his brother Thomas, a lawyer and amateur cellist who lived nearby in Lincoln's Inn Fields. In May 1747 Thomas called at the shop to inspect the latest set of cello sonatas:[7] 'Geminiani has just published 6 Solos for a violoncello, which I have lookd at at Walsh's, & am afraid they are above my skill, but they are certainly genuine.' He therefore presumably did not buy the Solos, and we might wonder what their commercial value was to Walsh: there were not many cellists in London, and most of the amateurs were probably less competent than Thomas Harris. In view of the small potential market, the case of these Geminiani sonatas is particularly intriguing. The composer published them in Paris as his Op.5, in an edition dated 1746. There was also another edition, with an Italian titlepage giving the place of publication as 'London', but with no date or publisher's imprint: this was not engraved in the current Walsh style, and the only surviving copy includes a British Privilege, dated 29 July 1730, giving Geminiani publication rights over his music. In a postscript to a letter written from The Hague on 10 January 1747, Geminiani complained thus to his former pupil Joseph Kelway:[8]

After writing the above, I discovered that I have been robbed by my engraver of four copies of the new solo sonatas, and I have been told that one of them has been sold to an Englishman, which makes me very afraid that it has got into the hands of Walsh. If this is true, it could be very prejudicial to my interests, so I ask you therefore to give me any information about this that you are able to learn.

We do not know which edition of the sonatas Thomas Harris saw at Walsh's, though the phrase 'they are certainly genuine' (concerning the music) perhaps suggests that he had some doubt about its provenance.[9] He had probably visited the shop after seeing the announcement for the publication of the sonatas in The Daily Advertiser on 5 May, which said that they were on sale from Kelway's house, but did not mention Walsh. Later in the year Geminiani seems to have accepted Walsh as one of the agents to take subscriptions for his forthcoming set of concertos, probably recognizing that this was inevitable in view of the hold that the publisher had over the London market. It is noticeable, nevertheless, that the relevant advertisement in *The General Advertiser* for 3 September 1747 did not include the Op.5 sonatas in the list of other works by Geminiani that were on sale at Walsh's. Walsh's practice of selling music editions from other British and foreign publishers, along with his own, gave a cover that could obscure the issue of piracy in the production of unauthorized editions, at least in the short term, while at the same time making a competitive pitch in claiming to provide a comprehensive service to London's musicians, amateur and professional.

However, the 'music shop' aspect of Walsh's business also left him directly accountable to the public for his own acknowledged publications. On this matter Thomas Harris's letters provide a rather surprising insight into the responsibility that the publisher was expected to fulfil. In 1728 and 1734 Walsh had produced some rather primitive collections of airs from Handel's current operas *Tolomeo* and *Arianna in Creta*, the latter not even as an independent publication but in a combined collection with arias from Handel's pasticcio *Arbace* and Porpora's 'Ariadne' opera for the rival company. In 1737 Walsh published more substantial — though still not 'complete' — editions of the music from Handel's operas, referred to in Harris's letter of 1 December: 'Walsh has printed the opera's of Ariadne and Ptolemy entire, of which before there were only favourite songs.' Five days later he wrote: 'Let me know ... if you have the favourite songs in those opera's which I am to buy; for if you will part with them, I believe Walsh will take them in exchange, as indeed he ought to do.'[10] This is all the more remarkable because *Arianna* and *Tolomeo* were not performed in Handel's current opera season of 1736–7, which must have limited the prospect of sales for the new editions.

We cannot be sure that music engraving and printing took place at Catherine Street, though it probably did, but it seems virtually certain that the ever-expanding stock of printing plates and printed music pages was stored there.[11] The scale of accumulated publication implies not only considerable storage space but also a considerable paper stock, and this leads us to an aspect of Walsh's activity that has received little notice hitherto: the sale of ready-ruled music paper. Handel's own surviving musical autographs written in London amount to about 7,000 leaves, and his performing scores now at Hamburg account for at least as many again. Large quantities of music paper went into the creation of library scores of Handel's music in manuscript copies, beginning with the Malmesbury collection in the second decade of the century and mushrooming with the Granville, Shaftesbury, Aylesford and Lennard collections (to give them their modern names) in the 1730s and 1740s. Most likely Walsh was the principal supplier of the good-quality paper that was used for this substantial London-based industry in manuscripts of Handel's music. The same papers are also found in repertories of other London-based composers, though not in such profusion since they mainly used poorer-quality paper types.

There are two specific hints of the scope of Walsh's activity as a seller of music paper. In 1717–18 Thomas Tudway, at Cambridge, was in the midst of his grand project to produce a multi-volume manuscript anthology of masterpieces of English church music to grace Lord Harley's library in his new country house at Wimpole.[12] His correspondence with Harley's steward in London records negotiations over the supply of paper for the project. First, on 17 November 1717:

My services to those friends you may meet with at St Paul's, as likewise to Mr Walsh, Let him know I shall want six quire of the same paper as hitherto, & that I desire him to get it ready to rule[;] against I send him notice by letter, I shall send him a specimen of size &c:[13]

and then on 1 December:

Pray favour me with telling Mr Walsh, that I make no scruple of paying down the money upon receiving my paper, but as to his chargeing me with twelve shillings, he is grossly mistaken; for I paid the balance of the account this last summer, when he was in Cambridg, & I have his acquitance in full;[14]

The matter of the account was settled by 19 January 1718, when Tudway wrote: 'Mr Walsh has done me the justice to own, that his demand above the 18s for the last paper, was a mistake', from which it seems that Walsh was charging 3 shillings per quire for ready-ruled music paper.[15]

We may wonder what Walsh was doing in Cambridge in 1717. My guess is that he had accompanied the court on King George I's brief visit to Newmarket and Cambridge early in October, even though that was not quite the 'summer' as described by Tudway. This would imply that at least some of the King's Musicians also travelled there, with the Instrument Maker in attendance. The excursion is not very well documented, and no travelling charges for musicians are recorded in the Lord Chamberlain's records, but if the Musicians did form part of the royal entourage then perhaps Walsh's court appointment carried real obligations. He was certainly in close touch with the Musicians themselves, since following the death of Henry Eccles in 1711 Walsh collected his final salary payment as executor.[16]

It is interesting that Tudway needed to send a specification of page size and layout for the ruled music paper, and this is echoed 27 years later in the letter from Walsh junior to James Harris (see Fig. 1):

I recd yours [i.e. your letter] & must desire you to send me half a sheet of Imperial paper for a patern. The Imperial paper will cost you 10s a quire[.] I never have any ready rul'd by me[.] On the receit of a patern will get it done with all expedition.

The London manuscripts of Handel's music on good-quality paper, whether autographs or copies, show a sequence of fairly standardized patterns of stave-rulings, and before seeing this letter I had assumed that the supplier had maintained a stock of music manuscript paper in readiness, but it now seems that the ruling was done to order. Since Tudway's music volumes are written on paper with the same types of watermarks and rastra as contemporary Handel autographs and copies, I think that we can regard Walsh as the general supplier around 1715–20. In 1743, in connection with Handel's composition of the 'Dettingen' music, John Christopher Smith wrote that 'by the paper he had from me I can guess that it must be almost finished', but my guess is that Smith had been supplied with the paper by Walsh:[17] given Smith's apparent role as manager for the considerable copying industry of Handel's music, it would not be surprising if he had acted as general distributor to the composer as well as his own copyists. The rather anomalous appearance of Italian papers in Handel's London autographs from around 1724–6 may reflect some interruption to the regular supply, or possibly a period when Handel had fallen out with Walsh and was reliant on a different London supplier. Rather less plausible as an explanation is the fact that Walsh was the subject of a court sentence in 1726 for non-payment of a stamp duty applicable to single-sheet songs, from which he received release the following year, for this did not involve actual detention in prison.[18]

The combined requirements for the production of music manuscript paper and printed editions must have prompted Walsh to be active in securing necessary paper supplies. There may possibly be information about the extent of Walsh's activity as an importer in the Excise records; that he was probably the direct agent, rather than dealing through intermediaries, is indicated by a petition to the Treasury in January 1734 from 'John Walsh of Catherine Street, in the Strand, music printer, concerning the wrong entry of paper at the Custom House'.[19] Good-quality paper was employed for both music manuscript and printed editions, but I have not found precise matches in the watermarks between the two types of sources, perhaps because of differences in size and format of the paper used. The printing paper of course needed to have a suitable absorbency for the type of ink, and the type of presses, that were used. The best, heavier, 'Dutch' paper was used more frequently as Walsh's editions increasingly printed the music on both sides of the page: the earlier single-sided aria collections are generally on thinner paper.

One striking feature is that the music was printed as separate leaves and bound by sewing at the inner margin; the presses of the time apparently could not cope with any sheet larger than a half-folio leaf.[20] This has some important consequences relating to the content of the music editions, particularly in the case of publications that had a long life, such as the two volumes of Handel's keyboard suites. The early editions of the Suites have a complex publishing history: in the 1730s Walsh took over the original edition of the First Collection, which he subsequently re-engraved, and produced a Second Collection whose content was partly related to a previous edition entitled *Pieces à un & Deux Clavecins Composées Par Mr Hendel.*[21] Surviving copies of the Suites have variations in the way of corrections and amendments to the printed music texts, and the quantity of apparently unrelated inconsistency might be explained by the circumstance that each copy was made up afresh from racks of the separate pages, in which individual bundles may have originated or been corrected at different times. The bibliographical diversity of musical content that may be found under one cover consequently defies simple classification by edition, impression and issue. The physical construction of the editions must also have made life difficult for the eighteenth-century musician, amateur or professional, who attempted to play the suites from a margin-sewn volume of nearly 100 pages in landscape quarto format and of substantial thickness, precariously balanced on the music-desk of a harpsichord.

It is not certain whether Walsh had a permanent staff of engravers in the house or whether he employed freelance journeymen, but there is a clear succession of engraving styles, suggesting that the publisher had a regular working relationship with a fairly small group of craftsmen. The short turn-round times implied by the proximity of publication dates to performance dates also suggests the existence of a permanent dedicated team.[22] The identification of 'Walsh engravers' on the basis of acknowledged publications is the main evidence for attributing other ventures to the same publisher, as for example the various issues that appeared with the anonymized imprint 'sold at the Musick Shops'. My impression is that, at least by the mid-1720s, Walsh had a regular team of engravers who worked mostly, possibly exclusively, for him, using pewter plates and punch-stamping in combination with engraving or etching. The identification of an 'engraving style' based on the consistent use of images from a particular set of punches of course relies on the punches rather than the user, but most likely each style probably represents an individual craftsman working with a separate and characteristic set of punches.[23] (The craft seems to have been an all-male activity.) Many of the page-images suggest that once an engraver had done the basic work, a second person reviewed the plate, making additions such as tempo indications or cues, and possibly also corrections.

David Hunter has identified six music-engraving styles in Walsh's editions up to the year 1726, a period that covers the first fifteen years of his Handel publications but is relatively thin compared with the quantity of Handel's music that Walsh issued during the following 35 years.[24] The 1720s saw the development of a characteristic Walsh house style in the music image, which can be traced through the publication history of the handsome two-volume collection of William Croft's church music, *Musica Sacra*.[25] Croft first announced the venture in March 1720, when he declared that the book of anthems, probably then planned as a single volume, had 'for some time past ... been Engraving in Score on Copper Plates' and was 'now finished and printing off; and will be ready to be deliver'd to such Persons as have desired, or may be desirous of having the same, before Easter next', but no such result followed.[26] My guess is that he initially intended to produce the publication independently, in collaboration with the printer Richard Meares, as he was currently also doing with the handsomely produced score of his Oxford doctoral odes, but that the project was delayed, and probably became unmanageable as the repertory of anthems for inclusion expanded. So instead Croft threw in his lot with Walsh, resulting in a proposal dated 25 March 1724, in which Croft announced that: 'I have appointed ... Mr *Walsh* to print my Anthems, as above; and I intend to correct the Errors of the Press with my own Hand before the said Anthems are published.'[27] The first volume of *Musica Sacra* appeared early in 1725, with a subscription list of 154 names and a dedication to the King; the second volume came out about a year later, with a dedication to the Prince of Wales. Volume 1 has 184 music pages. Of these, 54 pages, carrying 6 anthems, are in a fully engraved style and were presumably printed from the copper plates of 1720. Most of the remainder of the volume, and interleaved with the 'copper-plate' style for the first 101 pages, is in the 'Walsh' style, the work of a different engraver. The 1724 proposal makes no mention of copper plates, and it looks to me as if these new pages were worked on pewter. The proposal promised that 'To each Volume there will be one Anthem, with Accompanyments of Instruments', and Volume 1 concludes with two items that were probably engraved last: Croft's most recent orchestrally accompanied anthem, *Rejoice in the Lord, O ye righteous*', and the now-famous setting of the Burial Service, which had been performed at the Duke of Marlborough's funeral in 1722. The orchestrally accompanied anthem introduced a second new engraver. The two 'Walsh' engravers were entirely responsible for the music pages of Volume 2 of *Musica Sacra*, with the later engraver from Volume 1 doing a

*Fig. 2.* A page of music from the edition of songs from Handel's *Deborah*, in Walsh's 'engraving style A'. (Private Collection, reproduced by permission)

greater proportion of the work; however, the volume as a whole seems to reflect the co-operative activity of two men, each working with his own punches. The styles (which I have designated elsewhere as 'A' and 'B') are also familiar from Walsh's Handel publications in the 1730s,[28] and together constituted the house style on which the great expansion of the Handel issues developed, with various modifications such as the increasing employment of type-punches for the text-underlay (Fig. 2).

Tables 1 and 2 (see Appendix) summarize the repertory of Walsh's editions of Handel's music. For the first half of the publisher's relationship with Handel — that is, the first 25 years — various questions arise about the authority of Walsh's editions. 'Piracy' is rather a crude term here, because two distinct situations are involved: the reproduction of music that was also issued, under the composer's authorization, from another publisher, and the publication of music from a possibly authentic source but without the composer's permission or co-operation. We do not have any specific documentation on the second aspect, so Table 1 lists the works for which Walsh produced the first published editions, and Table 2 lists the works for which Walsh printed his own edition against an authoritative edition from another London publisher. (It is not appropriate to say 'after' another edition, because in some cases Walsh may have published first.)

The tables cover the principal publications of Handel's major works, but not the various parallel anthologies of arias or overtures. The publication dates are derived mainly from William C. Smith's surveys of advertisements in the London newspapers in connection with his catalogue of the editions, but these dates may sometimes be rather imprecise, reflecting what Walsh was minded to announce rather than what he published and when. The page-counts must also be regarded as approximate, for different issues even within a short time of the first publication have variations in both make-up and page-numbering. Sometimes, also, the 'Song' publications might or might not include the overture in score, or might incorporate the overture after it had been published separately. Nevertheless, the table gives a general overview of the repertory, the publication timetables and the relative bulk of the individual items — that is, the number of pages of music that you would get for your money.

The relationship between composer and publisher began positively, as Walsh senior seems to have been keen to secure a publication for Handel's first London opera, *Rinaldo*. The description of *Rinaldo* as a 'popular' work has been challenged,[29] but there is good reason to believe that it made a particular mark among the sort of people who went to the opera or who wanted to play through the latest songs from the shows for themselves — in other words, the sort of people who would buy music of the type that

Walsh sold. The edition of *Rinaldo* airs was advertised as 'exactly corrected by Mr. George Frederick Handell',[30] a claim that Walsh would not make again about his Handel editions for another 25 years. It also set the style that became standard for the 'Songs' publications, by printing a selection of arias in score, with the name of the original singer (rather than the name of the operatic character) in the headline to each. The subsequent productions of the opera company, worthy as they were, did not have the same cachet as *Rinaldo*, so it is not surprising that Walsh did not give them the same attention. What the composer thought is not known: perhaps publication was not a serious ambition for him at that time, and the printing of music from *Rinaldo* had sufficiently served its purpose in reinforcing his London reputation.

The initiation of the Royal Academy of Music, with its first operatic production in April 1720, marked a new beginning for Handel in London, and musical publications were a natural adjunct to the re-launch of his career. At this point, however, he seems not to have sought a renewed association with Walsh, preferring to proceed in a more independent manner, as Croft also was doing at the same time. The first set of keyboard suites, and the songs from his first Academy opera *Radamisto*, were 'Printed for the Author' and 'Publisht by the Author', respectively, and Handel, like Croft, used Meares as his publisher.[31] The music was sold by Meares and also by Christopher Smith 'at the Hand and Musick-Book in Coventry Street'; we may suspect that the publication projects were at least partly managed by John Christopher Smith, who a couple of years previously had come to London to assist Handel and became his principal music copyist. To the suites Handel added a preface beginning 'I have been obliged to publish some of the following lessons because surrepticious and incorrect copies of them had got abroad', probably a reference to the published collection already mentioned, the *Pieces à un & Deux Clavecins Composées Par Mr. Hendel*. This had appeared with a titlepage as if from Jeanne Roger of Amsterdam, but the music within was engraved in the current London style (clearly distinct from Roger's) and was littered with characteristically English movement names.[32] One would suspect piracy, but the titlepage could just be genuine, and this edition may have been a rare example of a genuinely collaborative enterprise between Roger and a London publisher, perhaps even Walsh.[33]

Returning now to Handel's own editions, the Suites (and, soon afterwards, *Radamisto*) included a copy of the Royal Privilege, dated 14 June 1720, giving '*George Fredrick Handel*, of our City of *London*, Gent. … Our Licence for the sole Printing and Publishing the said Works [of 'Vocal and Instrumental Musick'] for the Term of Fourteen Years' (Fig. 3). The

# GEORGE R.

GEORGE, by the Grace of GOD, King of *Great Britain France* and *Ireland*, Defender of the Faith : *&c.* To all to whom thefe Prefents fhall come, *Greeting*: Whereas *George Fredrick Handel*, of our City of *London*, Gent. hath humbly reprefented unto Us, That he hath with great Labour and Expence compofed feveral Works, confifting of *Vocal and Inftrumental MUSICK*, in Order to be Printed and Publifh'd ; and hath therefore befought Us to grant him Our Royal Priviledge and Licence for the fole Printing and Publifhing thereof for the Term of Fourteen Years : We being willing to give all due Encouragement to Works of this Nature, are gracioufly pleafed to condefcend to his Requeft ; And We do therefore by thefe Prefents, fo far as may be agreeable to the Statute in that behalf made and provided, grant unto him the faid *George Fredrick Handel*, his Executors, Adminiftrators and Affigns, Our Licence for the fole Printing and Publifhing the faid Works for the Term of Fourteen Years, to be computed from the Date hereof, ftriÀly forbidding all our Loving Subjeàs within our Kingdoms and Dominions, to Reprint or Abridge the fame, either in the like or any other Volume or Volumes whatfoever, or to Import, Buy, Vend, Utter or Diftribute any Copies thereof Reprinted beyond the Seas, during the aforefaid Term of Fourteen Years, without the Confent or Approbation of the faid *George Fredrick Handel*, His Heirs, Executors and Affigns, under their Hands and Seals firft had and obtain'd, as they will anfwer the contrary at their Perils : Whereof the Commiffioners and other Officers of Our Cuftoms, the Mafter, Wardens and Company of Stationers are to take Notice, that due Obedience may be rendred to our Pleafure herein declared. *Given at Our Court at St. James's the 14th Day of* June, 1720. *in the Sixth Year of Our Reign.*

## By *His Majefty's Command,*

# J. Craggs.

*Fig. 3.* Handel's first publication 'Privilege', dated 14 June 1720 (British Library, D.310.b.(1.))

description of Handel as being of the 'City of London' is interesting, since we do not know where he lived at the time. A more serious matter, of course, was the extent to which the 'Commissioners and other Officers of Our Customs, the Master, Wardens and Company of Stationers' were expected to enforce this Royal command. In 1721–3 Handel returned to Walsh as his publisher, but then went over to Cluer until 1730.[34]

Not surprisingly, the Privilege is attached to the copies of those editions that Handel authorized, with Walsh and then Cluer.[35] As can be seen from Table 2, this did not deter Walsh from putting out his own editions against those of Cluer, though with limited collections of songs rather than the handsome, if rather old-fashioned-looking, copper-plate full scores on smaller page-formats that Cluer produced. Here it is necessary to point out that some of Walsh's smaller collections were rather casually assembled from the plates of his mixed song-anthologies, such as the *Monthly Mask of Vocal Music* and *Apollo's Feast*: once a few songs had been engraved, these could be re-packaged under the name of the work. The inclusion of the Privilege stops rather abruptly after Cluer's edition of *Tamerlano* in 1724: perhaps in practice the monopoly was admitted to be a dead letter after about four or five years, or perhaps Handel simply ran out of copies of the Privilege. It may or may not be a coincidence that, just when the Privileges vanish, the Cluer editions go over to a pre-publication subscription system; the subscriptions were fairly successful for a couple of years but then diminished quite substantially, perhaps reflecting the loss of impetus that overcame the Royal Academy in its last seasons.

The early 1730s are the most obscure period in Walsh's relationship with Handel, and also an important period of change in the organization of the firm. Around 1730–1 Walsh severed his long-standing collaboration with the Hare family, which had continued with Joseph Hare after the death of his father John in 1725, and the managerial succession in the Walsh family itself probably began at about the same time. On 8 May 1731 Walsh senior surrendered his office as Instrument Maker to the King to his 21-year-old son; this was quite a rare occurrence since court posts were normally held for life at that time. A couple of technical innovations have reasonably been attributed to the influence of the younger man: the introduction of titlepages with variable passe-partout inserts, and of serial numbers for the publications (Fig. 4). The numbers are indicators of dates for new publications only for the period between summer 1733 and the end of 1740. My analysis suggests that Walsh allocated numbers to items in his back-catalogue, including music that originated from other publishers, in (or by) the spring of 1733.[36] The introduction of the numbers may have had an element of vanity, to emphasize the quantity of publications available

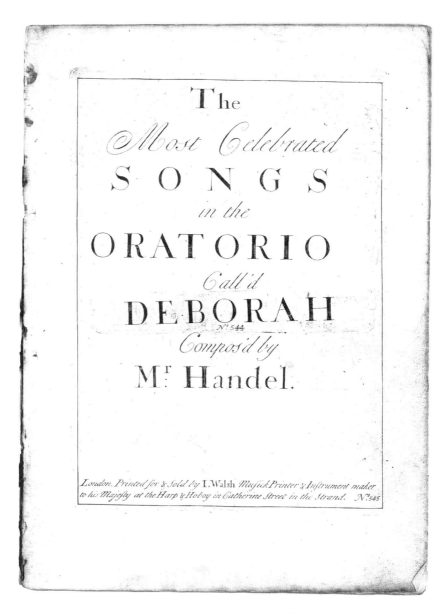

*Fig. 4.* Titlepage from Walsh's 1735 edition of songs from Handel's *Deborah*, incorporating a passe-partout title for the name of the work. (Private Collection, reproduced by permission)

and to assert the status of the Walsh house in relation to continental publishers, but they may also have been used to establish some control over the storage of the stock.[37] (Virtually nothing was dropped from the back-catalogue as new publications were introduced, so the stock was in a permanent process of expansion.)[38] The serial numbers were included in Walsh's 'Great Catalogue' from the early 1740s, although it was around this time that they were abandoned again for new publications, presumably because their usefulness had proved limited.[39]

The younger Walsh achieved a new working relationship with Handel, but not immediately. The editions from the period around 1732–4 are rather chaotic, suggesting a situation in which Walsh had access to Handel's music, but without co-operation or approval from the composer. The publications of the solo sonatas (subsequently called Op.1) and the trio sonatas Op.2 originally had titlepages that gave the appearance of publications from Jeanne Roger, and old publications at that, since Roger had died in 1722;[40] but the music within was in the current Walsh style, the work of engravers A and B. My guess is that Walsh pulled out a copy of *Pieces à un & Deux Clavecins* and used that as the model for the new titlepages, giving the impression that the editions had been published in Amsterdam a decade previously, but the engraver was not a very skilful forger in copying the forms of the capital letters. Before long, the 'Roger' imprint on the titlepages was covered with a Walsh label, and then the titlepage was replaced with one that had Walsh's own imprint.[41] The Walsh label on the 'Roger' titlepage read 'Sold by John Walsh', rather than 'Printed: and Sold by John Walsh', as if to leave the identity of the printer undefined, and the initial attempt to evade responsibility may have been motivated by the consideration that Handel's 14-year Privilege had not quite expired, but it is unlikely that London musicians were deceived for long. The publications of these instrumental collections of dubious provenance were accompanied during the same period by some pretty thin 'song' publications from Handel's major vocal works, with *Athalia*, *Ariodante* and *Alcina*, for example, being represented by no more than 31 pages each (see Table 1). The nadir is perhaps represented by *Deborah*, which comprised a mere seven airs, only three of which belonged to that oratorio; two of the other airs were from *Esther* and two from *Athalia*, headed simply as coming from 'the Oratorio'. The three works together had provided the repertory for Handel's substantial run of oratorios during March–April 1735, in the midst of his opera season at Covent Garden. In the case of one of the *Athalia* arias Walsh even misattributed one of the soprano numbers to the bass singer Gustavus Waltz. In newspaper advertisements Walsh was rather guarded about his Handel publications in 1733–4, usually leading with miscellaneous anthologies like *The British Musical Miscellany* and only mentioning Handel in a general list of composers of instrumental music, but beginning in December 1734 he began to emphasize his Handel repertory, advertising substantial all-Handel lists.[42]

It looks, therefore, as if Walsh junior wanted to become 'Handel's publisher', but it took some time before he could secure the composer's agreement. The mid-1730s saw the height of the competition between Handel and the Opera of the Nobility, and Walsh naturally published music from the Nobility's repertory as well as Handel's, with songs from operas by Porpora and Veracini as well as Farinelli's famous showpiece, Hasse's *Artaserse*. Handel may have been none too pleased to have his *Arianna* music appearing in a combined publication with Porpora's. But it is noticeable that for his edition of songs from Porpora's *Arianna* in 1734, and again with Porpora's *Polifemo* in 1735, Walsh used a titlepage which incorporated the rubric 'Note. Where these are sold may be had all Mr. Handel's Operas and Instrumental Musick.'[43]

The first explicit public evidence of a new formal arrangement between Walsh and Handel came on the titlepage of the Op.4 Organ Concertos, published in October 1738, which carried the following recommendation printed above Handel's name: 'These six Concertos were publish'd by Mr. Walsh from my own copy corrected by my self, and to him only I have given my right therein'.[44] However, the collaboration can reasonably be back-dated to 1736, when there was a sudden resurgence of publications of decent size, accompanied by pre-publication subscriptions. The advertisement for the first subscription, for *Atalanta*, announced that the music would be printed on 'the best Dutch paper', and that the price to subscribers would be half a guinea 'which will be one third cheaper than any opera yet printed in score'.[45] The radical result of the new relationship between Handel and Walsh, however, was the subscription publication of a complete full score of *Alexander's Feast* with all recitatives and choruses included. The publication did not deter Handel himself from continuing to perform the work, in contrast to *Acis and Galatea*, the only other comparable score published during Handel's lifetime, which was only released when the composer had finished with it. *Alexander's Feast* is shorter than Handel's regular operas and oratorios (in two parts rather than three), and was thus a practical proposition for performers outside London's theatre environment; nevertheless the production of the score, with an accompanying engraved portrait of the composer, took longer than anticipated, and the publication was subjected to a succession of delays.

Having established the marriage, Walsh wanted a licence, and a second Royal Privilege followed in 1739 (Fig. 5). By now Handel was

G E O R G E  R.

G EORGE the Second, by the Grace of God, King of *Great Britain, France,* and *Ireland,* Defender of the Faith, *&c.* To all to whom 'thefe Prefents fhall come Greeting. Whereas *George Frederick Handel,* of the Parifh of *St. George the Martyr Hanover Square,* in Our County of *Middlefex,* Efq; hath humbly reprefented unto Us, that he hath with great Labour and Expence compofed feveral Works confifting of Vocal and Inftrumental Mufick, and hath authorifed and appointed *John Walfh* of the Parifh of *St. Mary le Strand,* in Our faid County of *Middlefex,* to print and publifh the fame; and hath therefore humbly befought us to grant Our Royal Privilege and Licence to the faid *John Walfh,* for the fole Engraving, Printing, and Publifhing the faid Works for the Term of Fourteen Years; We being willing to give all due Encouragement to Works of this Nature, are gracioufly pleafed to condefcend to his Requeft; and We do therefore by thefe Prefents fo far as may be agreeable to the Statute in that Behalf made and provided, grant unto him the faid *John Walfh,* his Heirs, Executors, Adminiftrators, and Affigns, Our Licence for the fole Printing and Publifhing the faid Works for the Term of Fourteen Years, to be computed from the Date hereof; ftrictly forbidding all Our loving Subjects within our Kingdoms and Dominions to reprint or abridge the fame, either in the like or in any other Size or Manner whatfoever; or to import, buy, vend, utter, or diftribute any Copy or Copies thereof, reprinted beyond the Seas, during the aforefaid Term of Four- teen Years, without the Confent or Approbation of the faid *John Walfh,* his Heirs, Ex- ecutors, Adminiftrators, and Affigns, under their Hands and Seals firft had and obtained, as they will anfwer the contrary at their Perils; whereof the Commiffioners and Officers of Our Cuftoms, the Mafter, Wardens, and Company of *Stationers* are to take Notice, that due Obedience may be rendered to our Pleafure herein declared.

Given at Our Court at *St. James's,* the Thirty-firft Day of *October,* 1739, in the Thirteenth Year of Our Reign.

*By His Majefty's Command,*

Holles  Newcaftle.

*Fig. 5.* Handel's second publication 'Privilege', dated 31 October 1739 and naming Walsh as his authorized publisher (British Library, g.274.a)

resident at his house in Brook Street 'in the Parish of St. George the Martyr', and instead of receiving a personal licence the Privilege records that he had 'authorised and appointed *John Walsh* of the Parish of *St. Mary le Strand* ... to print and publish' his works. In a sense that marks the end of the story, since Walsh thereafter remained Handel's exclusive publisher, but it is the end of a beginning for a regular and constant stream of publications covering the remainder of Handel's creative life. As with Cluer's editions in the 1720s, the pre-publication subscription system inaugurated in 1736 seems to have had a limited life-span: it was gone after 1740, though advertisements for a couple of the later oratorio-type works mentioned subscriptions that were apparently either abandoned or not followed up. There is some uncertainty as to whether an advertisement for a subscription always implied the formal procedure that resulted in published lists of subscribers. In the case of the full score of *Acis and Galatea* in 1743, a 'subscription' apparently referred to a single payment of half a guinea: unusually, the work was alternatively offered in ten fortnightly parts at one shilling each, with a final payment of 1*s*.6*d*. in week eleven.

Walsh's personal commitment and loyalty to Handel during a difficult period in the 1740s, when the composer was opposed by London's 'opera party', is revealed in his autograph letter (Fig. 1), which was written just after the disappointing start to Handel's ambitious oratorio season at the King's Theatre in the autumn of 1744:

Mr Handel has perform'd twice, the gallery very full, the pit and boxes almost empty; a strong party against him supported by Lady Brown &c, & I am afraid but a small subscription. ... Pity so great a man should ever perform without crouded audience, who's musick will ever be in esteem & can never be perform'd to the advantage it is now.

In subsequent years James Harris and his family relied on Walsh for advance information about Handel's performing programmes, a subject about which the composer could be surprisingly uncommunicative. In February 1747 Thomas Harris wrote that he had 'called this morning on Walsh, who could not give me any better information, but promised to call this afternoon on Handel and learn all particulars', though the result was not entirely helpful: 'Handel will begin (if nothing prevents) on Wednesday se[v]enight with the Occasional Oratorio; I believe he does not know himself what he will go on with afterwards, for Walsh told me he could get nothing from him that he could understand.'[46]

Concerning the business dealings between Handel and Walsh, the extracts from the 'cash-book', as published by Macfarren, can be supplemented by reports of legal agreements that were produced during a court case in 1772 when Walsh's successors tried to prove their rights over various pieces of music.[47] Together, these provide evidence for about half of the transactions that we may suppose to have taken place. The sums recorded are given in column 6 of Table 1. After a couple of anomalous (and possibly incorrectly transcribed) entries, it appears that Handel was paid a regular 25 guineas per work, presumably for supplying copy and for perpetual publication rights. The payments resume in 1729–32 with *Partenope*, *Poro*, *Ezio* and *Orlando*: the rise in page-counts is in itself an indication that these editions were the result of some collaboration. I doubt if any entry is missing from the following years, until payments resume with the subscription editions from 1736 onwards, but the cash-book entries then run out and we are left with sporadic information about the later works, in an accidental pattern relating to the particular works that were involved in the court case. It appears that the going rate for the oratorios was only 20 guineas: I cannot explain the drop in the case of *Judas Maccabaeus*, for an edition that had more pages than *Joshua*. The arrangement continued even to Handel's last oratorio, in 1757.

Two questions arise: what was Handel's financial value to the publisher, and what did Handel actually supply to Walsh for the money he received? There was no constant relationship between the standard-rate payment to the composer and the price of the ensuing edition. With the publication of the *Atalanta* songs or the full score of *Acis and Galatea* at half a guinea the calculation is fairly easy: Walsh had paid off Handel when 50 copies or 40 copies had been accounted for, respectively, and with a subscription of 192 copies for *Atalanta* Walsh was doing very well before he put any copies on general sale. The *Grand Concertos* in 1740 were expensive at 2 guineas: the part-books comprised many pages, but they were 'Published for the Author', possibly under a special arrangement whereby Handel paid Walsh a fixed amount, rather than vice versa, and took the sales income himself. At the other extreme, the initial keyboard-score publication of the Op.4 Organ Concertos (a 25-guinea work) sold for 4 shillings, and the St Cecilia Ode for 3 shillings: Walsh would have had to shift 175 copies of the latter before he recouped a payment of 25 guineas to Handel. On the whole, the larger collections of opera songs appear to be expensive, even luxury, items, many of them priced at 16 or 18 shillings in the 1740s catalogue.

The subscription lists provide some leads into the people who purchased Walsh's Handel publications. The list for *Alexander's Feast* was headed by all seven of the King's children, but this was exceptional. No doubt there was a vanity market among connoisseurs whose copies would rarely leave the library shelves, but most names on the subscription lists that might be described as 'patrons' were of people who had known connections with Handel and a genuine interest in music.[48] Taking the subscription list for *Arminio* as an example, the names include Earl Cowper, the Marchioness of Carnarvon (i.e. one of the 'Chandos' family) and the Earl of Shaftesbury; further down the social scale there are William Freeman, Wyndham Knatchbull, Bernard Granville and Charles Jennens (with two copies each), and James Harris. Harris had a dual interest, as a connoisseur and as director of the Musical Society in Salisbury; in the latter role, he needed repertory for the fortnightly music meetings, and it is no surprise to find musical societies from Windsor and Oxford also in the subscription list. John Simpson the London music seller committed himself to 14 copies, obviously for resale, but Cross, the Oxford bookseller, accounted for only one copy. For the remainder, there is a surprisingly large number of professional musicians in the list, including Festing, Stanley, Pepusch, Gates and a couple of cathedral organists, but also a substantial collection of relatively unknown names, from London and elsewhere, not to mention a smattering of national and ethnic diversity with Baron Suasso, a couple of Mendez da Costas and Isaac Ximenes.

It is important to bear in mind that the aria collections in score, which carry most of the subscription lists, were only one of the uses to which Walsh put the music that he received from Handel, and even from these collections the plates could be re-used with additional paginations for general anthology publications. Sometimes the traffic went in the other direction, as songs from the anthologies were brought in to expand previously published collections. The most remarkable example of this probably occurred with the opera *Sosarme*, originally published as two song collections covering the overture and 15 movements (arias and duets), but then expanded by pulling in another 12 movements from the anthologies. The page-count went up from 53 (printed one-sided) to 83 (on two sides), but the price went up even more substantially: the original song collections probably sold for 5 shillings together, but the expanded edition was in the catalogue at 16 shillings.[49] Music clubs required scores from which they could copy out part-books for concert items, but a different format was needed for the domestic amateur: Joe or Joanna at home with their harpsichord or spinet, trying out the latest music with or without a vocal contribution, or with a violin or a flute taking the vocal part. It was for this market that Walsh produced the anthologies such as *Sonatas or Chamber Aires* and *Songs Selected from the Oratorios*. In the latter case the music, derived from the same copy-text as the scores, was re-engraved in oblong format, in simple practical arrangements on two staves, incorporating the leading orchestral lines with the vocal parts in the right hand, and with additional figurings to the bass part to indicate the harmony.

It is worth pausing for a moment at this point for a brief diversion on the strange case of *Messiah*. It seems that music copy for *Messiah* was handed over to Walsh in the 1740s and that a collection of songs was engraved but not issued. However, individual items appeared in the anthologies, though with a blank space where the name of the work should have been. The *Songs from Messiah* did not appear until after Handel's death: every surviving copy includes stamped figurings for the sharp, of the type used by Walsh from about 1760 onwards, instead of the engraved sharp signs from the original plates. It is no surprise that in the 1772 court case Walsh's successors were unable to produce the agreement for *Messiah*: it looks as if Handel never made the agreement.

The music copy that Handel routinely supplied to Walsh presumably comprised manuscript full scores, and we can trace likely errors in these sources through some of the details of Walsh's editions. Barry Cooper has suggested that *Alexander's Feast* was engraved directly from Handel's performing score (now in the collection at Hamburg), but I think this improbable, not least because Handel needed the score for his own performances during the engraving period.[50] More likely, Walsh's copy was another manuscript taken from the performing score. With nearly all of the works, indeed, the publication date is so close to Handel's performance dates, even sometimes in the midst of them, that a separate copy must have been needed for Walsh. At the same time we may marvel at the speed with which a small engraving team could turn round a substantial collection of songs in order to catch the tide from the launch of a new opera or oratorio.

In 1785 Charles Burney included the following tantalizing statement in his 'Chronological List of Handel's Works':

The late Mr. Walsh, of Catherine-Street, in the Strand, purchased of HANDEL, for publication, transcripts of the manuscript scores of almost all the works he had composed in England; and Mr. Wright, of the same place, successor to Mr. Walsh, is still in possession of these manuscripts, many of which have never yet been published.[51]

It is possible that the manuscript scores that Wright owned are today to be found as a major part of the 'Lennard' Collection at Cambridge, but whether they are also the copies that were the subject of Handel's original agreements with Walsh is more doubtful.[52] They carry no engravers' annotations from the Walsh period, and the paper characteristics of the volumes for many works indicate later dates of origin than the relevant first publications.[53] More seriously, such full scores, even if delivered unbound, would not have been practical copy for the engravers who set up collections of individual songs. It is apparent, from the surviving evidence of the agreements and the 'cash-book', that Handel was paid much more for *Alexander's Feast*, published complete with recitatives and choruses, than for the usual song collections, and it seems logical to suppose that one of the reasons for this was that he supplied a more substantial manuscript copy. (We have to take on board the probability that Walsh's payments to Handel included cover for manuscript copying charges, or the alternative possibility that the manuscripts were returned to the composer as his property after Walsh had used them.) It seems likely that the copy that Handel usually provided looked much more like what was published — that is, anthologies of selected airs in full score, probably with the names of the singers included. But apparently, as with many other pieces of evidence about Walsh's practical dealings with Handel, not a leaf of such copy seems to survive today. On the other hand, we do have Walsh's music editions themselves, of considerable and complex bulk, to keep us occupied.

## *References*

1.  Concerning the family history of the Walshes, including the various properties that they occupied and transcripts of the wills, see James S. Hall, *A Chronology of the Life and Works of John Walsh ... and his Son* (typescript, 1956, copy in the Gerald Coke Handel Collection).

2.  Hampshire Record Office 9M73/G610, letter dated 27 November 1744; transcription with commentary in Donald Burrows and Rosemary Dunhill, *Music and Theatre in Handel's World: The Family Papers of James Harris 1732–1780* (Oxford, 2002), pp. 207–8.

3.  G. A. Macfarren, *A Sketch of the Life of Handel, with particular notices of the works selected for each day's performance, at the Centenary Festival in the Crystal Palace* (London, 1859), p. 22; Macfarren's list was included in Otto Erich Deutsch, *Handel: A Documentary Biography* (London, 1955), p. 468.

4.  Andrew Ashbee, *Records of English Court Music* (9 vols, Snodland and Aldershot, 1986–96), vol. ii, p. 46.

5.  Ashbee, vol. ii, p. 150: the '1712' Birthday Ball presumably refers to the celebrations on 6 February 1713 by the modern calendar.

6.  Advertisement in *The Daily Advertiser* 29 October 1744 (Deutsch, *Handel*, pp. 596–7).

7.  Letter from Thomas Harris to James Harris, 12 May 1747: see Burrows and Dunhill, p. 242. In quotations from English eighteenth-century documents, capitalization has been modernized, but not punctuation or word-forms.

8.  Original in Italian; for the full text, and further background on the publication history of the sonatas, see Enrico Careri, *Francesco Geminiani (1687–1762)* (Oxford, 1993), pp. 36–7.

9.  In 1741 Harris had also seen at Walsh's a French essay that Geminiani had published to accompany the launch of his treatise *Guida Armonica*, in this case an item that Walsh would not have been tempted to republish himself: see the letter of 5 December 1741, Burrows and Dunhill, p. 128.

10. Letters from Thomas Harris to James Harris, 1 and 6 December 1737, Burrows and Dunhill, pp. 39–40.

11. 'Engraving' is used here as a general description, covering the various processes including stamping and etching. In the course of Walsh's court proceeding in 1726, reference was made to music by Walsh printed 'in the parish of Harrow on the Hill': see William C. Smith, 'New evidence concerning John Walsh and the duties on paper, 1726', *Harvard Library Bulletin* vi (1952), pp. 252–5. This was almost certainly a legal diversion asserting that the printing had taken place beyond the jurisdiction of London and Westminster.

12. The volumes are now Lbl [British Library] Harley MSS 7337–7342.

13. Lbl Harley MS 3782, f. 83.

14. ibid., f. 85.

15. ibid., f. 87.

16. Ashbee, vol. ii, pp. 106, 174.

17. Letter from John Christopher Smith to the Earl of Shaftesbury, 28 July 1743, printed in Betty Matthews, 'Unpublished Letters Concerning Handel', *Music & Letters*, xl (1959), pp. 265–6.

18. I thank my colleague David Mateer for drawing attention to the misconception about Walsh's 'imprisonment', which is stated as fact in the biographies of Walsh in *The New Grove* and *The Oxford Dictionary of National Biography*, and derives from Smith's article cited in note 11, above. I also thank Olive Baldwin and Thelma Wilson who, following the conference, checked the parish records of St Mary-le-Strand and found that Walsh attended Vestry meetings throughout the relevant period. For a survey of the paper types in Handel's autographs, see Donald Burrows and Martha J. Ronish, *A Catalogue of Handel's Musical Autographs* (Oxford, 1994).

19. Reference in William C. Smith, *A Bibliography of the Musical Works published by John Walsh 1695–1720* (The Bibliographical Society, 1968), p. ix.

20. This is true of a range of Walsh's Handel editions that I have examined, from *Rinaldo* to *Jephtha* (and including *Alexander's Feast*), on the evidence of watermarks. The rare exemplars in the Gerald Coke Handel Collection of Walsh's editions of Handel's Solos and Op.2 Trio Sonatas in their original condition (uncut, sewn in paper covers) show unequivocally that the music pages are single leaves, and that the titlepage, forming a wrapper, was only printed on half of the folio, which could easily have been folded when placed in the flat-bed press.

21. Concerning the bibliographical history of the Suite publications, see Terence Best's commentary to Klavierwerke I–IV, *Hallische Händel-Ausgabe* IV/7 (Kassel, 2000), pp. 41–8.

22. Presumably the engravers would have claimed that they were operating under the protection of Walsh as a publisher, in case of legal claims over piracy.

23. Allowance must be made for the possibility that individual punches might be replaced or exchanged from time to time without affecting the set (and therefore the style) as a whole.

24. David Hunter, *Opera and Song Books published in England 1703–1726: a Descriptive Bibliography* (London, Bibliographical Society, 1997): see especially the index to 'Engravers and engraving styles' on p. 516. Hunter excluded the Handel publications from his survey, on the grounds that they are covered in William C. Smith, *Handel: A Descriptive Catalogue of the Early Editions* (2nd edn, Oxford 1970); Walsh's Handel

publications from the period have the same engraving styles as his other publications, but the application of Hunter's analysis to them awaits attention.

25. The following description incorporates the results of recent work that I have undertaken during the preparation of a collected edition of Croft's orchestrally-accompanied church music for the *Musica Britannica* series.

26. See H. Diack Johnstone, 'Music and Drama at the Oxford Act of 1713', in Susan Wollenberg and Simon McVeigh (eds.), *Concert Life in Eighteenth-Century Britain* (Aldershot, 2004), p. 207.

27. An apparently unique copy of the proposal is now at New York Public Library (JOG 72–104); I thank Dr H. Diack Johnstone for this reference. For the publication dates of *Musica Sacra*, see Donald Burrows, *Walsh's editions of Handel's Opera 1–5: the texts and their sources*, in Christopher Hogwood and Richard Luckett (eds.) *Music in Eighteenth-Century England: Essays in Memory of Charles Cudworth* (Cambridge, 1983), p. 81, note 5.

28. See Donald Burrows, *Walsh's editions of Handel's Opera 1–5*, pp. 79–102; 'A' and 'B' are illustrated on pp. 84–5.

29. See David Hunter, 'Bragging on *Rinaldo*: ten ways writers have trumpeted Handel's coming to Britain', in Hans Joachim Marx (ed.), *Göttinger Händel-Beiträge*, x (2004), pp. 113–31, in which Hunter also challenges the excessive claims for the profits that Walsh made from his *Rinaldo* edition (pp. 118–21).

30. *The Evening Post*, 28 April–1 May 1711.

31. The Suites were apparently printed by Cluer, but marketed through Meares.

32. The style is similar, but not identical, to the styles designated 'Walsh 2 & 3' in Hunter, *Opera and Song Books*, so I am more cautious in attributing the printing to Walsh than Terence Best was in *HHA* IV/7 (see note 21, above), p. 47.

33. The letter-forms on the titlepage are in the current Roger style, though 'Jeanne Roger' is usually in block capitals: compare, for example, the titlepage to the set of concertos by Albinoni and Tibaldi, with the titlepage serial number 439 (copy in Lbl). An entry for Handel's Suites with the serial number 490 (as on the *Pieces à un & Deux Clavecins*) appears in the 1737 catalogue from Roger's successor Le Cène: see the catalogue facsimile in François Lesure, *Bibliographie des éditions musicales publiées par Estienne Roger at Michel-Charles Le Cène* (Paris, 1969). At that time Le Cène was probably still selling the *Pieces* along with a later edition of the Suites. Walsh used the same serial number for his publication of the second set of suites, *c*.1733. Although engraved in a 'London' style, the *Pieces* were printed on conjunct leaves, unlike Walsh's editions.

34. John Cluer died in 1728, which probably explains why J. C. Smith seems to have taken a hand in the management of the publication of *Lotario* in 1730, probably in collaboration with Cluer's widow.

35. The titlepages of the editions involved (*Floridante, Ottone, Flavio*) read 'Publish'd by the Author. Printed and Sold by John Walsh'.

36. The serial numbers are rather difficult to interpret, partly because the same titlepages (incorporating numbers) were sometimes used for different publications. My analysis suggests that Walsh began, probably in the summer of 1733, by numbering his back-catalogue in genre groups (flute music 1–129, violin music 130–66, keyboard music 167–203, church music 205–16, operas 219–86, cantatas and songs 287–338, sonatas and concertos in approximately alphabetical order 339–456; there are some anomalies probably resulting from the difficulties of covering all of the stock systematically), and that new publications begin in order from 487 or 488. By contrast, the Roger/Le Cène

numberings cover a longer time-span and can thus provide more evidence of publication dates: see Lesure, *Bibliographie*.

37. Apparent illogicalities in the number sequences may reflect the pre-existing storage arrangement.

38. The need for further storage may account for Walsh's occupation of an additional property in Halmet Court (probably backing on to the Catherine Street property) between 1740 and 1756, and then his removal to two adjacent houses in Catherine Street in 1757.

39. The so-called 'Great Catalogue', an independent publication of 28pp., entitled *A Cattalogue of Musick: Containing all the Vocal, and Instrumental Musick Printed in England. For John Walsh*, survives in a single copy (Lbl C.120.b.6); the latest items listed date from about 1741, but the copy appears to be a revision from an earlier edition. The system of serial numbers may have been abandoned because no gaps had been left for the addition of new publications in each genre.

40. The serial numbers on the bogus 'Roger' titlepages (534, 535) had been used in 1727 by Roger's successor for editions of music by Vivaldi and Schikhard.

41. The 'Walsh' editions of the Solos also re-arranged the musical content. The history of Walsh's editions of Handel's instrumental music from this period is described in Burrows, *Walsh's Editions* (see note 28, above) and the articles referred to in note 42, below.

42. See Donald Burrows, 'Handel, Walsh, Sonatas and Concertos in the early 1730s', *The Handel Institute Newsletter*, vol. 17, no. 1 (Spring 2006), pp. 1–4. After writing that article I discovered one Walsh advertisement devoted to Handel's publications in March 1733: see Donald Burrows, 'Walsh's edition of Handel's "Solos"', *The Handel Institute Newsletter*, vol. 19, no. 1 (Spring 2008), pp. 5–6.

43. See William C. Smith and Charles Humphries, *A Bibliography of the Musical Works published by the firm of John Walsh 1721–1766* (London, 1968), items 1218, 1220.

44. Handel's statement of approval seems to have been made in response to a pirate edition of one or more of the concertos, which appears to be referred to in a letter of 24 January 1736 from the Earl of Shaftesbury to James Harris: see Burrows and Dunhill, *Music and Theatre*, p. 12.

45. Advertisement in *The London Daily Post, and General Advertiser*, 14 May 1736; Deutsch, *Handel*, p. 408.

46. Letters of 26 February and 3 March 1747, Burrows and Dunhill, *Music and Theatre*, p. 235, 236.

47. See Ronald J. Rabin and Steven Zohn, 'Arne, Handel, Walsh, and Music as Intellectual Property: Two Eighteenth-Century Lawsuits', in *Journal of the Royal Musical Association*, vol. 1, part 1 (1995), pp. 112–45.

48. For more detail on the subscribers to two collections of Handel's opera songs, see David Hunter and Rose M. Mason, 'Supporting Handel through Subscription to Publications: the Lists of *Rodelinda* and *Faramondo* compared', *Notes*, lvi (1999–2000), pp. 27–93.

49. The titlepage for the Second Collection of songs included 'Price 2s 6d' and I assume here that the First Collection, with a comparable number of pages, was offered at the same price. The 'catalogue' referred to is Walsh's 'Great Catalogue': see note 39, above.

50. See Barry Cooper, 'The Organ Parts to Handel's *Alexander's Feast*', *Music & Letters* lix (1978), pp. 159–79, at pp. 164–6; the similarity of readings referred to by Cooper is evidence of a relationship in filiation between the performing score and the printed

edition, but does not prove that the former was the source for the latter. See also Donald Burrows, 'The Composition and First Performance of Handel's *Alexander's Feast*', *Music & Letters* lxiv (1983), pp. 206–11.

51. Charles Burney, *An Account of the Musical Performances in Commemoration of Handel* (London, 1785), p. 44.

52. See Donald Burrows, 'The Lennard Collection', in Terence Best (ed.), *Handel Collections and their History* (Oxford, 1993), pp. 108–36.

53. The manuscript scores of *Floridante*, *Ottone* and *Flavio*, for example, operas that were the subject of authorized Walsh editions in the 1720s, have watermarks from the period *c*.1736–41.

# Appendix

## Walsh's Handel Editions

The editions are arranged in order of publication, based mainly on William C. Smith, *Handel: A Descriptive Catalogue of the Early Editions* (2nd edn, Oxford 1970). Dates are given in modern form, with the year beginning on 1 January; dates derived from thrice-weekly newspapers are given as the latest (e.g. 8–11/3/38 as 11/3/38).

**Table 1.** *Original editions: principal works by Handel for which Walsh produced the first published editions*

Column 1: Works are named by their original titles, though Italian operas were usually published with an 'Englished' form (e.g. 'Xerxes' for *Serse*).    * issued with 1720 privilege; ** issued with 1739 privilege; ** issued with 1760 privilege

Column 2: Usually the date of first performance. Dates in square brackets relate to relevant revivals or periods of composition.

Column 4: 'Songs' = collections of movements in score; 'Score' = full score of complete work including recitatives and choruses; K/Score = 2-stave keyboard score; 'Parts' = part-books.

Page-counts are given in brackets; 'ff.' indicates folios printed one side only.

Column 5: CB = date from Walsh 'cash-book' (Macfarren, *Sketch*, p. 22); A = agreement date (Rabin and Zohn, 'Arne, Handel, Walsh')

Column 6: Payment recorded in source (column 5), with guineas equivalent in brackets.

Column 7: Number of subscribers in printed subscription list /number of copies subscribed for.

| Work | Performance | Publication | Format | Cashbook /Agreement | £ (= gns) | Subscription |
|---|---|---|---|---|---|---|
| *Rinaldo* | 24/2/11 | 24/4/11 | Songs (65)[1] | | | |
| *Floridante** | 9/12/21 | 28/3/22 | Songs (81)[2] | 1721 (CB) | 72.0.0.[?:error] | |
| *Ottone** | 12/1/23 | 19/3/23 | Songs (92)3 | 1722 (CB) | 42.0.0 (=40) | |

| Work | Performance | Publication | Format | Cashbook /Agreement | £ (= gns) | Subscription |
|---|---|---|---|---|---|---|
| Flavio* | 14/5/23 | 21/6/23 | Songs (64) | 1723 (CB) | 26.5.0 (=25) | |
| Tolomeo | 30/4/28 | 14/9/28 | Songs (23 ff.)[4] | | | |
| Partenope | 24/2/30 | 4/4/30 | Songs (99) | 1729 (CB) | 26.5.0 (=25) | |
| Ormisda (pasticcio) | 4/4/30 | 25/4/30 | Songs (23 ff.) | | | |
| Venceslao (pasticcio) | 11/1/31 | 27/1/31 | Songs (16 ff.) | | | |
| Poro | 2/2/31 | 2/3/31 | Songs (82) | 1730 (CB) | 26.5.0 (=25) | |
| Ezio | 15/1/32 | 14/2/32 | Songs (91) | 1732 (CB) | 26.5.0 (=25) | |
| Sosarme | 15/2/32 | 11/3/32 | Songs (53 ff.)[5] | | | |
| Solos (= Op.1) | | c.1732 | Score (63)[6] | | | |
| Esther | [2/5/32] | 25/11/32 | Songs (30) | ? (A) | | |
| Catone (pasticcio) | 4/11/32 | 25/11/32 | Songs (20 ff.) | | | |
| Amadigi and Teseo | [1715/1713] | c.1732 | Songs (uncertain) | | | |
| Orlando | 27/1/33 | 6/2/33 | Songs (90) | 1732 (CB) | 26.5.0 (=25) | |
| Trio Sonatas Op.2 | | c.1733 | Parts (66)[7] | | | |
| Suites II | [by 1720] | c.1733 | K/Score (83)[8] | | | |
| Utrecht Te Deum and Jubilate | 7/7/13 | ?end 1733[9] | Score (71) | ? (A) | | |
| Water Music | 17/7/17 | ?end 1733[10] | Parts (35) | | | |
| Arbace (pasticcio) | 5/1/34 | 5/2/34 | Songs (19)[11] | | | |
| Arianna | 26/1/34 | 6/4/34 | Songs (29)[12] | | | |
| Concertos Op.3 | | [7/12/34][13] | Parts (c.110) | | | |

| Work | Performance | Publication | Format | Cashbook / Agreement | £ (= gns) | Subscription |
|---|---|---|---|---|---|---|
| Il Pastor Fido | [9/11/34] | 30/11/34 | Songs (47)[14] | | | |
| Six Fugues ('Op 3') | | by 17/5/35[15] | KJ/Score (23) | | | |
| Deborah | [26/3/35] | by 17/5/35 | Songs (21) | | | |
| Athalia | [1/4/35] | by 17/5/35 | Songs (29) | | | |
| Ariodante | 8/1/35 | 13/9/35 | Songs (31)[16] | | | |
| Alcina | 16/4/35 | 30/8/35 | Songs (23)[17] | | | |
| Atalanta | 12/5/36 | 9/6/36 | Songs (83) | 1736 (CB) | 26.5.0 (=25) | 154/192 |
| Arminio | 12/1/37 | 12/2/37 | Songs (91) | 1736 (CB) | 26.5.0 (=25) | 110/145 |
| Giustino | 16/2/37 | 26/3/37 | Songs (104) | 1736 (CB) | 26.5.0 (=25) | 105/111 |
| Berenice | 18/5/37 | 18/6/37 | Songs (82)[18] | 1737 (CB) | 26.5.0 (=25) | |
| Faramondo | 3/1/38 | 4/2/38 | Songs (91) | 1737 (CB) | 26.5.0 (=25) | 75/87 |
| Alexander's Feast | 19/2/36 | 8/3/38 | Score (193) | 1737 (CB) / 27-4-37 (A) | 105.0.0 (=100) | 124/146[19] |
| Alessandro Severo (pasticcio) | 25/2/38 | 8/3/38 | Songs (advertised, no copy known) | | | |
| Serse | 15/4/38 | 30/5/38 | Songs (107) | 1738 (CB) | 26.5.0 (=25) | |
| Organ Concertos Op.4 | [1735-6] | 4/10/38[20] | KJ/Score (48) | 1738 (CB) | 26.5.0 (=25) | |
| Trio Sonatas Op.5 | | 28/2/39 | Parts (78) | 1738 (CB) | 26.5.0 (=25) | |
| Saul | 16/1/39 | | 12/3/39 | Songs (47)[21] | | |
| Ode for St Cecilia's Day | 22/11/39 | 13/12/39 | Songs (23) | | | |
| Concertos Op.6** | [1739-40] | 21/4/40 | Parts (c.350) | | | 100/122 |

| Work | Performance | Publication | Format | Cashbook /Agreement | £ (= gns) | Subscription |
|---|---|---|---|---|---|---|
| L'Allegro | 27/2/40 | 15/3/40 | Songs (65)[22] | ? (A) | | |
| Organ Concertos 2nd Set** | [1739] | 8/11/40 | K/Score (61) | | | |
| Imeneo | 22/11/40 | 18/4/41 | Songs (32) | | | |
| Deidamia | 10/1/41 | 29/1/41 | Songs (89)[23] | | | |
| Coronation Anthems | [11/10/27] | [1742-3] | Score (98)[24] | | | |
| Funeral Anthem | [17/12/37] | [1742-3] | Score (54)[25] | | | |
| Acis and Galatea | [1732-41] | 28/11/43 | Score (89)[26] | 20-9-43 (A) | £21 (=20) | |
| Samson | 18/2/43 | 9/4/43 | Songs (91)[27] | 9-3-43 (A) | £21 (=20) | |
| Semele | 10/2/44 | 25/2/44 | Songs (85)[28] | | | |
| Joseph | 2/3/44 | 19/5/44 | Songs (85)[29] | | | |
| Hercules | 5/1/45 | 8/1/45 | Songs (97) | | | |
| Belshazzar | 27/3/45 | 18/5/45 | Songs (86) | | | |
| Occasional Oratorio | 14/2/46 | 3/4/46 | Songs (71) | | | |
| Judas Maccabaeus** | 1/4/47 | 30/4/47 | Songs (73) | 1-4-47 (A) | £15.15 (=15) | |
| Joshua** | 9/3/48 | 2/4/48 | Songs (66) | 9-3-48 (A) | £21 (=20) | |
| Alexander Balus** | 23/3/48 | 5/5/48 | Songs (94)30 | 23-3-48 (A) | £21 (=20) | |
| Susanna** | 10/2/49 | 8/3/49 | Songs (94) | | | |
| Solomon** | 17/3/49 | 17/4/49 | Songs (80) | | | |
| Fireworks Music | 27/4/49 | June/49 | Parts (37) | | | |
| Messiah | [23/3/43] | c.1749[31] | Songs (70) | ? (A) | | |

| Work | Performance | Publication | Format | Cashbook /Agreement | £ (= gns) | Subscription |
|---|---|---|---|---|---|---|
| *Theodora* | 16/3/50 | 20/6/51 | Songs (93)[32] | | | |
| *The Choice of Hercules* | 1/3/51 | 4/5/51 | Songs (41) | | | |
| *Jephtha* | 26/2/52 | 4/4/52 | Songs (91) | | | |
| *The Triumph of Time and Truth* | 11/3/57 | 16/4/57 | Songs (67) | 12-3-57 | £21 (=20) | |
| Organ Concertos Op.7*** | [1740-51] | 23/2/61 | KJScore (51) | | | |
| Dettingen Te Deum | 27/11/43 | 1/4/63 | Score (92)[33] | | | |

**Table 2.** *Walsh editions of works that were authoritatively issued by other publishers*

All works published as 'Songs', except Suites II as K/Score.   ^ = 'Sold at the Music[k] Shops' imprint, without Walsh's name

| Work | Date (Walsh edition) | 'Official' Edition | | | |
|---|---|---|---|---|---|
| Muzio Scevola | 2/8/22 (21 ff.) | Meares | 23/8/22 | (22 ff.) | |
| Giulio Cesare | c.1724^ (24 ff.) | Cluer* | 24/7/24 | (118) | |
| Tamerlano | c.1724^ (17 ff.) | Cluer* | 14/11/24 | (89) | |
| Rodelinda | c.1725^ (18 ff.) | Cluer | 22/2/25 | (180) | subscription 120/162 |
| Alessandro | c.1726^ (11 ff.)[34] | Cluer | 6/8/26 | (113) | subscription 80/106 |
| Scipione | c.1726^ (13 ff.) | Cluer | 27/5/26 | (102) | subscription 58/80 |
| Admeto | 14/9/28 (20 ff.) | Cluer | 24/6/27 | (127) | subscription 57/93 |
| Siroe | 14-9-28 (22 ff.) | Cluer | 13/7/28 | (105) | |
| Lotario | 1730^ (20 ff.) | Cluer | Feb.1730 | (125) | 'and sold by Christopher Smith' |
| Radamisto | 1730-31 (71) | Meares* | 15/12/20[35] | (81) | 'Published by Author; sold C. Smith' |
| Suites I | c.1736 (94) | Cluer* | 14/11/20 | (94) | 'Printed for the Author, only to be had at C. Smith's' |
| Riccardo Primo | c.1750 (23) | Cluer | 17/2/28 | (116) | 'and sold by C. Smith' |

Sources:  George A. Macfarren, *A Sketch of the Life of Handel* (London, 1859), p. 22 ('Cash-book')
William C. Smith, *Handel: A Descriptive Catalogue of the Early Editions* (2nd edn, Oxford 1970). In notes, 'Smith 3' (etc.) refers to Smith's classification
Ronald J. Rabin and Steven Zohn, 'Arne, Handel, Walsh, and Music as Intellectual Property: Two Eighteenth-Century Lawsuits', in *Journal of the Royal Musical Association*, vol. 1, part 1 (1995), pp. 112-145 ('Agreements')
Donald Burrows, 'Handel, Walsh, Sonatas and Concertos in the early 1730s', *The Handel Institute Newsletter*, vol. 17, no. 1 (Spring 2006), pp. 1-4

*References for Tables 1 and 2*

1. Smith 3, 21/6/11, has 67 pp.; additional songs (9 ff., Smith 7) also published with 1731 revival
2. also 4 additional songs (11+ 3 pp., Smith 2), following December 1721 revival
3. also 4 additional songs (9 ff, Smith 4 and 5), following March 1723 revival
4. later, expanded, edition 1737 (65 pp., Smith 6)
5. 1st collection 11/3/32 (26ff.), 2nd collection 29/4/32 (23+4 ff.); subsequent combined and supplemented edition *c.*1733 (83 pp., Smith 4)
6. 'Roger' edn 62 pp., 'Walsh' edn 63 pp.
7. 'Roger', then 'Walsh', titlepages
8. music partly based on *Pieces à un & Deux Clavecins* (Walsh, with 'Roger' titlepage, *c.*1719-20), newly engraved
9. advertised 23/2/34 as 'just publish'd'; subsequent issue (?*c.*1745) as vol. III of church music
10. advertised 7/12/34, but listed on 'Walsh' Op. 2 titlepage and Castrucci Sonatas (Jan. 1734, latest on list)
11. soon afterwards issued in combined edition with Porpora and Handel 'Arianna' operas
12. 2 collections: 23/2/34 (18 pp., following *Arbace* and Porpora songs) and 6/4/34 (21 pp., including overture); expanded edition 1737 (88 pp., Smith 5)
13. probably prepared earlier: first state of titlepage mentions royal wedding of March 1734
14. 2 collections, 25+22 pp., later combined *c.*1735 (Smith 3)
15. see Burrows, 'Handel, Walsh, Sonatas and Concertos' for this and the next two items
16. including overture (5 pp.), possibly not included in first issue
17. including overture (4 pp.), preceded by earlier 'Musick Shops' issue without overture; followed in 1735-6 by further collections, combined edition (91 pp.) in 1737
18. proposals for subscription advertised 20/5/37, but not followed up
19. 2nd edition 17/2/39, subscriptions 125/147; proposals for subscription advertised 20/5/37
20. accompanying part-books published on 2/12/38
21. 1st collection 12/3/39 (17 pp.); 2nd collection + overture 17/3/39 (20+11 pp.); combined edition 19/3/39
22. 1st collection 15/3/40 (36 pp.); 2nd collection 7/5/40 (29 pp.); combined edition 13/5/40. Additional songs published *c.*1742 (19 pp., Smith 6)
23. 1st collection 29/1/41 (35 pp.); complete 21/2/41
24. originally without The King shall rejoice, 66 pp.; then as 'Vol. I' of church music; advertised on Water Music (26/2/43) as 'Four Coronation Anthems'

25. originally published with *The King shall rejoice* (pp. 55-86), then issued separately as 'Vol. II' of church music, and advertised on Water Music (26/2/43)

26. with choruses, replacing (and re-using) Walsh's previous edition of Songs, 18/10/22 (36 ff.)

27. issued in 3 parts: Part I (30 pp.) 19/3/43; Part II and overture (36+7 pp.) 2/4/43; Part III (18 pp.) 9/4/43; collected edition advertised 15/7/43

28. 1st set 25/2/44 (?pp. 1-32); 2nd set 2/3/44 (?pp. 33-54); 3rd set (?pp. 55-85, to complete) 10/3/44; subscription advertised 13/2/44, but not followed up

29. Act I (32 pp.) 19/5/44; complete 24/5/44

30. 2 sets combined; first set advertised 19/4/48 (33 or 36 pp.), 'remainder next week'

31. prepared, but not issued until after 1760

32. proposal for subscription 4/5/51, but not followed up

33. as Vol. IV of church music

34. also edition by Benjamin Cooke, 2 collections 4/8/26 (11+16 ff., Smith 3, 5)

35. announced ('is engraving finely on copper plates') 2/7/20; engraved by T. Cross

# The Sale Catalogue of Carl Friedrich Abel (1787)

### STEPHEN ROE

IN THE MID-1780S, the Foundling Hospital was on the very northern edge of the metropolis, just off the road to the village of Highgate. To the north was the parish church of St Pancras, where in early January 1782 the body of Johann Christian Bach was interred in a grave no longer marked. Carl Friedrich Abel, Bach's oldest friend in London, was not at the funeral, though he had sent provisions to Bach's sick bed in his friend's last days.[1] Whatever detained Abel from being there, Bach's death was of great moment to him and influenced his remaining five years of life.

They had been friends since Bach arrived in London from Milan in 1762, belonging to the circle of mostly German musicians at the court.[2] Both were chamber musicians to Queen Charlotte and both were the dominant forces in English musical life from the mid-1760s onwards. The founding of the Bach-Abel concerts in 1765, at various locations around London, and from 1775 at their final home in the wonderfully-decorated Hanover Square rooms, was their main joint achievement. They lived together in Soho probably until the early 1770s. Both were freemasons in the same lodge;[3] and both dandled the young Mozart on their various knees in 1764 and 1765. Mozart had transcribed one of Abel's symphonies, later erroneously sanctified with a Köchel number, K.18. If there was a difference between the two musicians, it was that Bach was very much at home as an opera composer, whereas Abel wrote none.

In that respect, Abel resembles Johann Sebastian Bach, with whom he probably studied in Leipzig. Abel's relationship with the Bach family goes back to his infancy. He was born in Cöthen in 1723, the year Johann Sebastian moved from there to Leipzig. The Abel dynasty was not as fecund or as important as the Bachs, but certainly prominent in the musical and artistic world of Germany in the seventeenth and eighteenth centuries. Abel's father, Christian Ferdinand, was a musician at the court of Anhalt-Cöthen when J. S. Bach was appointed there in 1717 and they became friends, Bach becoming godfather to Christian Ferdinand's eldest daughter in 1720. It was a talented family: in addition to Carl Friedrich, his eldest brother Leopold August (1718–94) was a violinist and composer and two brothers made their living as artists. The instrument for which the Abel dynasty was renowned, from the sixteenth century, was the viola da gamba.

It seems likely that Christian Ferdinand performed the gamba parts in Bach's works for the instrument written at Cöthen. It is often asserted that Bach wrote his cello suites for Christian Ferdinand, though in fact it is not known if he even played the instrument. Nevertheless, until the twentieth century, the greatest solo music for a bass string instrument after Bach was composed by Christian Ferdinand's son, the London Abel, Carl Friedrich.

Christian Ferdinand was certainly Carl Friedrich's first teacher of his instrument and no doubt of music too. Burney, who knew Abel well, claims that on his father's death in 1737, the young musician went to Leipzig as a 'disciple of [Johann Sebastian] Bach', where he acquired mastery of 'musical science in harmony, modulation, fugue and canon, which he had acquired under his great master'.[4] There is no evidence, however, that the young Carl Friedrich was ever attached to the Thomasschule and if he were strictly a pupil of Johann Sebastian, it must have been in private. Abel evidently shone in Leipzig as a viola da gamba player and he may have been an early performer of J. S. Bach's three gamba sonatas (BWV 1027–29), now redated to before 1741. Abel's training was later extended by experience under Hasse in Dresden, one of the liveliest and most glittering courts in Europe, where Carl Friedrich was a gamba player in the orchestra from as early as 1743. Abel stayed there till the mid-1750s, after which, he wandered westwards and having visited Mannheim, Frankfurt and Paris, settled in London in late 1758 or early 1759, giving his first documented public concert just before the death of Handel on 5 April 1759.

Abel was a captivating performer on the gamba and all accounts draw attention to his mastery and the powerful emotion he could summon up in his celebrated adagios. It was an instrument at the end of its musical life — Burney said that it died with Abel — so Abel's achievement is all the more extraordinary.[5]

Although London was the base for J. C. Bach and Abel, they travelled extensively and frequently in England, to Bath and Salisbury — Abel appeared at the festival in Salisbury as early as 1759 — but especially in Europe.[6] We know of several trips by Bach to Paris, Germany, the Netherlands and to Italy, but much less has been unearthed about Abel's European activities. He seems to have had regular jaunts in Paris to buy claret:[7] he was known for his love of wines and liquor in general, in later years apparently to excess. We know that he stayed in Germany for a time between 1782 and 1784, but the range of Abel's travels around Europe has yet to be adequately explored.

Angelo points out that Bach and Abel were unusual among musicians in their interest in art and in their number of artistic friends.[8] Abel came from a family of gifted painters as well as musicians. Both Bach and Abel

*Fig. 1.* Carl Friedrich Abel, by Thomas Gainsborough, 1777 (Courtesy of the Huntington Library, Art Collections, and Botanical Gardens, San Marino, California)

knew many of the great figures of the day, including Sir Joshua Reynolds and Zoffany, Cipriani and Bartolozzi, whose designs were used on the engraved music and concert tickets of both musicians. The painter who was closest to them was Thomas Gainsborough, who was passionately interested in music. Gainsborough too was a gamba player, much admired in some quarters,[9] who at one stage possessed five instruments, one supposedly given to him by Abel in exchange for paintings and drawings.[10] Gainsborough painted Bach once (two copies survive in London and Bologna); he drew Abel on several occasions and executed two full-length portraits, the more famous being the masterly painting of Abel composing, with his Pomeranian dog and his instrument, exhibited at the Royal Academy in 1777. This picture, which surely is one of the greatest portraits of any musician, is now in the Huntington Library and Museum, San Marino, California (Fig. 1).[11] The other portrait apparently dates from the mid-1760s and shows Abel, again with his instrument and looking much younger. This, and a sketch for it, is in the National Portrait Gallery.[12] Angelo describes the profusion of Gainsborough drawings in Abel's home, the walls 'covered with them, slightly pinned to the paper hangings'.[13]

Bach and Abel would have known Gainsborough in Bath, which they often visited. The artist only moved permanently from Bath to London in 1774, and it is from this date that Gainsborough was a permanent feature of Bach and Abel's life in London. Gainsborough also contributed to the lavish decorations in the Hanover Square concert rooms. Although the concerts were initially successful, it is generally believed that both composers' finances were considerably stretched by the outlay and expense of the building. Bach's bank account tells a sorry story in his last years and it seems that at his death on 1 January 1782, he had little to pass on to his widow Cecilia Grassi. Abel continued the concert series in 1782, but afterwards left London to see his family in Germany and to work at the Prussian court and apparently to escape his creditors. He returned to resume an active role in the London musical life for the 1785 concert season. His death on 20 June 1787 was unexpected: Gainsborough, in a letter to Henry Bate Dudley, wrote: 'tis not a week since we were gay together, and that he wrote the sweetest air I have in my collection of his happiest thoughts ...'.[14]

Abel, unlike Bach, died without a will and without an obvious heir in England. He had at least two brothers still living, Leopold August, the musician at Ludwigslust in Mecklenburg-Schwerin, and Ernst Heinrich, the artist. The latter, who apparently had worked in London and Paris before settling in Hamburg, was evidently a main beneficiary of the auction of Abel's estate, which took place on 12 and 13 December 1787 at

Mr Greenwood's Rooms, Leicester Square. A single copy of the sale catalogue has survived in the library of the Frick Collection, New York; a black
and white photographic copy of this can be consulted in the Library of the
National Gallery, London.[15] While it has occasionally been used in the
context of Gainsborough studies, the catalogue has not been really looked
at from a musical point of view. It is a fascinating document, which illumi-
nates Abel the composer, musician, art-lover and the man. Abel is revealed
as a man of wide interests and culture, with a large number of objects
collected from around Europe, a major collection of paintings and drawings and a tantalizing amount of music, both printed and manuscript. The
sale catalogue amplifies Abel's biography and sets new directions to explore
in the study of his life and times and that of his contemporaries.

There were no specialized music auctions in eighteenth-century
London, at least not to the extent of later centuries. Indeed, book auction
houses such as Leigh and Sotheby sold other things too if they could, such
as antiquities, drawings, coins and medals, musical instruments, prints,
medical instruments and paintings. The larger art auctioneers, such as
Abraham Langford in Covent Garden, might describe themselves as
'auctioneers and book-sellers', but they seemed to sell everything, including
houses and land, the paintings from Handel's estate in 1760, and also
William Gostling's great music and book collection in 1777. Gostling's
sale catalogue was the first English auction catalogue devoted to music.
Abel's auctioneer dealt more with pictorial art. John Greenwood was an
extraordinary figure, a portrait painter and a contemporary of Abel, born
in Boston, Massachusetts.[16] He settled permanently in London in 1764,
after some years in Surinam, then Holland and Paris. After working as a
painter, agent and dealer, he set up as an auctioneer. By 1783 his rooms
were based in the heart of artistic London, Leicester Square. The saleroom
was large and on the south side of the square, with a communication
through to Whitcomb Street. The square itself was still dominated by
Leicester House, once home of the Princes of Wales, where George III had
grown up. On the west side lived Sir Joshua Reynolds, whose house later
became the premises of the book auctioneers, Puttick and Simpson.
Hogarth once lived on the other side and in 1790 his widow sold prints
and drawings through Greenwood's rooms.[17] Later, Sir Thomas Lawrence's
first London home was in the square. Leicester Square was, in all respects, a
very good place to open a saleroom.

Abel's sale catalogue, published here for the first time (see Appendix),
is a quarto of just eight type-set pages, similar in size and format to Greenwood's later catalogue for Mrs Hogarth. It is almost, though not entirely,
devoted to the sale of Abel's possessions; at the end of the catalogue there

are 21 lots of paintings, the 'Property of Mr Allen, going Abroad'. The catalogue is divided into sections relating to 'Music', containing 22 lots of printed music arranged in fairly large lots (numbered 1–21*, with lots 21 and 21*); then follow 17 lots of 'Manuscript Music' (22–38); a 'Musical Instruments' section of 12 lots (39–49*, with lots 49 and 49*); 'China' follows (50–56), with a mixed section of 'Trinkets, Plate, and Jewels' (57–92) concluding the first day's sale. The second day resumed at midday with pictures, starting with 'Loose Prints, Drawings, and Pictures' (lots 1–14), 'Prints and Drawings, framed and glazed' (15–52), and some paintings by various artists to conclude Abel's section (53–79). The catalogue ends with Mr Allen's paintings.

Descriptions in eighteenth-century catalogues are brief and those in book catalogues often very summary, with phrases such as 'three boxes of books' and 'ten others' being common. Greenwood's catalogue is more informative than many: a high proportion of items can be actually identified. In the music section, the detail is such that some items are described as unpublished. This suggests that the vendors, probably Abel's brother, may have supplied the auctioneers with additional information about the provenance and identification of many of the musical items and paintings. As with a modern catalogue, this evidence is used to boost their sale: an unpublished manuscript of Abel was evidently more interesting than a published source. The catalogue gives more detail than, for example, Christie's sale of John Stanley's instruments and music in 1786, where little of the printed or manuscript music can be identifed with certainty.[18]

There are numerous typographical and factual errors in the descriptions of the music. In particular, the cataloguer shows ignorance of foreign names. He is on surer ground (just) with the paintings. More items may have been in the sale than are described in the printed catalogue. In eighteenth-century auctions, it was quite common for lots to be added at the last moment, after the catalogue had been printed, and the auctioneer would mark up his own catalogue in manuscript with these additional lots. Many such catalogues have survived to show that this was very common practice. There were clearly some late additions in the Abel catalogue, but the additional lots 21* and 49* were squeezed into the catalogue before the typesetter had completed his work and there are no manuscript annotations at all in the surviving exemplar.

As usual, there are no illustrations of any of the lots. The only surviving catalogue of this period to contain engravings of books is the famous La Vallière sale (1783) in Paris, with its five pages of plates and an engraved plate depicting the deceased owner.[19] John Stanley's catalogue (1786) contains a very elaborate engraved memorial to the musician by Benjamin

West, engraved by Bartolozzi; it is not uncommon for sale catalogues to include such portraits. Some catalogues also contain introductions or laudatory prefaces, not so very different (at least in intention) from their modern equivalents. Sadly, neither portrait nor preface is included in the case of Abel.

The titlepage of the catalogue describes the sale as being sold 'by Order of the Administrator', confirmation that Abel died intestate, though it provides no information about his heirs. Administration of the 'Goods, Chattels and Credits of Charles Frederick Abel late of the Parish of Saint Mary le Bone' was granted on 25 September 1787, the estate being managed by a lawyer, George William Sottan, acting on behalf of 'Ernst Heinrich Abel the natural and lawful Brother and next of Kin ... now residing at Hamburg'.[20] No other inventories of Abel's possessions are known. The catalogue contains no details about buyers' names or prices achieved: it was not the auctioneer's own copy and there are no annotations at all, but we can piece together some information relating to the purchasers in 1787 from the evidence of later ownership.

What the catalogue does provide is an unparalleled insight into the life, career and life-style of a major figure in English musical and intellectual life at the end of the eighteenth century. It allows us to piece together the contents of Abel's music room, reveals his interests, which stray far beyond music, shows us the instruments he owned and played and what he had on his walls and on his shelves, and above all enables us to explore the repertory of the Bach-Abel concerts in a little more detail. We know little about the concert programmes of the 1760s and 1770s, apart from a few details from contemporary accounts and non-specific references in newspaper advertisements. The presence of so much printed music in Abel's sale catalogue gives us perhaps the best view of the performance materials he owned, while Abel's character explodes out of the lapidary descriptions.

The catalogue is also interesting for what is left out. It is significant that neither of the two great Gainsborough portraits of Abel is here. *Pace* the Huntington online catalogue, the great portrait is not lot 42, which was in fact a portrait in crayon of Abel playing the gamba. The reason for the absence of the portrait from the catalogue, assuming that it was once in Abel's possession, is that it was acquired by Queen Charlotte, and appeared in Christie's catalogue of her sale after her death.[21] When J. C. Bach died, the queen acquired a number of items, including the autographs of his Milan church music and one or two other items, most now in the Royal Music Library, in the British Library. The queen does not appear to have owned any of Abel's manuscripts: there are no known Abel autographs in the Royal Library and indeed, as we shall see, only one identified autograph in a British collection. The early provenance of the National Portrait Gallery painting of Abel (1765) is unknown. It may perhaps be the portrait which in January 1788 sold for 'only nine guineas … the work set a few weeks later above the orchestra in the Concert Room at Hanover Square in place of a bad painting of Apollo'.[22] In any event, it cannot be matched to anything in Abel's sale catalogue. The National Portrait Gallery chalk sketch for it evidently remained with the painter's unmarried daughter Margaret (1752–1820) and again was not in the Abel sale.[23]

Although there are only 22 lots of printed music, the heavy lotting up disguises a larger quantity, possibly as many as 200 separate items, which evidently made up Abel's working library as a teacher, composer and concert promoter. Many of the musical editions here are identifiable through *RISM*, though not in every case down to the issues and publishers. Almost all the music is contemporary and dates from the span of Abel's career in London and a little earlier. Most seems to have been printed in London. Abel was no antiquarian — few were at this stage. Indeed it was only gradually that music of older times was republished in London in the eighteenth century. With the exception of reprints of music of Handel and Purcell, most of the music published in London in the second half of the eighteenth century was new.

There is little obvious printed viola da gamba music in the catalogue. There does not seem to have been a single substantial publication for the instrument in London in the second half of the century. Abel published none in London for certain: one single copy survives of a collection of *Six easy Sonattas* attributed to him, allegedly printed in Amsterdam, but we cannot be certain of the validity or even authenticity of this issue.[24] It might have been expected that the leading gamba player of his age would have some music for the instrument, perhaps printed in France, given Abel's close links with the French capital.[25] In lot 12 lurks something described as 'concertos by Rameau', which refers to the *Pièces de Clavecin en Concerts* published in Paris in 1741 for violin or flute, viol and keyboard.[26] But these were also published in London and it is Walsh's London edition of 1750 that is referred to here, as it has the word 'Concertos' rather than Concerts on the titlepage.[27] This edition offers 'viola' as the second instrument, though the score certainly seems to allow for a viola da gamba, even if the separate parts do not.

The gamba music owned by Abel must have been in manuscript, the form in which his own compositions circulated and largely remained. Despite the presence of several other gamba players in London, not least Gainsborough, numbers were too small to include even the option of a viol da gamba on the titlepages of printed music, even at a time when multiple choices of instruments on a titlepage, such as 'German flute or violin', 'Harpsichord, Piano Forte or Organ', were commonplace. None of the other cellist/gamba players in London contemporary with Abel published anything other than cello music. It is interesting that the only work by J. C. Bach published for viol da gamba was illicitly printed by Longman, Lukey and Co. in 1773; Bach went to court to assert his copyright.[28] He did not feel it necessary to publish it himself and his known gamba music, like Abel's, evidently only circulated in manuscript.[29]

Many of the editions listed in the catalogue are by people who worked with Abel in London: Bach, of course, but Barthélemon, Eiffert, Cervetto, Kammell, Syrmen, Schetky, Agus, Giordani, Borghi and Benser, to take names at random, all worked in London and many of them appeared at the Bach-Abel concerts. Many of them too, received payments from Bach's bank account. Several, including Cervetto junior, were evidently pupils of Abel. Much of the music was published in London, many items by Robert Bremner in the Strand, who produced editions of Abel's music throughout his career. Indeed if a work by Abel was not published at some stage by Bremner, then questions need to be asked about the authority of the edition, or even its authenticity.[30]

Although the catalogue is peppered with spelling errors and the lotting is a little haphazard, there is a modicum of order, beginning with the theoretical books and moving in Lot 2 to five ruled books of manuscript paper (blank one assumes), then to operas and church music. Lot 3 is interesting in that it includes the only two operas published by Bach in a relatively complete form and in full score. *Amadis des Gaules* was written for Paris in 1779 and published posthumously with a preface, in some copies at least, signed by Bach's widow, stating that the first production in Paris mangled the text so much that Bach had wanted his original published but had died before it had appeared.[31] The likelihood is that this copy might have been given to Abel by Bach's widow; indeed many of the volumes here may have been presentation copies, but this probably seemed of no importance to the cataloguer and goes unstated.

Lot 4 is inaccurately printed: it should read *Mattutino de' Morti* by Perez. Both Bach and Abel were subscribers to this edition, printed by Abel's publisher Robert Bremner in 1774, which was a highly sumptuous and expensive production.[32] Burney, also a subscriber, refers to the score in his *History* describing the music accurately as 'grave, ingenious and expressive'.[33] He might also have added 'expensive'. When so little music appeared in full score, the printing of these Latin offices of the dead seems an extravagance. No performance of it appears to be recorded. Even more remarkable is that it was reissued three years later by Preston. This second edition retailed at £1.11.6d., a large amount of money and indicative that good engraved music was a luxury commodity. To put this in perspective, two portraits by Sir Peter Lely sold at Langfords on 1 April 1773 for 19s.[34] Printed music in the 1770s could cost more than paintings by distinguished artists.

There is a collection of cello pieces in lot 5. These are sonatas or solos for cello and continuo in a similar style and form to much of Abel's own gamba music. No doubt much of this printed music was easily adaptable for Abel's own instrument. Of the authors here, Philip Peter Eiffert, a cellist, was a friend of both Bach and Abel and played at their concerts. Cervetto jun. was James Cervetto, who had been a child prodigy on the cello; like Bach and Abel, he was a chamber musician to the queen and, with John Crosdill, whose name will feature later, was probably the cellist for whom Bach and Abel wrote their music. Antonín Kammell was a Bohemian, violinist and pupil of Tartini, who lodged with Bach and Abel on his arrival in London; Bach helped him to transport timber from the Waldstein estates in his native land to be made into masts for ships.[35] Kammell was also a stalwart at the Bach-Abel concerts and was a close enough friend of J. C. Bach to name his son after him. Kammell is not known to have published any solos for the cello, so these pieces are likely to be for the violin.

Lot 7 contains six symphonies by Richter, the first of a number of Mannheim composers listed. Bach had great connections with the court there, visiting it at least twice. But these works were probably not collected on a German trip, for Richter's symphonies were published by Walsh in 1760.[36] '3 concertos in 6 parts by Benda', lot 8, are not composed by any of the more important members of this musical dynasty, but by Friedrich Ludwig Benda (1752–92), who worked as a violinist and composer at Lud-wigslust with Carl Friedrich Abel's brother. The concertos were published in 1783, when Abel was in Germany.[37] The presence of these concertos in Abel's papers suggests that he *did* visit his brother in Ludwigslust in the mid-1780s, where he probably met Benda.

Lot 8 also contains printed music by the lady violinist Maddalena Syrmen, *née* Lombardini, who was the star of the Bach-Abel concerts in the 1771 series. She published her violin concertos in London (as Op.3, c.1770) and the rather peculiar description 'set to music by Giordani' means in fact that they were arranged for keyboard by him.[38] Lot 9 is particularly interesting with the 'German Opera by Holtzbauer'. The cataloguer prob-ably could not transcribe the German title of the Singspiel *Günther von Schwarzburg*, which had been published by Holzbauer in Mannheim in 1776 and is considered to be one of his major achievements.[39] Mozart saw it in Mannheim in 1777 and was pleased with what he heard. This is an extremely rare volume and one suspects may have been acquired by Abel, who did not participate much in the opera house, through some direct connection with the composer. Sold with the score were periodical overtures. This was a type of publishing popularized by Bremner, to bring out a series of individual symphonies in separate parts (symphonic scores were not printed at this time) by various composers, including Abel, once a month. It was an idea much in vogue in Paris and was taken up by Bremner in London in the 1760s. The works are probably Dittersdorf's *Periodical Overture* no. 38 and no. 61, though Bremner's prints give the title of overture rather than symphony;[40] and Jommelli's Overture is either no. 14 or no. 19 in the periodical series.[41] The parting shot of 'periodical overtures in 8 parts, by different authors' suggests that Abel acquired the whole series. If so, one can postulate the use of the periodical overtures at the Bach-Abel concerts. The Haydn Periodical Overture in lot 21 was perhaps one of the symphonies known to have been performed at the Bach-Abel concerts in their last years and reflecting the increasing popularity of the composer in London in the 1780s, a popularity which was to reach its apogee with the composer's visit just over three years later.

The high proportion of chamber music in the following lots is also indicative of its use in Abel's concerts and at court, where Bach and Abel had to charm the queen and the royal family with regular doses of new music and teaching material. Lot 16 contains some interesting items: the 'Five sonatas and 1 duetto by Benser' are by a composer who evidently was a friend and possibly pupil of J. C. Bach and whose first names were hitherto unknown.[42] They are John Daniel: he was involved in the legal case — fought separately by Bach and Abel — against Longman, Lukey and Co., and he signed his full name in an affidavit by Bach.[43] The six sonatas by Abel are probably one of the five sets of accompanied sonatas he published in London. The set by Reichardt, the exact edition and works are unidentifiable, is interesting as it was published in Berlin, and not in London, and may have been acquired by Abel there in the 1780s. Reichardt was also a writer on music and he describes Abel's drunken escapades on his visit to Berlin and his inordinate affection for Rhineland wines.[44] The '3 ditto' by Cramer are almost certainly the accompanied sonatas Op.2, by William Cramer, with whom Abel lodged between 1776 and 1779.[45] Cramer's son, Johann Baptist Cramer, the famous piano virtuoso, was a composition pupil of Abel, studying 'Canto Fermo, Counterpoint, Thorough Bass [from Corelli's and Handel's works principally] and also the elements of Fugue writing'.[46] The child prodigy made his debut on stage when Abel resumed his concert career in London in 1785 and began his studies with him in the same year.

Most of Abel's own music is crammed into two lots, 19 and 20, and the cataloguer has clearly not made much effort to distinguish what is what. If the 26 books of lot 19 refer to the individual orchestral parts, then some of the overtures are likely to be incomplete. Abel published 36 symphonies in six sets during his years in London. Lot 18 contains a reference to Mozart's four sonatas. These are the *Four Sonatas for the Harpsichord, with Accompaniment for a Violin. Composed by Wolfgang Mozart, seven years of age* (K 6–9; London, 1764). This is most interesting and in present-day terms by far the most valuable of all the printed music in this collection; indeed only four copies in various states of completeness now survive in libraries.[47] It was an edition almost certainly published on demand and possibly only in a print run of tens. It is a strange publication, amateurish by the standards of Bach and Abel's published work. The four sonatas are numbered in pairs, 1 and 2 and 1 and 2, a reflection that the set is made up of two sets of sonatas published in Paris as Opp.1 and 2 and amalgamated with a new English title by Leopold Mozart in 1764.[48] One wonders why he bothered translating the title: several of Bach and Abel's editions had French titles, as did Mozart's next London publication, the accompanied sonatas dedicated to Queen Charlotte, Op.3, which is a far more assured production, replete with an effusive dedication to the queen, presumably penned by Leopold Mozart.[49] Oddly, there appears to have been no copy of this publication in Abel's collection. Abel's copy of the *Four Sonatas*, was, to use contemporary auction language, a tremendous association item. Probably this was a gift, at least from Leopold, if not from Wolfgang, to one of the two men who took such an interest in the gifted child during their months in London. The Mozarts certainly possessed printed music by Bach and Abel; and we know that Wolfgang copied out Abel's symphony Op.7 no. 6. This manuscript was transcribed in London, almost certainly copied from Abel's score, as it was not published until 1767, two years after the Mozarts had left the city. Interestingly, Mozart's manuscript contains clarinets rather than the oboes of the publication, probably reflecting Abel's original conception of the symphony. There were also exchanges of music between Bach and the Mozarts, for it is little known that an autograph manuscript of a sonata by Bach survives in Leopold Mozart's music library.[50]

The lots relating to manuscripts are tantalizing. Very little of Abel's music exists in his handwriting and surprisingly no letters from him are recorded. There is a thematic catalogue of his music (hereafter WKO) prepared by Walter Knape, Abel's lone modern biographer, but sadly Knape is totally unreliable on the subject of the composer's hand.[51] Manuscripts which are *not* autograph, are consistently described as autograph, and vice versa. Of the illustrations of Abel's handwriting in Knape, only one is actually autograph, the manuscript of the Quartet Op.15 no. 1, which Knape characteristically calls 'probably autograph'.[52]

Abel's signature appears on the legal documents in his dispute with Longman, Lukey and Co. and it is an extremely characterful hand (Fig. 2).[53] The handwriting is poised and elegant and suggests that Abel too had the artistic talent of his brothers and forebears. It is difficult to make out Gainsborough's depiction of Abel's handwriting in the Huntington portrait of the composer. The letter A of Allegro is similar, but the musical handwriting is different, Gainsborough using a somewhat old-fashioned clef. Gainsborough does transcribe some of Abel's music, in E major, as yet unidentified, but very much in Abel's style.

There are three collections of autograph gamba music. The first is the Countess of Pembroke manuscript in the British Library (Add. MS 31,697), so called because of a clipped signature of 'Eliza: Pembroke' halfway through the manuscript. She was the wife of the tenth Earl of Pembroke (1738–1831), a lady-in-waiting to Queen Charlotte and a regular acquaintance of Abel. The manuscript seems to have been assembled in the nineteenth century and has been much interfered with, making it difficult to ascertain its original structure. The first thirteen pages, comprising two sonatas and two unallocated minuets are in Abel's hand; a movement in G major in 2/4 (p. 8) is in a copyist's hand. The remaining 29 sonatas are scribal, with the possible exception of alterations to the titles of the last two. The second manuscript is in the Drexel collection at New York Public Library (MS 5871) and contains a large collection of movements grouped by key and almost certainly used as teaching material by Abel. The third is an interesting, partly autograph collection of works, including some new pieces, sold at auction at Sotheby's in 1994 and now in a private collection in the USA.[54] This manuscript also derived from the collection of Lady Pembroke and the preliminaries are signed by her.

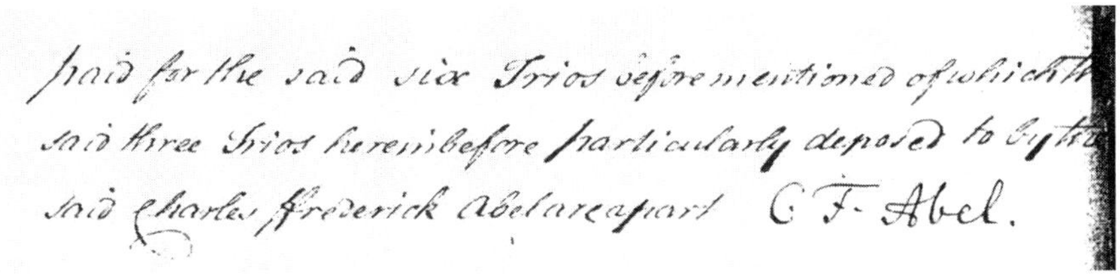

*Fig. 2* Abel's signature, 12 May 1773 (The National Archives, C.31/188, p. 97)

Abel's sale catalogue does not help with identifying the various works in question and in determining what is autograph and what is not. Lot 22, 'solos by Abel and Giardini', presumably refers to two batches of material. Giardini was a rival of J. C. Bach and their relationship during the early part of Bach's career was not cordial. He appeared in the Bach-Abel concerts, but his involvement in the rival concerts at the Pantheon from 1774 to 1779 may have caused friction. The relationship between Abel and Giardini probably varied, though Abel did own Giardini's portrait executed by Ernst Heinrich Abel (Second Day's Sale, lot 25). Giardini's solos were published in various editions and all the known works are for the violin. Abel's solos are almost certainly for the viola da gamba. It is possible that some or all of the three surviving manuscript collections formed part of this lot and may have been acquired by Lady Pembroke at the auction, although they may also have been gifts or commissions.

Lots 23, 'Scores by Mr. Abel', 24, 25 and 27 are too vague to identify. Lot 26, 'Trios, chiefly by Mr. Abel', may well be the original manuscripts of the *Six Sonatas for 2 Violins...Op.III*, published in London in 1765, or indeed for the accompanied sonatas. Paisiello's opera *Nitteti* (lot 28) was written for St Petersburg in 1777 and the presence of this score, with another item of Russian provenance, will be discussed later. Lot 32, 'Concertos by Mr. Abel', may relate to his sets of keyboard concertos published in London. But the last five lots of this section are the most interesting and revealing.

Lot 34. *Mr. Abel's last solos and concertos, for the viola da gambo.* No manuscripts or editions survive of any concertos for the viola da gamba by Abel, though contemporary concert advertisements do indicate their existence. Of the solos, the auctioneer distinguishes between 'solos' in lot 22 and 'last solos' in lot 34, which again suggests that the auctioneer had some knowledge of the dates. We know that Abel was performing and composing right up to his death, and the auctioneer must have been aware of this, or the manuscripts must have been dated or dateable. None of the surviving autographs is dated.

35. *Galatea by Bach.* This is a lost work by Christian Bach dating from 1764 and we know that it was first performed at Bach and Abel's initial collaboration in a concert in the Great Room in Spring Gardens, on 29 February 1764. It was a serenata in two parts, to a libretto by Metastasio. The libretto was published, but none of the music appears to have survived.[55] Presumably this manuscript was left behind by Bach when he ceased to live with Abel in the early 1770s.

36. *The famous Miserere by Leo* was indeed a famous work in the eighteenth century. Written by the Neapolitan opera composer Leonardo Leo

in 1739, it was extremely popular throughout Europe. Burney remarks that '[Leo's] celebrated *Miserere*, in eight real parts, though imperfectly performed in London at the Pantheon, for Ansani's benefit, 1781, convinced real judges that it was of the highest class of choral composition.'[56]

37. *The last concerto which Mr. Abel composed, designed for the present King of Prussia.* Again, this presupposes some knowledge by the auctioneer of the dating of the piece and its place in the composer's output. Abel went to Germany at the end of the 1782 concert series. But his connection with Berlin probably preceded the visit in 1782. For in 1781, he had published in London a sumptuously produced collection of string quartets later given the opus no. 15.[57] These were very lavish, without opus number and with no publisher's name, indicating perhaps the special nature of the collection and the special dedicatee, the hereditary prince of Prussia, who acceded to the throne on the death of Frederick the Great in 1786 as Frederick William II (1744–97). The prince played the cello and loved music; he had a private orchestra and Haydn and Mozart wrote quartets for him with prominent cello parts. A musician in the eighteenth century would not dedicate anything to anyone without permission and without a reason, especially to someone as well-placed as the heir of Frederick the Great. Abel may have visited Berlin before 1782 or had contacts there who were able to ensure that his offer of dedication would be accepted. With the quartets Op.15, Abel was following a similar path to that trodden by J. C. Bach, whose *Six Quintettos*, published first without the opus no. 11, with a lavish titlepage and dedication leaf to the Elector Palatine in Mannheim, were definitely printed after Bach's visit there in 1772, as alluded to in the dedication. It seems probable, therefore, that Abel visited Berlin before 1782.

A set of parts for a cello concerto in C major — the cello being the prince's instrument — survives in the Königliche Hausbibliothek, Berlin (Staatsbibliothek zu Berlin, K.H.M.20). Although described by Knape as 'zweifellos Autograph', the manuscript is in the hand of a single copyist, who is also responsible for other manuscripts by Abel in Berlin (see below).[58] There is no doubt that this is the concerto written for 'The present King of Prussia'. It is probable too that the copyist worked with Abel in London and that the composer brought the manuscript with him to Berlin. Some of the paper used in the other Berlin Royal Library manuscripts of Abel came from Britain and it is likely that this may also be true of the paper of the cello concerto.[59] There are two noteworthy features of this manuscript. The cadenzas in the solo cello part are added on tipped-in sheets of a different paper type, and they are in Abel's hand, marked for performance, proving that this manuscript can be firmly associated with the composer. Secondly, this concerto is unusually in four movements, with the third, the 'Rondeau di Minuetto', inserted at the last moment, all the instrumental parts being adjusted accordingly. While this concerto can certainly be identified with lot 37 in the sale, it is highly unlikely that the Berlin parts were sold in London. They were surely retained in Berlin after Abel's return home, which explains their place in the Royal Library. It may be surmised that the manuscript of lot 37 was probably the autograph score, now lost.

38. *Symphonies by Abel, his last work, unpublished.* Abel's last published symphonies were the *Six Overtures* Op.17, which Bremner produced in the mid-1780s. All Abel's published symphonies are for an orchestra in eight parts, with strings, two oboes and two horns. However, in Berlin there are five manuscripts in parts of four symphonies in eight parts (two in B flat, one in C and one in E flat) and one in D major in ten parts.[60] These are the prime candidates for the unpublished symphonies of lot 38. The manuscript parts are written in a variety of hands and on a variety of papers, perhaps indicating haste in their production. One of the hands is the scribe of the cello concerto, which also suggests that they date from the same time, late in Abel's career.[61] Many of the parts are written on fine English Whatman paper. Knape describes these parts as all autograph, but they are not. Only the two oboe parts of the Symphony in C, KVO.38 (Berlin K.H.M.9) are in Abel's hand, and they are on British paper. Two instrumental parts of the D major symphony bear the pencilled names of 'Napier' and 'Mr Hindmarsh'. Napier was a music publisher and viola player; John Hindmarsh a London violinist.[62] All the evidence suggests that these parts were prepared in London and possibly even used in concerts before Abel took them to Berlin, where, like those for the cello concerto, they remained; the references in the sale catalogue for lot 38 probably again relate to lost full scores.

The presence of the manuscripts of the symphonies and the cello concerto in the Berlin Royal Music Library, together with the dedication of the quartets Op.15 to the Crown Prince of Prussia, indicate that Abel's trip to Berlin in or around 1782 was carefully planned and prepared. It may not, therefore, have been quite the flit that gossipy accounts suggest and it may have been preceded by at least one other visit, which had established his reputation there. These unpublished pieces are not the only manuscripts of Abel in Berlin. Four overtures of the Op.17 set are present in parts in the Staatsbibliothek: these share a number of the hands and similar paper to the manuscripts discussed above, and it seems likely that they arrived in Berlin at the same time and were part of the repertoire of his compositions performed there.[63] The Op.17 set was not published until Abel returned to London.[64] There is no information as to the purchaser of the music in the catalogue and none of the five unpublished symphonies was printed until the twentieth century. Nevertheless, there was an excited account in the *Daily Universal Register* two days after the sale: 'We are happy to hear, that the last symphonies, concertantes, and favourite concertos for the violoncello, by the late celebrated Mr Abel, are not likely to be buried in oblivion; as the manuscript copies have been purchased, and will most likely to be published.'[65] They were not.

\* \* \*

The musical instruments section of the sale catalogue is revealing. There is some significant detail here, as well as interesting omissions. Given that Abel is known to have played the pentachord, a five-string cello in public in his earliest years in London and he is likely to have played also the four-string variety, why are there no cellos offered for sale in the catalogue? Were they disposed of before the sale? Or were they additional lots not in the catalogue? Did Abel play the cello regularly enough in his later years to own one? Or had he disposed of them earlier? Abel is not generally known as a violinist. Yet he had four valuable instruments: an Amati violin (lot number 41), a fine-toned Italian violin (46), one by Guarneri (47), and one by Jacob Stainer dated 1675 — presumably on a label inside the violin (48). While any active musician is likely to have collected instruments for others to play, the number and quality of the violins here lead one to believe that Abel must also have performed on it himself. After all, his father and brother also played the instrument. There is also a viola, called tenor here (lot 42), and some very fine gambas, perhaps the one in the Huntington Gainsborough portrait, 'capital' in its mahogany case and Abel's 'best instrument' (44), with an old gamba (40) and a third (lot 45). Gainsborough is reputed to have spent 40 guineas on a gamba in Abel's sale, though it is not known which instrument he purchased.[66]

There is quite a lot of interesting detail in the contents of the mahogany box with its 'strings, ivorys for rosin, 16 bridges for bass viols' (39), and there were plenty of music stands for chamber music evenings. In addition to playing the gamba, Abel performed on the harpsichord in the concerts of his early years and in his performances at court, and he certainly directed from the instrument. Bach and Abel moved in the circle of the keyboard manufacturers. Bach's central role in the development of the piano in London is pinpointed by Burney, so it is not surprising that Abel should own a fine-toned forte piano by Buntebart, the German instrument manufacturer.[67] Bach's dealings with him are revealed in his bank account between 1776 and 1779.[68] Shudi too was a great harpsichord manufacturer resident in London for many years and it is not surprising that Abel would have a fine example, as in lot 49 with its 'exceeding fine and sweet' tone.

While this description may be attributed to auctioneer's hyperbole, it also suggests some deeper knowledge, at least of the consignors of these items for sale. The guitar is interesting (lot 49*). There is no music by Abel for the instrument, but it was of course much in vogue in amateur circles and the instrument is specified in some contemporary publications and manuscripts. The presence of the lute (40) is notable, so old-fashioned as to be thrown in with the old gamba and music stands.

The china, plate, trinkets and jewels contain many choice items. Abel had lived in Dresden during the 1740s and 1750s, an important decade in porcelain manufacture there. Although of course Abel could have acquired this porcelain at any time, from the descriptions of the designs in the catalogue, it is clear that many of the items here were not made after about 1755, which would coincide with his time in the city.[69] Though if he had bought the china there and then, it would have had to have been transported across Europe in his peregrinations in the late 1750s.

Among the 'Trinkets, Plate and Jewels', there are some quite mundane things, such as the '12 sticks of sealing wax'. This was a real clear-out sale, though not perhaps as much as Leopold Mozart's auction in Salzburg earlier in the year, where clothes, wigs and household linen, amongst many other things, were sold.[70] Money scales would have been very useful for dealing with foreign currency, as they were for Leopold Mozart. The surviving formal images do not show Abel in spectacles. But Thomas Rowlandson's caricature entitled 'Concerto Spirituale with Bach and Abel', which in fact shows Fischer with Abel in later life fighting his way through some tricky score, red-faced, emboldened by drink and resplendent in his 'temple spectacles' — as opposed to glasses that fitted just on the nose (lot 62).[71] Lots 63, 90 and 91 are telescopes, the first an achromatic telescope by Ramsden and two others by Dollond and Watkins. Astronomy was the rage in London, and the city could boast William Herschel, who was also a musician and almost certainly known to Abel, and his sister Caroline, who was a singer as well as helping out her brother in astronomy, and a friend of the royal princes and princess, Abel's pupils. London was also the centre of telescope manufacture: for example, Jesse Ramsden's achromatic telescope, an instrument which used different types of glass cut to produce a plain, uncoloured image. Ramsden arrived in London at the same time as Abel and set up in business in 1762. His achromatic telescopes were very highly prized for their craftsmanship. Captain Cook used a Ramsden telescope with optics by John Dollond on the Transit of Venus expedition in 1769. Abel clearly owned the best and presumably most expensive telescopes in town, and he had three of them.

Lot 70 is a steel sword and belt, possibly that depicted in Nixon's caricature portrait and followed by a pair of curious pistols by 'Ruchenreuter' (lot 71).[72] The cataloguer means Kuchenreuter, the family of gunsmiths in Regensburg since the sixteenth century. Travelling as much as he did, Abel would probably have needed some protection: Bach, Abel and Gainsborough had indeed been held up by a highwayman outside Hammersmith on 7 June 1775.[73]

There are three other items of interest in this section. First, the portrait of the Empress of Russia, Catherine the Great (lot 66). Unfortunately, the catalogue does not reveal whether or not this was a miniature or merely a plaque. Did Abel have any connection with the Russian court that he should receive the royal portrait, and should this be viewed in relation to the Paisiello score of *Nitteti*, written in St Petersburg in 1777? There were connections between the musical life of London and St Petersburg; Giardini would die in Moscow. There is insufficient information to suggest that Abel ever went to Russia, but enough perhaps to say that he had contacts or connections. Nor should it be forgotten that the Russian empress was of German birth and a princess of Anhalt-Zerbst, not so far away from Abel's early homes. Lot 68 is a miniature of Queen Charlotte. Quite a number of these survive and she often gave them out to her favourites.[74]

Eleven snuff boxes are described here (lots 59–61; 71–75), the last four being the most splendid and described by the cataloguer in considerable detail. Abel was evidently very fond of them, as both the Gainsborough portraits show him with them: the earlier portrait (1765) seems to show a lacquered box, which does not seem to correspond to anything in the Greenwood catalogue; the Huntington portrait contains a particularly fine example. All contemporary accounts stress that Frederick William of Prussia presented Abel with one, and we must accept this at face value. However, the 'exceeding curious gold box with Chinese figures, mounted with brilliant diamonds, present from the King of Prussia', is more in the style of Frederick the Great, who owned the finest collection in Europe. This style of snuff box went out of fashion in the 1760s and it is especially interesting that although one single design is known for a box in *chinoiserie* style, no actual example has survived.[75] Abel's seems to have been a particularly interesting and valuable item. Clearly the snuff box in the Huntington portrait (1777) was of such importance to Abel that it was depicted by Gainsborough. It is oval in shape and therefore not lots 72 and 73; nor does it appear to be lot 75. Abel may of course have parted with it before he died. If the snuff box with Chinese figures was the one in Gainsborough's portrait, the splendid and curious box of lot 74, then Abel must have received it prior to his journey to Berlin in the 1780s. Perhaps

Abel was given another snuff box by Frederick William on his visit to Berlin in the 1780s?

We have noted the absence of the great Gainsborough portraits from the sale catalogue, but this is partly compensated for by the estimated 120 paintings, drawings and engravings of the second day's sale. This is a bare minimum as some of the lots of loose prints contain multiples. Several paintings at least were very large in size, so one must conclude that Abel's house was sizeable and the walls covered in paintings. The collection is wide-ranging, dating from the sixteenth to the eighteenth century, with a strong preponderance of pastoral landscapes and a lot of cows and cattle. In fact Abel's taste in paintings seems to have been wider than his musical taste, where the music seems only to be contemporary. The number of items listed here supports Angelo's description of Abel's home as being covered in works of art.

The portraits of famous contemporaries included the intensely musical Lord Clive and his son, and Alderman Beckford, who as Mayor of London would have been known to Abel. There is no record of the intensely unmusical Samuel Johnson having much to do with Bach or Abel, but perhaps Abel admired the famous portrait by Reynolds sufficiently to own a copy of it (lot 49). Lot 6, the proofs of the Bartolozzi frontispiece, is for the quartets Op.8, dedicated to George III, and lavishly decorated.[76] Lot 14 contains quires of printing paper, an indication that when a composer advertises his works as 'printed for the author', it probably means that he provided the paper as well.

The section entitled 'Prints and Drawings, framed and glazed' reveals Abel's connection with the artists Cipriani and Bartolozzi, who were friends of Bach and Abel. Their designs and engravings decorated many first editions, particularly the issues printed for the author, such as the first editions of J. C. Bach's keyboard sonatas Op.5 and Abel's Op.8 quartets. These titles and frontispieces were never merely decorative, but must be considered part of the overall aesthetic effect of the editions, in which music, art and engraving came together. They were expensively produced and expensive to buy. With their keen artistic sense, Bach and Abel attracted the best artists to embellish their works and utilized them probably more than any other composer in London. This concern for overall artistic effect transferred to their concert tickets, which were also beautifully done and were evidently collected even at this early time. The Bach-Abel concerts were subscription concerts at 5 guineas a season per person in 1765. At others, a single ticket was 10s. and 6d., half a guinea, the cost of an edition of sonatas of Bach and Abel. A collection of 'six tickets of Mr Giardini's' sold for £2.6s. at a sale by Hutchins (22 March 1786, lot 230), indicating the interest in these attractive items.[77] You could attend the concert and later recoup some of the expenditure by selling the tickets as works of art. Their emphasis was on fine performances in beautiful surroundings adorned with paintings by Gainsborough and others. This luxury extended to the concert tickets, which, keeping their value, remained collectors' items. Many of them were still being offered for sale at the sale of the Queen's relics in 1819.

Abel owned several drawings by his brother, presumably Ernst Heinrich, who was to benefit from the sale. The portrait of Giardini, who had left London in 1784 for Italy, suggests that the portraitist had visited London somewhat earlier, probably to stay with his brother. The importance of Abel as a collector lies in his closeness to Gainsborough, of whose work he owned at least 40 examples, not including the two great portraits. Although many of these were drawings in chalk or crayon, there were several oils (from lot 37 onwards). At least three can now be identified: Lot 44, the portrait in oils of the favourite dog and puppy, now known as the Pomeranian Bitch and Puppy, is the delightful painting now in Tate Britain, thought to date from 1777, the time of the Huntington portrait of Abel with the dog.[78] A biographer of the painter mentions that when the portrait first arrived at Abel's house 'the deception was so complete that the elder subject, irritated by the presence of a supposed rival, flew at her own resemblance with such fury that it was found necessary to place the picture in a situation where it was free from her jealous anger'.[79] Abel and Bach evidently both loved dogs, to the extent that when Bach's beloved 'Pomy' disappeared, he put a notice in *The Public Advertiser* offering a reward to the finder.[80] The purchaser of the painting at the sale was almost certainly Abel's pupil and friend John Crosdill, the cellist: he was listed as the owner when the painting was exhibited for the first time in 1814, as one of 69 paintings by Gainsborough shown at the British Institution.[81]

The other two oil paintings which we know belonged to Abel and which can be identified are, firstly, the landscape described by its owner Mrs Piozzi as the 'beautiful Picture here which Mr. Piozzi and I mean As a Nuptial Present to Sophia ... a Gainsborough, scarce five Feet by four — The Subject Cattle driven down to drink, and the first Cow expresses something of Surprize as if an otter lurked under the Bank. It is A *naked* looking Landscape — done to divert *Abel* the Musician ... and the Dog is a favourite's Portrait'.[82] This painting is now at Bowood House, Wiltshire. The Piozzis were the first recorded owners and it seems likely they purchased it at Abel's sale (lot 47). John Crosdill is again the likely purchaser of another landscape, 'upright half-length ... with a group of cattle' (lot

45), which again was exhibited in 1814 as 'an upright landscape, with cattle', and is now in the National Gallery of Ireland.[83] Many cattle roamed over Abel's walls.

The other paintings and drawings of Gainsborough in Greenwood's catalogue are more difficult to track down, though Thomas Rowlandson later made engravings of four landscapes in Abel's collection, all issued on 21 May 1789. The originals of these drawings would all appear to be lost, with one exception. They comprise:

1. 'Wooded Landscape with Figures and Cows', drawing, grey wash heightened with white over off-set outline; now in British Museum, G.g3–393. This was engraved by Rowlandson 'late in the collection of Charles Frederick Abel'.[84]
2. 'Wooded Landscape with Faggot Gatherers, Cows and Sheep'; Hayes, *Drawings*, no. 680.
3. 'Wooded Landscape with Faggot Gatherers and Cows'; Hayes, *Drawings*, no. 681.
4. 'Upland Landscape with Herdsman and Cattle'; Hayes, *Drawings*, no. 682.

One further entry in the catalogue deserves some consideration: could lot 40, 'The portrait of a gentleman, friend to Mr. Abel, by Gainsborough', be J. C. Bach? There is no evidence that Bach's widow Cecilia Grassi took this remarkable and celebrated painting with her when she returned to Italy on his death; it does not seem to have been acquired by the Queen, as it was not in her sale, and it seems to have remained in England. The early provenance is completely unknown: it was evidently acquired at some stage by Thomas Mudge (1789–1839), grandson of the Royal Clockmaker Thomas Mudge 1715/16–94) or by his widow, Anna Robson. The stretcher bears the seal of the Robson family and is inscribed: 'The Property of Mrs Mudge/widow of Mudge/and of her daughter Charlotte'.[85] It is quite possible that Mudge junior and senior would have known Bach at court and acquired the painting in his memory.

The remainder of Abel's art collection is rather more varied, with two drawings by the fashionable English painter and draughtsman John Hamilton Mortimer (1740–79), whose 'Banditti' (lot 53) and scenes from Shakespeare were very popular in his day (a scene from *The Tempest*, lot 71) and frequently appear in engravings. Many of the painters are pastoralists, with cattle featuring prominently. Abel might well have known the artist Claude-Joseph Vernet (1714–89) who lived in Paris from 1753; similarly, Charles Amadée Philipp van Loo (1719–95), who is notable for his portrait of the young Marquis de Sade.[86] One interesting name here is that of Philip James de Loutherberg, a pupil of van Loo, who came to London with a letter of recommendation to David Garrick. He became a friend of Gainsborough and so would certainly have been known to Bach and Abel. De Loutherberg experimented with scenic effects in the theatre 'and his Eidophusikon, sequences of moving scenery on a model stage accompanied by dramatic sound effects and music by Dr Arne took London by storm in 1781.'[87] Abel owned 'A sea storm' by Loutherberg (lot 70), an event depicted apparently very excitingly in the Eidophusikon and which must therefore be deemed a speciality of the artist.

Abel's collection was very much that of a gentleman of his day, not perhaps in the major league of art collecting (apart from his Gainsboroughs), but evidently knowledgeable and a connoisseur. The tranquillity of the pastoral scenes was occasionally broken by the odd rape or battle scene, with Guercino's Cleopatra (lot 64) as one of the high spots. A version of this scene, depicting her bare-breasted and with an asp, survives in Genoa.[88]

The catalogue opens up our view of the composer, his heartfelt gamba playing and music supported by a hinterland of art, based on his family tradition. A musician who probably played the violin as well as the gamba and harpsichord. But did he regularly play the cello? An active musician, whose repertoire included many of the masters of Europe, but few of the past. A man for whom the world of science and the wider arts, as well as wine, were of great importance. A man who travelled, probably more than we have known so far, who had some connection with Prussia and perhaps Russia and who maintained a connection with his homeland and family. We have only sampled the auction catalogue and dipped our metaphorical toe in the water with it. There is much more to do, especially in relation to the other paintings not by Gainsborough, to identify those which may survive in other collections. One word needs to be said about the last 21 lots, the 'Property of Mr. Allen, going Abroad', whose collections included works by Titian, Rubens and Caracci. But also lot 6, a portrait of Captain Coram, framed and glazed, by William Hogarth, presumably a copy of the wonderful portrait presented by the artist to Thomas Coram, the founder of the Foundling Hospital, which in the mid-1780s was on the very edge of the metropolis.

The auction sale catalogue of C. F. Abel

5 sheets    Box A vi    6   7

# A CATALOGUE

### Of the CAPITAL COLLECTION of

## Manuscript and other MUSIC,

An exceeding valuable and fine-toned Viol de Gamba, a Forte-Piano by Buntebart, a Violin, &c. a Number of fine Drawings, and Four Pictures by Mr. GAINSBOROUGH; several Gold Snuff-Boxes, and Watches, Plate, Trinkets, fine Dresden China, &c. of

## CHARLES FREDERICK ABEL, Esq; DECEASED,

### MUSICIAN TO HER MAJESTY.

Which *(by Order of the Administrator)* will be SOLD by AUCTION,

## By Mr. GREENWOOD,

### At his ROOMS in LEICESTER-SQUARE,

On WEDNESDAY the 12th of DECEMBER, 1787, And following DAY, at TWELVE o'Clock.

## Also, a small Select COLLECTION of PICTURES,

*The Property of Mr. ALLEN, going Abroad;*

### CONSISTING OF

The choicest Works of MORTIMER, and other esteemed Masters,

To be viewed on MONDAY the 10th, and Catalogues had.

☞ CONDITIONS of SALE AS USUAL.

Printed by H. REYNELL, No. 21, Piccadilly, near the Hay-market.

A

# CATALOGUE, &c.

---

## FIRST DAY'S SALE,

### Wednefday, December the 12th, 1787.

## MUSIC.

LOT
1 TREATISE on Harmony, in 2 parts, and 20 other fmall books
2 Five ruled books for mufic, and favorite fongs in the Opera of Adriano in Syria, by Bach
3 Amadis des Gaules by Bach, Theorie by Rodolphe, La Clemenza Scipione, by Bach
4 Matlutino de Morti by Peren, and 6 books of fongs by Barthelemon, &c.
5 Solos for the Violoncello by Eiffert, 6 Solos by Cervetto, jun. 6 ditto by Flackton, 6 duets by Kammel, 8 duets by Paxton, and Scotch fongs by Bremner
6 Two fets Bremner's Scotch fongs, Englifh and Italian fongs by Barthelemon, 12 folos by Cervetto, folos by Eiffert, Galeotti fonate, 6 folos by Borghi, and finfonias by Baron Bagge
7 Six fymphonies by Bach, 6 ditto by Richter, Concertos by Benda, 6 concertos by Bach, and 6 ditto by Giordani, for the harpfichord
8 Six concertos in 9 parts by Syrmen, and 3 concertos in 6 parts by Benda, and 6 concertos by Syrmen for the harpfichord, fet to mufic by Giordani
9 German Opera by Holtzbauer, periodical fymphonies by Ditters, periodical overtures by Jomelli, and periodical overtures in 8 parts, by different authors
10 Six Quintetti by Zannetti, 6 quartettos by Pieltain, 6 quartettos by Canales, 6 ditto by Schetky, 6 ditto by Toefchi, and 6 fonates by Bach

LOT

11 Trios by Baron Bagge, fonatas by Zanetti, trios by Agus, fonatas by Cirri, trios by Kammel, and trios by Giardini

12 Trios by Kammel, trios by Agus, concertos by Rameau, concertos by Bach, concertos by Schevanberger, mifcellaneous quartetts, and 6 fonatas by Abel

13 Trios by Kammel, overtures in 6 parts by Jomelli, 6 fonatas by Abel, 6 fonatas by Bach, Abel, Kammel, and 6 folos by Falco

14 Handel's Opera Songs, ditto felected from his Oratorios, 2 numbers of Falco's folos, 12 fonatas by Jordani, and the fcore of the 12 concertos compofed by Corelli

15 Six fonatas by Chalon, felect concert pieces by Bremner, 6 divertiffements by Boutmy, 6 fonatas by Boccherini, 6 ditto by Clementi, 6 ditto by Count Bruhl, 6 ditto by Wagenfeil, and 6 ditto by Abel

16 Five fonatas and 1 duetto by Benfer, 6 divertiffements by Boutmy, felect concert pieces by Bremner, 6 fonatas by Abel, 6 ditto by Reichardt, 3 ditto by Cramer, 6 ditto by Sejan, and 6 ditto by Martini

17 Six fonatas by Eaftcott, jun. fei foli by Falco, 3 fonatas by Cramer, 6 ditto by Count Bruhl, 6 ditto by Abel, 3 trios by Frike, and a fet of leffons for the harpfichord by Arnold

18 Leffons for the harpfichord by Arnold, 6 fonatas by De Virbes, 10 ditto by J. Burlon, 6 ditto by Benfer, 4 ditto by Mozart, 6 ditto by Richter, and 6 overtures in 8 parts by Abel

19 Twenty-fix books by Abel, of 6 overtures in 8 parts, with a thorough bafs

20 Sundry fymphonies, quartettos, and concertos by Abel

21 Periodical overtures in 8 parts by Haydn, overtures by Bach, 6 fonatas by Richter, ditto by Benfer, &c.

21* Six overtures in 4 parts by Lewis Borghi

## MANUSCRIPT MUSIC.

22 Solos by Abel and Giardini

23 Scores by Mr. Abel

24 Symphonies by different authors

25 Scores by ditto

26 Trios, chiefly by Mr. Abel

27 Concertos and fymphonies by different authors

28 Nitteli, an Opera by Paifiello

29 Trios, fonatas, &c. by different authors

30 Ditto ditto

31 A duet by Paifiello, and fymphonies by various mafters

32 Concertos by Mr. Abel

33 A parcel of fymphonies by Abel and other mafters

34 Mr. Abel's laft folos and concertos, for the viola de gambo

35 Galatea by Bach

36 The famous miferere by Leo

37 The laft concerto which Mr. Abel compofed, defigned for the prefent King of Pruffia

38 Symphonies by Abel, his laft work, unpublifhed

## *Musical Instruments.*

LOT
39 A mahogany box, with a parcel of strings, ivorys for rosin, 16 bridges for bass viols,
    2 pocket music stands, 6 bows, and a table stand
40 Four mahogany music stands, an old viol de gambo, and a lute
41 An amati violin, exceeding fine, and bow
42 A tenor and bow, the case to be sold with the violin
43 A fine toned forte piano, by G. Buntebaart, made for Mr. Abel
44 A capital viol de gamba, in a mahogany case, his best instrument
45 A ditto
46 A fine toned Italian violin
47 A ditto ditto, by Granarius
48 A capital ditto by Stainer, 1675
49 An exceeding fine and sweet toned double keyed harpsichord, by B. Schudi
49* An exceeding fine large guitter, inlaid with mother-o'pearl

## C H I N A.

50 A tureen, cover and dish, 2 oblong dishes, five round ditto, 40 table plates, 12
    soup ditto, and 14 desert pieces of blue and white Dresden china
51 A tea set, painted in flowers, of Dresden china, containing 12 tea cups, 6 coffee
    cups, 18 saucers, sugar dish and cover, slop bason, cream pot, tea pot and cover
52 A handsome coffee pot and stand, japanned china
53 A caudle cup, saucer and cover, painted in flowers, Dresden china
54 A ditto, most beautifully painted with Cupids and flowers
55 A tea set of Dresden china, each piece painted with different flowers from Nature,
    containing 12 tea cups, 6 coffee cups, 18 saucers, sugar dish and cover, slop bason,
    cream pot, tea pot, cover and stand
56 Thirty-five Dresden china handles for knives and forks

## *Trinkets, Plate, and Jewels.*

57 Two small marble busts on pedestals, a drinking glass in a case, a pair of scissars, and
    2 knives
58 A pair of money scales, tortoiseshell toothpick case, 2 small magnets, a green shag-
    reen toothpick case, silver toothpick in it, and leather ink horn
59 Stone whistle, 3 snuff boxes, 2 oval miniature frames, and 12 sticks of sealing wax
60 Agate snuff box, silver ditto, and a round tortoiseshell snuff box
61 A tortoiseshell snuff box with a miniature picture, mounted with gold, and an oval
    tortoiseshell ditto
62 A pair of temple spectacles, and a small reading glass, mounted with mother o' pearl
    and silver
63 An acromatic telescope by Ramsden
64 Free-mason's badge and apron, a worked pocket book and purse

LOT

65 A pair of agate sleeve buttons, mounted with gold, a Scotch pebble seal, mounted with ditto

66 The portrait of the Empress of Rusia

67 A pair of silver shoe and knee buckles, and a stock buckle

68 A very small miniature of her Majesty, in a case

69 An exceeding fine joint with a gold head

70 A steel sword and belt

71 One pair of exceeding curious pistols, by Joh. And. Ruchenreuter

72 A round gold chased snuff box, different coloured gold

73 A noble ditto, with emblematical enamelled compartments, in a green shagreen case

74 An exceeding curious gold box with Chinese figures, mounted with brilliant diamonds, present from the King of Prussia

75 A beautiful gold snuff box, with six miniature landscapes, after Teniers

76 A gold toothpick case

77 A silver gilt repeater, by Archambo

78 A gold watch by Roth, London

79 A gold horizontal stop watch, Lepine, a Paris

80 Six tea spoons, a pap spoon, 6 bottle marks, a pair tea tongs, and 2 silver tops of castors

81 Soup ladle, at per oz.

82 A ditto scolloped, ditto

83 A silver snuffer stand, and steel snuffers, ditto

84 A wine strainer, ditto

85 Seven table spoons, at per oz.

86 Fifteen ditto, ditto

87 Eighteen 4-pronged forks, ditto

88 A coffee can, ditto

89 Four fluted pillar candlesticks, ditto

90 A telescope by Dolland

91 A ditto by Watkins

92 Three leather trunks

## End of the First Day's Sale.

# SECOND DAY'S SALE.

## Thursday, December the 13th, 1787.

### Loose Prints, Drawings, and Pictures.

LOT

1 PORTRAIT of Mr. Abel, copper plate, and 37 impressions
2 Various portraits, and a number of sketches
3 Twelve miniatures
4 Portrait of the late Lord Clive, his son, and six other portraits
5 Alderman Beckford, by Bartolozzi, and 9 others
6 Frontispiece to Abel's quartettos, by Bartolozzi, proofs
7 Cipriani's drawing book, engraved by Bartolozzi
8 Two landscapes by Gainsborough, in chalks
9 Two ditto      ditto
10 Two ditto      ditto
11 Two ditto      ditto
12 Two ditto      ditto
13 Four ditto      ditto
14 A leather case with some ruled paper, blotting book, and 6 quires printing paper

### Prints and Drawings, framed and glazed.

15 Six Cipriani and Bartolozzi tickets
16 Two boys at play, and Guerchino's daughters, by Bartolozzi
17 A bust of Mr. Cramer, a frame with some casts, and a portrait
18 A Magdalen, a high-finished miniature
19 A woman with a vase, and the companion, by Bartolozzi
20 Clytie, a fine proof by Bartolozzi

LOT
21 A young Bacchus, red and white chalk, by Cipriani
22 Six portraits drawn in chalk, by Mr. Abel's brother
23 Six ditto by ditto
24 Three ditto by ditto
25 Two ditto, the portrait of Giardini, and a lady
25 La Hogue and the Boyne, fine proofs, elegantly framed
26 Two landscapes by Gainsborough
27 Two ditto ditto
28 Two ditto ditto
29 Two ditto ditto
30 Two ditto ditto
31 Two ditto ditto
32 Two ditto ditto, in colours
33 Two ditto ditto, on blue paper
34 Two ditto ditto, on white paper
35 Two ditto ditto, in oil
36 One ditto ditto, ditto
37 Two landscapes by Gainsborough, and 1 historical by ditto
38 A painting of a girl with a book in her hand
39 An emblematical basso relievo, by the famous Gerhart
40 The portrait of a gentleman, friend to Mr. Abel, by Gainsborough
41 Mr. Abel's portrait in crayons
42 A ditto, playing the Viol de Gamba, by Gainsborough
43 The portrait of a gentleman and two horses, by H. Barron
44 The portrait of a favorite dog and puppy, by Gainsborough
45 An upright half length landscape, with a group of cattle, by ditto
49 Morning, a beautiful landscape with figures and horses, by ditto
47 Evening, the companion, with a drove of cattle, and a shepherd and shepherdess, dogs, &c. by ditto
48 An Italian bishop after Titian, very fine
49 The portrait of Dr. Johnson, after Sir J. Reynolds, ditto
50 Robinetta, after ditto
51 An arch girl, the companion, ditto
52 St. John, after Guido

| | LOT | |
|---|---|---|
| MORTIMER ——— | 53 | Banditti, a fine pen and ink drawing |
| VISCHER ——— | 54 | The rat-catcher, a fine print by |
| VERNET ——— | 55 | A calm, with Nymphs bathing |
| DE HEUSCH ——— | 56 | A pair of agreeable landscapes and figures |
| SWANEVELD ——— | 57 | A ditto, in the stile of Claude |
| VAN GOOL ——— | 58 | A farm yard with cattle, highly finished |
| Ditto ——— | 59 | The inside of a barn, the companion |
| V. DER HAAGEN — | 60 | A beautiful landscape and figures |
| G. FLINCK ——— | 61 | The head of a high priest, very fine |
| ROTTENHAMER — | 62 | A battle piece |
| Ditto ——— | 63 | A rape, the companion |
| GUERCHINO ——— | 64 | Cleopatra |
| ITALIAN ——— | 65 | The triumph of Venus |

| | LOT | |
|---|---|---|
| CALAVARI | — | 66 A Venetian sea port |
| VAN LOO | — | 67 Acis and Galatea |
| SOLIMENI | — | 68 A classical story |
| B. PETERS | — | 69 A view of Rotterdam |
| LOUTHERBOURG | — | 70 A sea storm |
| MORTIMER | — | 71 A scene in the Tempest |
| ZUCCARELLI | — | 72 A landscape and figures |
| ARTOIS | — | 73 Ditto |
| M. RICCI | — | 74 Ditto |
| Ditto | — | 75 A pair ditto, views in Italy |
| V. DE VELDE | — | 76 A ditto with cattle |
| ASSELIN | — | 77 A ditto with figures and cattle |
| D. HALS | — | 78 A lady at work |
| L. JORDANO | — | 79 The conversion of St. Paul, a very large and capital picture |

## The sole and genuine Property of Mr. Allen, going Abroad.

| | | |
|---|---|---|
| ROOSE of Tivoli | — | 1 A landscape and cattle |
| LE MOINE | — | 2 Venus attired by the Graces |
| LAMBERT & HOGARTH | | 3 A view of the Thames from Greenwich |
| RUBENS | — | 4 A small whole length portrait, and the head of a woman |
| CARRACCI | — | 5 An ecce homo |
| HOGARTH | — | 6 The portrait of Captain Coram, framed and glazed |
| FYT | — | 7 Hunting a stag |
| MORTIMER | — | 8 A dead partridge |
| Ditto | — | 9 Ditto |
| GUIDO | — | 10 Taking down from the Cross |
| MORTIMER | | 11 Banditti in a cave, a fine drawing with a pen |
| F. LAURA | — | 12 Two beautiful historical subjects |
| TENIERS | — | 13 A procession in Flanders |
| MORTIMER | — | 14 A sketch, from Spencer's Fairy Queen |
| TITIAN | — | 15 The portrait of Charles the Vth. |
| BORGINIONE | — | 16 A battle piece, a fine spirited picture |
| DE VLIEGER | — | 17 A calm, with variety of shipping, capital |
| VAN DYK | — | 18 A dead Christ in the lap of the Virgin |
| MORTIMER | — | 19 The deluge, a finished sketch |
| Ditto | — | 20 Sextus, the son of Pompey, applying to Erictho, to know the fate of the battle of Pharsalia |
| Ditto | — | 21 Edward the Confessor putting away his mother;—the picture for which he gained the premium, and esteemed the best and most capital performance by this master |
| | | 22 An easel and a frame |

## F I N I S.

## References

*Note:* This is an updated and expanded version of the paper given at the Foundling Museum on 2 December 2007. It was illustrated with many slides which are not possible to reproduce here. I have tried to include details of locations and references should the reader wish to view the illustrations.

It is a pleasure to acknowledge the kind assistance of the following friends and colleagues:. John Arthur, Nicolas Bell, Darin Bloomquist, Julia Clarke, Heath Cooper, Roland Folter, Michael Harris, Paul Hayday, Sebastian Kuhn, Elias N. Kulukundis, Ulrich Leisinger, Giles Mandelbrote, Malcolm Marjoram, Robin Myers, Frances Roe, Mary Roe, Arturo Solf Diaz, Lindsay Stainton, Charlotte Verrall and Wayne Williams. I am especially grateful to Peter Holman, who lent me an early draft of his chapter on Abel from his forthcoming work on the viola da gamba and its performers, which was indeed most helpful.

1. *Court and Private Life in the Time of Queen Charlotte, being the Journals of Mrs Papendiek, Assistant Keeper of the Wardrobe and Reader to Her Majesty. Edited by her Granddaughter, Mrs Vernon Delves Broughton*, 2 vols (London, 1887), i. 150–1.
2. For biographical information about Bach and Abel, see C. S. Terry, *John Christian Bach*, 2nd edn, ed. H. C. Robbins Landon (London, 1967) and H. Gärtner, *John Christian Bach, Mozart's Mentor and Friend*, transl. R. G. Pauly (Portland, Oregon, 1994) and W. Knape, *Karl Friedrich Abel* (Bremen, 1973).
3. E. Warburton, 'Johann Christian Bach und die Freimauer-Loge zu den Neun Musen in London', *Bach Jahrbuch*, lxxviii (1992), pp. 113–17. Many members of Bach and Abel's circle were members at the Lodge of the Nine Muses, including the artists Bartolozzi and Cipriani, the oboist, composer and son-in-law of Gainsborough, Johann Christian Fischer, and Bach's solicitor Augustus Greenland. The meetings took place at the Thatched House Tavern, an important venue for concerts at the time.
4. C. Burney, *A General History of Music*, 4 vols (London, 1776–89), iv. 679.
5. Ibid., iv. 679, Burney in fact quotes this from an obituary of Abel in the *Morning Post* of 22 June 1787.
6. D. Burrows and R. Dunhill, *Music and Theatre in Handel's World* (Oxford, 2002), p. 345.
7. *The John Marsh Journals*, ed. B. Robins (Stuyvesant, NY, 1998), p. 197.
8. H. Angelo, *Reminiscences of Henry Angelo, with Memoirs of his late Father and Friends*, 2 vols (London, 1830), i. 184.
9. 'His performance on the Viol de Gamba was, in some movements, equal to the touch of Abel. He always played to the feelings', obituary of Gainsborough, *The Morning Herald*, 11 August 1788, quoted in J. Hayes, *The Landscape Paintings of Thomas Gainsborough*, 2 vols (Ithaca, New York, 1982), i, p. 145. Angelo, *Reminiscences* (i. 184ff.) and William Jackson, *The Four Ages, together with Essays on Various Subjects* (London, 1798), pp. 148–54, are more caustic on the subject.
10. See the obituary of Gainsborough by Henry Bate Dudley in *The Morning Herald*, 25 August 1788, where it is stated that Abel gave the artist a gamba 'in return for two valuable landscapes and several beautiful drawings'.
11. The Huntington Library, Art Collections, and Botanical Gardens, San Marino, California: accession no. 25.19. The online catalogue gives incorrect information about the immediate provenance of this portrait. It is not in Abel's sale catalogue.

12. National Portrait Gallery 5947 (portrait); 5081 (sketch); reproduced in J. Ingamells, *Mid-Georgian Portraits* (London, 2004), pp. 2–3.

13. Angelo, *Reminiscences*, i. 190.

14. J. Hayes (ed.), *The Letters of Thomas Gainsborough* (New Haven and London, 2001), p. 164.

15. *A Catalogue of the Capital Collection of Manuscript and other Music, An exceeding valuable and fine-toned Viol de Gamba, a Forte-Piano by Buntebart, a Violin, &c. a Number of fine Drawings, and Four Pictures by Mr. Gainsborough ... Sold by Auction, by Mr. Greenwood, At his Rooms in Leicester-Square*, 12 & 13 December 1787 (The Frick Collection and Art Reference Library, New York; Lugt no. 4232).

16. C. L. Kingsford, rev. R. H. Saunders, 'John Greenwood', *ODNB* (Oxford, 2004).

17. *A Catalogue of the Pictures and Prints The Property of the Late Mrs Hogarth, Decd. ... Sold by Auction by Mr. Greenwood By Order of the Executrix ... 24ᵗʰ April, 1790*. The catalogue is printed in an anonymous editorial, 'Mrs Hogarth's Collection', in *The Burlington Magazine*, lxxxv, no. 499 (October 1944), pp. 237–9.

18. *A Catalogue of all the capital Musical Instruments, Extensive and Valuable Collection of Manuscript, and, other Music, by the most eminent Composers, late the Property of John Stanley Esq., M.B. deceased* (Christie's, London, 24 June 1786).

19. *Catalogue des Livres de la Bibliothèque de feu M. le Duc de la Vallière ... dont la Vente se fera dans les premiers jours du mois de Décembre 1783* (Paris, G. de Bure, 1783).

20. The National Archives, PROB 6/163, f. 214. I am most grateful to Peter Holman for informing me of this document.

21. 25 May 1819, lot 93: 'A whole length portrait of the celebrated musician Abel, engaged in musical composition, his viola da gamba resting on his knee'. The painting sold for £63.

22. J. Lindsay, *Gainsborough: his life and art* (London, 1982), p. 194.

23. Ingamells, *Portraits*, p. 3.

24. *Six Easy Sonattas for the Harpsichord or for A Viola Da Gamba Violin or German Flute with a Thorough-Bass Accompaniment Composed by C. F. Abel*. The surviving copy at the Sächsische Landesbibliothek, Dresden Mus.3122–R–2, has a label with the imprint 'A Amsterdam Chez J. J. Hummel: Marchand de la Musique Prix f 2.10'. Given that the titlepage is in English, it is likely that the edition was published in England and that Hummel was merely the seller. Strangely, this edition is not included in *RISM*. A facsimile of the original and a modern edition. ed. L. and G. von Zadow, with an introduction by Michael O'Loghlin, was published by Edition Güntersberg, Heidelberg, in 2005. Had the original edition been published by Bremner, Abel's usual publisher, there might be some grounds for regarding it as authentic.

25. Peter Holman points out that in a lecture to the Musical Society in 1889, Edward Payne exhibited copies of printed gamba music by the early eighteenth-century composer and gamba-player Louis de Caix d'Hervelois (*c.*1670–80–*c.*1760), claiming that they were once owned and annotated with fingerings and notes by Abel. In the ensuing discussion he added: 'There are two volumes — one was bought in London, and the other seems to have been in Germany for nearly a century', (see E. J. Payne, 'The Viola da Gamba', *Proceedings of the Royal Musical Association*, xv (1888–9), pp. 91–107. D'Hervelois published six collections for the viola da gamba, the last appearing in Paris in 1750. No recorded copy survives with Abel's annotations.

26. J. P. Rameau, *Pièces de Clavecin en Concerts, avec un Violon ou une Flûte, et une Viole ou un deuxième Violon* (Paris, for the author, 1741).

27. *Five Concertos for the Harpsicord Compos'd by Mr Rameau. Accompanied with a Violin or German Flute or two Violins or Viola, with some Select Pieces for the Harpsicord alone* (London, J. Walsh, 1750).

28. No copy of the printed sonata for gamba and keyboard seems to have survived. However, see note 30 for manuscript sonatas. A copy of another disputed work in the same court case, *A New Lesson for the Harpsicord*, turned up in a Sotheby auction in London: *Continental Books, Manuscript and Music*, 22 November 1984, lot 399. See also S. Roe, *The Keyboard Music of J. C. Bach* (New York, 1989), p. 85, and J. Small, 'J. C. Bach goes to law', *Musical Times*, cxxvi (1985), pp. 526–9.

29. The only known manuscripts of this type were discovered in a mixed collection of autographs and copyist's manuscripts of music, mostly by J. C. Bach, sold at Sotheby's, London, *Continental Printed Books, Manuscripts and Music*, 29 May 1992, lot 463, which contained a manuscript (with autograph title) of a Sonata in F major for pianoforte and viola da gamba, a Sonata in B flat (an arrangement of Op.10 no. 1) and another in G (arranged from Op.10 no. 3), in the hand of Muzio Clementi.

30. For a contemporary confirmation of this, see C. F. Cramer, *Magazin der Musik*, I (1783), p. 553, quoted in Roe, *Keyboard Music*, p. 71.

31. J. C. Bach, *Amadis des Gaules* (Paris, Sieber, *c.*1782). There is a facsimile edition of the British Library copy, without Cecilia Bach's preface, and with an introduction by Anthony Ford (Gregg International Publishers Ltd, 1972). Interestingly this edition was later owned by Abel's pupil J. B. Cramer and is signed by him on the titlepage 'JB Cramer 1804'.

32. D. Perez, *Mattutino de' Morti composto per commando di Sua Maestà Fedelissima Don Giuseppe I°* (London, R. Bremner, 1774). Among the other subscribers were Joah Bates, Barthélemon, Hawkins, Napier and the publisher Peter Welcker.

33. Burney, *History*, iv. 571.

34. *A Catalogue of the Large and Capital Collection of Pictures … of James West, Esq … sold by Auction by Messrs. Langford*, London, 1 April 1773: lot 3, 'Sir P Lely Portraits of Earl and Countess of Carlisle'.

35. See M. Freemanová and E. Mikanová , ' "My honourable Lord and Father…" 18th-century English musical life through Bohemian eyes', *Early Music*, xxxi/2 (May 2003), pp. 211–31.

36. F. X. Richter, *Six Symphonys in eight Parts for Violins, Hoboys and French Horns with a Bass for the Harpsicord and Violoncello … Opera Seconda* (London, J. Walsh, 1760).

37. F. L. Benda, *III Concerti per il violino principale, accompagnati da due corni, due oboi, due flauti, due violini, due viole, violoncello obligato, e basso ripieno* (Leipzig, Engelhardt Benjamin Schwickardt, no date [1783]).

38. *Six Concertos for the Harpsichord or Piano Forte… adapted for the Harpsichord by Sigr. Giordani* (London, [*c.*1773]; reissued Longman and Broderip, [*c.*1785]).

39. I. Holzbauer, *Günther von Schwarzburg. Ein Singspiel in drei Aufzügen* (Mannheim, for the author, 1776).

40. C. D. von Dittersdorf, *The Periodical Overtures in 8 parts … no. 38 … no. 61* (London, R. Bremner … Preston, no date [early 1770s or early 1780s]); *RISM* D 3280 and 3281; one must posit a lost Bremner edition of no. 61, as Preston took over Bremner's plates when the original publisher went out of business; several works were published as *Symphonies Périodiques* in Amsterdam and Paris, see *RISM* D3267–9; 3270–5.

41. N. Jommelli, *The Periodical Overture in 8 parts. … number XIV … XIX* (London, R. Bremner, no date [late 1760s]), *RISM* J595 and 597.

42. J. D. Benser, *Five Sonatas and One Duetto for the Piano Forte or Harpsichord &c. with an Accompaniment for a Violin or German Flute ... Opera V* (London, for the author, no date).
43. Document dated 22 March 1773, The National Archives C 31/187 Hil., p.430 r.
44. J. F. Reichardt, *Musikalischer Almanach* (Berlin, 1796), unpaginated, section XI 'Anekdoten aus dem Leben merkwürdiger Tonkünstler', no. 5.
45. W. Cramer, *A first Sett of three Sonatas for a Violin with an Accompanyment for a Violoncello ... Op.II* (London, Welcker, no date).
46. J. B. Cramer, *The Adagios, the Compositions of the late C. F. Abel ... published by the surviving and grateful pupil* (London, 1820). This also contains, in addition to a brief memoir by Cramer himself, a short biography of Abel by the late Charles Burney.
47. *RISM* M 6463 actually lists only three copies, but a fourth was acquired by the Bodleian Library, Oxford, from the collection of the late Albi Rosenthal in 2006.
48. W. A. Mozart, *Sonates pour le clavecin qui peuvent se jouer avec l'accompagnement de violon*, as Op.1 and 2, 2 vols. KV 6 and 7; and 8 and 9 (Paris, 1764), *RISM* M 6461 and M6464.
49. W. A. Mozart, *Six sonates pour le clavecin qui peuvent se jouer avec l'accompagnement du violon ou flaute traversière ... oeuvre III* (London, 1765), *RISM* M6346.
50. See S. Roe, 'Neuerkenntnisse zu einigen autographen Notenhandschriften von Johann Christian Bach', *Bach-Jahrbuch*, lxxxv (1999), pp. 179–90.
51. W. Knape, *Bibliographisch-thematisches Verzeichnis der Kompositionen von Karl Friedrich Abel* (Cuxhaven, no date [1971]) Works are numbered with the prefix WKO.
52. Knape, *Verzeichnis*, p. 118.
53. The National Archives C.31/188, p. 97.
54. *Continental Manuscripts and Music* (Sotheby's, London, 26 May 1994), lot 97.
55. Libretto published by J. Haberkorn (London, 1764), facsimile reproduction in E. Warburton (ed.), *The Collected Works of Johann Christian Bach* (New York, 1984–1999), p. xlv.
56. Burney, *History*, iv. 545.
57. *Six Quatuors pour Deux Violons, Alto, et Violoncello obligés Dediés avec le plus profond Respect à Son Altesse Royale, Monseigneur Le Prince de Prusse* (London, printed for the author).
58. Knape, *Werkverzeichnis*, WKO 60, p. 91.
59. For example, several instrumental parts of the Symphony in B flat (WKO 38), are written on paper with the watermark 'J. Whatman', K.H.M.9. The hand of the cello concerto scribe is also found on several of the instrumental parts of this and other symphonies here.
60. Symphony in C (WKO 37), Staatsbibliothek zu Berlin K.H.M.8; in B flat (WKO 38), K.H.M.9; in E flat (WKO 39), K.H.M.10; in B flat (WKO 40), K.H.M.12; and in D (WKO 41), K.H.M.13.
61. For a facsimile of this hand, see Knape, *Werkverzeichnis*, p. 62, Sinfonia concertante in D; and p. 98, Cello Concerto in C.
62. P. Highfill, K. A. Burnim and E. Langhans, *A Biographical Dictionary of Actors, Actresses, Musicians, Dancers, Managers and other Stage Personnel, 1660–1800*, 16 vols (Carbondale and Edwardsville, 1973–93), entry for 'William Napier', x. 411–12, and 'John Hindmarsh', vii. 326.

63. Symphony in D, Op.17 no. 3, K.H.M.6; Symphony in C, Op.17 no. 4, K.H.M.5; Symphony in X, Op.17 no. 5; K.H.M.14 and Symphony in G, Op.17 no. 6, K.H.M.7, with an additional Symphony Concertante in D (WKO 42), K.H.M.11.

64. See Knape, *Werkverzeichnis*, p. 48.

65. *The Daily Universal Register*, 23 June 1787; this information is kindly provided by Peter Holman.

66. From the obituary of Gainsborough in *The Morning Herald*, 25 August 1788. Information from Peter Holman.

67. See Charles Burney's article, 'Harpsichord' in A. Rees, *Cyclopaedia or Universal Dictionary of Arts, Sciences and Literature* (London, 1819).

68. Discussed in S. Roe, *Keyboard Music*, p. 204.

69. I am very grateful to Sebastian Kuhn for this information.

70. See R. Angermüller, 'Leopold Mozarts Verlassenschaft', *Mittellungen der Internationalen Stiftung Mozarteum* xli, 3–4 (1993), pp. 1–32.

71. 'Concerto Spirituale with BACH and ABEL'. Reproduced in Ingamells, *Portraits*, p. 23. The performers are J. C. Fischer, playing the oboe and Abel, in temple glasses, on the viola da gamba.

72. Reproduced Ingamells, *op. cit.*, p. 4. This pen and wash drawing is in the National Portrait Gallery 5178 and is entitled 'A Solo on the Viola di Gamba Mr Abel'.

73. Gainsborough and Bach were separately robbed at Gunnersbury Lane, Hammersmith, on 7 June 1775. See the online *Proceedings of the Old Bailey*, 12 July 1775, t17750712–25. Bach and Gainsborough were relieved of watches. Abel himself does not appear to have been robbed, though he was present, according to Lindsay, *Gainsborough*, p. 124.

74. See *George III & Queen Charlotte, Patronage, Collecting and Court Taste*, ed. J. Roberts (London, 2004), pp. 47–52.

75. Information from Julia Clarke. The surviving design is at the Staatliche Museen zu Berlin, Kupferstichkabinett KdZ 11161, and this is reproduced in W. Baer, *Prunk-Tabatieren Friedrichs des Grossen* (Munich, 1992), p. 20.

76. *Six Quartettos for two Violins, a Tenor and a Violoncello obligati ... Opera VIII* (London, Bremner, [1769]).

77. The third evening's sale of *A Catalogue of a Most Curious and Valuable Collection of Prints, Drawings, Books of Prints and Portfolios collected ... by the late Jonathan Blackburne Esq ... Sold by Auction by Mr Hutchins*.

78. Tate Britain no. 05844. Reproduced on the website at www.tate.org.uk.

79. W. T. Whitley, *Thomas Gainsborough* (London, 1915), p. 363.

80. *Public Advertiser*, 11 March 1771.

81. Anon., *An Account of All the Pictures Exhibited at the Rooms of the British Institution from 1813–1823* (London, 1824), pp. 264–5.

82. Hester Lynch Piozzi, in a letter dated 17 October 1807, written to her daughter Hester Maria Thrale. See *The Piozzi Letters. Correspondence of Hester Lynch Piozzi, 1784–1821 (formerly Mrs Thrale), iv. 1805–1810*, ed. E. A. Bloom and L. D. Bloom (Newark, New Jersey, 1996), p. 153; see also notes 10 and 12, pp. 154–5. See also Hayes, *Landscape Paintings*, ii, no. 110, pp. 456–7, as 'Wooded Landscape with Drover and Cattle, Rustic Lovers and Distant Mountains'.

83. *An Account of All the Pictures Exhibited at the Rooms of the British Institution*, pp. 262–3. The owner is given as 'J. Crosdell [sic] Esq.'; National Gallery of Ireland no. 796, 'Open Landscape with Herdsman, his Sweetheart and a Herd of Cows'; Hayes, *Landscape Paintings*, ii. no. 90, pp. 432–3.

84. See J. Hayes, *The Drawings of Thomas Gainsborough*, 2 vols (London, 1970), no. 679.
85. See Ingamells, *Portraits*, p. 22.
86. Reproduced in *Sade Surreal-Der Marquis de Sade und die erotische Fantasie des Surrealismus in Text und Bild*, ed. T. Bezzola, M. Pfister and S. Zweifel (Zurich, 2001), p. 126. Apparently an oil painting of Sade by van Loo once existed. See *Sade-Surreal*, p. 129.
87. Hayes, *Letters*, p. 106.
88. 'Cleopatra morente', Galleria del Palazzo Rosso, Genova. This painting is visible at: www.museopalazzorosso.it.

## Bibliography

[C. F. Abel], *A Catalogue of the Capital Collection of Manuscript and other Music, An exceeding valuable and fine-toned Viol de Gamba, a Forte-Piano by Buntebart, a Violin, &c. a Number of fine Drawings, and Four Pictures by Mr. Gainsborough … Sold by Auction, by Mr. Greenwood, At his Rooms in Leicester-Square, 12 and 13 December, 1787*

*An Account of All the Pictures Exhibited in the Rooms of the British Institution from 1813–1823* (London, 1824)

H. Angelo, *Reminiscences of Henry Angelo, with Memoirs of his late Father and Friends*, 2 vols (London, 1830)

R. Angermüller, 'Leopold Mozarts Verlassenschaft', *Mitteilungen der Internationalen Stiftung Mozarteum*, xli, 3–4 (1993), 1–32

Anon., 'Mrs Hogarth's Collection', *The Burlington Magazine*, lxxxv/499 (1944), 237-9

W. Baer, *Prunk-Tabatieren Friedrichs des Grossen* (Munich, 1992)

H. Belsey, *Thomas Gainsborough, a Country Life* (Munich, 1988)

C. Burney, *A General History of Music*, 4 vols (London, 1776–89)

C. Burney, 'Harpsichord', in A. Rees, *Cyclopaedia or Universal Dictionary of Arts, Sciences and Literature* (London, 1819)

D. Burrows and R. Dunhill, *Music and Theatre in Handel's World* (Oxford, 2002)

J. B. Coover, *Private Music Collections Catalogs and Cognate Literature* (Warren, Michigan, 2001)

C. Cudworth, 'Gainsborough and Music', *Gainsborough, English Music and the Fitzwilliam* (Cambridge, 1977), 11–16

D. Fraser, *Frederick the Great* (London, 2000)

M. Freemanová and E. Mikanova, ' "My honourable Lord and father …" 18th-century English Musical Life through Bohemian Eyes', *Early Music*, xxxi/2 (May 2003), 211–31

H. Gärtner, *John Christian Bach, Mozart's Mentor and Friend*, translated by R. G. Pauly (Portland, Oregon, 1994)

J. Hayes, *The Drawings of Thomas Gainsborough*, 2 vols (London, 1970)

J. Hayes, *The Landscape Paintings of Thomas Gainsborough*, 2 vols (Ithaca, New York, 1982)

J. Hayes (ed.), *The Letters of Thomas Gainsborough* (New Haven and London, 2001)

R. Head: 'Corelli in Calcutta: Colonial Music Making in India during the 17th and 18th Centuries', *Early Music*, xiii/4 (Nov 1985), 548–53

F. Herrmann, *Sotheby's Portrait of an Auction House* (London, 1980)

P. Highfill, K. A. Burnim and E. Langhans, *A Biographical Dictionary of Actors, Actresses, Musicians, Dancers, Managers and other Stage Personnel, 1660–1800*, 16 vols (Carbondale and Edwardsville, 1973–93)

J. Ingamells, *Mid-Georgian Portraits* (London, 2004)

W. Jackson, *The Four Ages, together with Essays on Various Subjects* (London, 1798)

W. Knape, *Bibliographisch-thematisches Verzeichnis der Kompositionen von Karl Friedrich Abel* (Cuxhaven, no date, [1971])

W. Knape, *Karl Friedrich Abel* (Bremen, 1973)

J. Lindsay, *Gainsborough: His Life and Art* (London, 1982)

[Marsh] *The John Marsh Journals*, ed. B. Robins (Stuyvesant, New York, 1998)

[Papendiek] *Court and Private Life in the Time of Queen Charlotte, being the Journals of Mrs Papendiek, Assistant Keeper of the Wardrobe and Reader to Her Majesty. Edited by her Granddaughter, Mrs Vernon Delves Broughton*, 2 vols (London, 1887)

E. J. Payne, 'The Viola da Gamba', *Proceedings of the Royal Musical Association*, xv (1888–9), 91–107

*The Piozzi Letters. Correspondence of Hester Lynch Piozzi 1784–1821 (formerly Mrs Thrale)*, iv (Newark, New Jersey, 1996), ed. E. A. Bloom and L. D. Bloom

J. F.Reichardt, *Musikalischer Almanach* (Berlin, 1796)

J. Roberts (ed), *George III & Queen Charlotte, Patronage, Collecting and Court Taste* (London, 2004)

S. Roe, *The Keyboard Music of J. C. Bach* (New York, 1989)

S. Roe, 'Neuerkenntnisse zu einigen autographen Notenhandschriften von Johann Christian Bach', *Bach-Jahrbuch*, lxxxv (1999), 179–90

M. Rosenthal and M. Myrone, *Gainsborough* (London, 2002)

*Sade Surreal-Der Marquis de Sade und die erotische Fantasie des Surrealismus in Text und Bild*, ed. T. Bezzola, M. Pfister and S. Zweifel (Zurich, 2001)

S. Sloman, *Gainsborough in Bath* (New Haven, 2002)

J. Small, 'J. C. Bach goes to law', *Musical Times*, cxxvi (1985), 526–9

W. C. Smith and C. Humphries, *A Bibliography of the Musical Works Published by the Firm of John Walsh* (London, 1968)

C. S. Terry, *John Christian Bach*, 2nd edn, ed. H. C. Robbins Landon (London, 1967)

E. Warburton (ed.), *The Collected Works of Johann Christian Bach* (New York, 1984–99)

E. Warburton, 'Johann Christian Bach und die Freimauer-Loge zu den Neun Musen in London', *Bach Jahrbuch*, lxxviii (1992), 113–17

W. T. Whitley, *Thomas Gainsborough* (London, 1915)

C. Wolff, *Bach, Essays on his Life and Music* (Cambridge, Mass., 1991)

C. Wolff, *Johann Sebastian Bach, the Learned Musician* (New York, 2000)

# Artaria Plate Numbers and the Publication Process, 1778–87

### RUPERT RIDGEWELL

DESPITE THE FACT that a large proportion of his output was published in Vienna from 1781 until his death ten years later, Mozart's contacts with publishers and his attitude towards publication generally remains a problematic area in his biography. Publishing matters are only rarely alluded to in Mozart's family correspondence and only a very few letters written directly to publishers are known to survive. Indeed, only one of these is addressed to a Viennese publisher. Most likely any dealings with publishers were conducted in person, especially in the periods when Mozart lived in the centre of Vienna, within easy walking distance of most of the firms that issued his music. Even if Mozart sanctioned many Viennese editions, the extent of his control over them is difficult to gauge from the musical text alone. Without any independent verification it is impossible to know for sure whether Mozart read and corrected proofs of his editions or whether his corrections were actually carried through. In some cases, it is quite clear that engraving errors persisted into the published copy. Yet early editions sometimes display readings that one can only assume came directly from the composer. Amidst the confusion, editors have tended to treat these sources with a high degree of caution, even if they have to be accepted when an autograph source is lacking.

The problems are compounded by the fact that many early Viennese editions went through various different states in the course of their lifetime. By the end of the eighteenth century Viennese publishers had generally adopted the process of music engraving. This allowed alterations to be made to the engraved surface of the plate whenever they were deemed necessary. Often the changes were limited to matters of presentation, but sometimes they impinged on the musical text, for example when individual plates wore out and had to be replaced. The extent of these variants only started to become clear in 1986 with the publication of Gertraut Haberkamp's important study of Mozart first editions.[1] But even though Haberkamp examined sometimes up to 30 copies of each edition, these can only represent a fraction of the total number that were printed. Who is to say that copies of the earliest state of any particular edition actually survived the random selection of history?

Early Mozart editions are clearly important not only as textual sources, but also as vehicles through which the music reached a wider public in the composer's lifetime and beyond. Indeed the very fact that many of them were reprinted in different states is itself suggestive of a demand for copies. With the process of music engraving, sets of plates could be held in storage over long periods of time and copies could be printed as and when they were required. The publisher was therefore in a position to respond to demand, rather than having to predict exactly how many copies would be needed in advance of publication. The different states of an edition reflect this process of engagement with the market as the edition was reprinted over time. Textual matters thus overlap with the issue of reception and the role of the publisher as mediator between the composer and the musical public. Yet here again our knowledge is clouded and incomplete. While it is certainly true to say that Mozart benefited from a major expansion in music printing in Vienna during his lifetime, this development is commonly explained rather vaguely with reference to the changing demography of music consumption and specifically a demand for sheet music from a burgeoning middle class. This may well be true in raw outline, but it hardly accounts for the dissemination of a particular repertory or the decision to publish music by certain composers, or in particular genres, rather than others. The problem is again a lack of information, this time surrounding the operational and financial side of the publisher's business. As I. R. Willison has written, 'To be able to understand how the system of texts, books, readers, and consequences has operated in particular epochs and cultures, the book historian has to depend on the hard evidence of price, print runs etc., which can only be done by seeking out and engaging with the surviving records of publishers, printers, and other agents in the book industry, that are scattered and fragmentary.'[2] In truth we know very little about the size and frequency of print runs, the identity of engravers and printers, the capacity of printing workshops, the cost of paper and other raw materials, the average shelf-life of a set of plates, the nature of the market for sheet music, and the reach of distribution networks generally in the late eighteenth century.

The Artaria firm was arguably the most important music publisher in Vienna at the end of the eighteenth century. The business was established by a family of Italian dealers from the town of Blevio, in the Lombardy region of northern Italy, principally the cousins Carlo (1747–1808) and Francesco (1744–1808), and the latter's brother, Ignazio (1757–1820). During the 1780s and 1790s, the firm became the leading publisher of music by Mozart and Haydn, and many of its editions are primary sources for the works of both composers. This article stems from an attempt to explain a deceptively simple bibliographical problem, which nevertheless raises fundamental questions about the operation and administration of Artaria's business in the 1780s. The problem relates to Artaria's edition of two Mozart sonatas for piano duet (K.381 and 358), which was first advertised by the firm on 24 May 1783 and labelled opus 3. On the basis of her study of eleven extant copies, Haberkamp was able to identify three different states of this edition, the first of which is identifiable from the complete absence of a plate number.[3] The number '25' was subsequently engraved on the titlepage and each of the 34 music plates that comprise the edition and appear in each subsequent print run, as far as these may be determined. The reason for the initial omission of the plate number appears to point to a lack of rigour in Artaria's application of plate numbers in the early 1780s, but it has never been satisfactorily explained. Was it simply an oversight on the part of the engraver that was only detected after the first run of copies had been printed, or does it indicate something unusual about the production of this particular edition? This begs another question: where precisely did the application of the plate number fit in the normal process of production, from the initial receipt of a manuscript to the point at which the edition was made available?

The possibility that the edition was somehow 'abnormal' may be considered in conjunction with Mozart's only known comment on the state of Viennese music engraving, found in a letter addressed to the music publisher Jean-Georges Sieber:

You probably know of my pianoforte sonatas with violin accompaniment which I have had engraved here by Artaria & Co. I am not very well pleased, however, with local publishing and, even if I were, I should like some of my compositions once more to find their way into the hands of my fellow-countrymen in Paris.[4]

This passage is usually understood to reflect Mozart's eagerness to gain favour with Sieber: by criticizing the situation in Vienna, he hoped to improve his prospects of sealing an advantageous agreement for publication of three new piano concertos (K.413–415) with the Parisian publisher. As he says in the letter, 'Artaria wants to publish them, but you alone, my friend, have priority'.[5] Taken literally, the reference to Viennese publishing could have several different connotations. It could mean, for example, that Mozart was unhappy with the quality of the engraved image, perhaps because details of his notation were not adequately reproduced or the music was not laid out to his satisfaction. Or it might hint at a general dissatisfaction with Viennese publishing, stemming perhaps from low levels of remuneration. Although the letter refers only to Artaria's first Mozart edition, of the violin sonatas Op.2 (K.296, 376–80), it is significant that it was written on 26 April 1783, a month before Artaria advertised the opus 3 sonatas in the *Wiener Zeitung*. By this time, production of the edition was presumably well advanced. The initial absence of a plate number could, therefore, reflect a wider problem or irregularity surrounding the edition's preparation, which was uppermost in Mozart's mind when he came to write to Sieber. It could, for example, be construed as a sign that proofs were not issued, since one might expect the lack of a number to be spotted on the proof and corrected. We clearly need to probe the wider context of Artaria's business practice in order to understand how the plate number system operated: who was responsible for allocating the numbers, at what point in the process were they assigned, and how unusual was it for an edition to go to the press before the number had been engraved on the plates?

*Plate numbers and the publication process*
Plate numbers can present a number of pitfalls for the unwary bibliographer. What may appear to be a simple numbering system may in reality bear little relation to the context of its application. False conclusions may be drawn regarding the chronology and dating of a firm's editions if the purpose of the plate number system and its position in the sequence of events leading to publication is not fully understood. The most obvious function of a plate number is to act as a unique identifier for the edition and was typically engraved in a central position at the base of each plate. For the publisher, it offered a simple method for keeping a set of plates together and for allocating any stray plates to the correct edition. This was particularly useful when a set of plates was sent to the press, where more than one edition might be in progress at the same time and the danger of mixing up different sets of plates was high. Perhaps more importantly, it would have also provided a useful tool at the point of assembling copies of an edition, to ensure that printed sheets relating to different editions were not confused.

The point at which a plate number was assigned to an edition and then engraved on the plates themselves depended on the degree to which the firm's administrative functions and production methods were co-ordinated. The sequence of events may vary between publishers, reflecting different practices, or within a single publishing house, as the process was refined or in reaction to events. The plate number may, for example, have been assigned when a work was accepted for publication, either when the manuscript was actually received or perhaps even earlier, when an agreement with the composer to provide a work had been finalized. Alternatively the plate number may have been allocated only at the point of engraving — after any preliminary work, such as copying parts or marking up the manuscripts for engraving, had been carried out. The engraver himself might even have been responsible for assigning the number in this instance, if he was working alone and could keep track of all the editions being published. If a particular firm employed several engravers, however, someone with an overview of the process probably administered the system, to minimize the possibility of duplication. Plate numbers might have been allocated either before the music was sent for engraving — in which case one would expect to find that the music engraver was responsible for punching the numbers on the plates — or after the music had been engraved and before the edition was printed. In this case, the number would have been punched centrally as the plates were received, probably using a different set of number punches from those used by the music engraver.

The evidence of surviving editions bears witness to the different practices employed by publishers since the beginning of the eighteenth century. The first publisher known to have adopted a numbering system was Estienne Roger in Amsterdam, who was active as a music publisher from 1696 until his death in 1722. Roger implemented his system belatedly, in either 1712 or 1713, by assigning numbers to existing editions in stock (apparently at random) before continuing the sequence as new publications appeared.[6] In London, the firm of John Walsh introduced a numbering system from about 1727 or 1728 and in Paris the Flemish engraver Anton Huberty applied plate numbers to his editions in a rather haphazard fashion in the late 1760s.[7] Huberty's experiment appears to have been shortlived, for although he was active as a music publisher in the French capital for twenty years from 1756 onwards, his editions bearing plate numbers are thought to date from about 1768 until only 1771. In Vienna, the major firms of Artaria, Torricella and Hoffmeister all used plate numbers in the 1780s, but Torricella's use of the system is especially difficult to comprehend. Alexander Weinmann, whose catalogue of Torricella's output appeared in 1962, identified only nine publications with plate numbers, in a range from 1 to 38, but even these do not appear to have been assigned sequentially.[8] Plate number 1, for example, was allotted to an edition of six trios for keyboard and violin by Luigi Boccherini (G.25–30), published in October 1781.[9] Plate number 2, on the other hand, was engraved on an edition of six duets for two violins by Franz Anton Rosetti, which appeared some three months before the Boccherini (it was advertised in the *Wiener Zeitung* on 14 July 1781), while plate number 4 was assigned to an edition of six keyboard sonatas by Giovanni Matielli advertised earlier still, on 31 January 1781. As O. W. Neighbour and Alan Tyson have commented in relation to British publishers, irregularities to do with plate numbers of one sort or another are the rule, rather than the exception, and are to be expected in almost every case.[10]

In 1942 Kathi Meyer and Inger M. Christensen published a ground-breaking article in *Notes for the Music Library Association* listing Artaria editions and their plate numbers as a tool for dating extant copies.[11] Their work was based on the premise that Artaria plate numbers were, by and large, assigned sequentially to editions as they were released, providing a useful (though not infallible) guide to the chronology of the publisher's output.[12] Compiling their list from copies held by the New York Public Library and from published descriptions of Artaria editions,[13] they identify a sequence of plate numbers dating from the beginning of Artaria's music business in 1778 onwards, and list publications for which plate numbers had not yet been established. Rather than insisting on a seamless continuity, the authors warn that 'the order of plate numbers cannot always be relied upon to supply accurate dates' and they note that parallel sequences of numbers were sometimes used by the publisher simultaneously. A case in point is Artaria's series of opera arias, the 'Raccolta d'arie', which was issued with its own sequence of numbers from 1786 onwards. The authors also acknowledge the limitations of reconstructing the list from evidence drawn from extant copies alone and state that 'an ideal aid for the dating of 18th century music would be photostatic copies of the plate books of the publishing houses which are still in existence and have preserved their records'.[14]

Since the publication of Meyer and Christensen's article, knowledge of Artaria's output has been amplified considerably through the work of Alexander Weinmann, who published the first full catalogue of the firm's music editions in 1952 (it was reprinted with some additional material in 1978).[15] The catalogue remains the most complete listing of Artaria's publications from plate number 1 (assigned to an edition first published in 1778) to 3176 (1858), but it was never intended to be a full descriptive bibliography of the firm's output. Weinmann does not distinguish between different states of an edition, transcribe titlepages, or give any indication of the physical state of each edition beyond a brief statement of the number of individual parts. Nor does he give any indication of contents, apart from the basic title and (where relevant) opus or composer catalogue number, and price. Weinmann's information was drawn from three main sources: unpublished listings of the firm's publications, one by plate number and the other arranged alphabetically by composer, compiled by Franz Artaria in the late nineteenth century; contemporary advertisements placed by the firm in the Viennese press; and sample copies of Artaria editions held mostly by Viennese libraries. Franz Artaria's listings form part of a larger collection of material deriving from the firm's archive now held by the Wienbibliothek im Rathaus.[16] They cannot, however, be said to relate directly to the production of the firm's output, or rather to the administrative apparatus that would have been built up internally to control the production process, since they were written at least 40 years after Artaria stopped publishing new editions. Their status therefore remains in some doubt.

Different problems are associated with Artaria's advertisements in the Viennese press, which Weinmann cited as an aid to dating editions. Given that Viennese publishers were not obliged to deposit their publications with a regulatory body like the Stationers' Company in London (whose registers provide a reasonably good guide to the dating of many English editions from the 1760s onwards), newspaper advertisements are very often the only independent documentary sources for establishing publication dates. Although Artaria did not advertise every new edition, the coverage provided by the firm's notices in the *Wienerisches Diarium* (in 1778 and 1779) and *Wiener Zeitung* (from 1780 onwards) is nevertheless quite extensive. The degree to which an advertisement date is equivalent to the point at which an edition was *first* made available to the public is an issue that demands closer scutiny. To take only one notable example, Weinmann dates Artaria's very first edition — of Paolo Bonaga's Six String Trios Op.1 — on the basis of an advertisement that appeared on 12 August 1778. But the text of that notice tells a slightly more complicated story. The edition was initially made available by subscription only, in order to 'estimate the number of copies [required] for here and foreign countries more precisely and to reduce the costs to customers'. Subscriptions were invited until the end of September and the first copies would be made available on 15 October.[17] The edition was therefore scheduled to appear two months later than the entry in Weinmann's catalogue implies.

Weinmann's third main source was the rich holdings of the main Viennese repositories of printed music, notably the archive of the Gesellschaft der Musikfreunde, the music collections of the Österreichische Nationalbibliothek, and the Wienbibliothek im Rathaus, as well as his own extensive collection.[18] Together these certainly account for the most concentrated holdings of Artaria editions anywhere in the world, with at least one copy of a large proportion of the firm's output and sometimes multiple copies. They would form the cornerstone of any attempt to compile a full bibliography, together with other library and archival collections located mainly in Europe and North America. For Weinmann's purposes, copies located in Vienna provided a sufficiently large pool of evidence to match entries in Franz Artaria's listings with newspaper advertisements and the numbers that appear on the editions themselves. But they would not have been sufficient to build up a full picture of the firm's publishing practices in order to distinguish between the different states of the same edition. For that reason, Weinmann probably did not encounter the numberless state of the edition of Mozart's duet sonatas Op.3, copies of which are not found in Vienna. Likewise, he would have been left unaware of other similar oddities or irregularities, if they were not actually present in the copies at his disposal.

In order to gain a fuller picture of Artaria's use of the plate number system, we need to consider afresh the archival, documentary and bibliographical evidence that surrounds the publication of Mozart's opus 3 sonatas and other editions that appeared in the early 1780s.

*Archival evidence*

The survival of material from the Artaria archive is due to the longevity of a firm that continued to trade uninterrupted until the 1920s. In 1936, a large portion of the administrative archive was sold to the Wiener Stadt- und Landesbibliothek (now the Wienbibliothek im Rathaus), while part of the firm's collection of music manuscripts found its way by a circuitous route to the Staatsbibliothek zu Berlin. The scope of the administrative archive is remarkably wide and includes ledgers, account books, contracts, catalogues, letter books, press cuttings, and hundreds of incoming letters covering the entire span of the firm's existence, from its foundation in Vienna in 1768 onwards. The earliest listings of Artaria's music publications are to be found in two inventory ledgers compiled in 1784 and 1787, labelled 'no. 3' and 'no. 4' respectively (numbers '1' and '2' are lost). As the numeration implies, the compilation of an inventory was a regular activity in the firm's business cycle, providing a full report of the firm's assets and liabilities at the end of each period of ownership in the firm (typically every three or four years). The ledgers reflect the fact that Artaria maintained two retail outlets in the 1780s: a shop located on the Kohl- markt in the centre of Vienna and a subsidiary outlet in Mainz. Each ledger therefore includes separate listings of stock held at the two premises, covering the entire gamut of the firm's commercial interests in art engrav- ings, books, paintings, maps, and music. Music published by Artaria accounts for substantial portions of each inventory, with sections covering the firm's stocks of unsold printed copies in Vienna and Mainz and the associated sets of engraved plates, which were stored in Vienna. These two elements represented a significant financial investment by the firm, in terms both of the cost of raw materials — editions of some major instrumental works, such as string quartets, symphonies or concertos, required upwards of 100 plates — and the labour costs associated with engraving and printing. The archival record does not, unfortunately, extend to material relating directly to the various strands of activity leading to publication, such as contracts with engravers or printers. The contents of the inventory ledgers therefore have to be considered in isolation from any other supporting or related documentation.

Ledger 3 consists of a leather-bound volume of 60 folios, paginated consecutively from fol. 2r to fol. 58v. The ledger corresponds to the financial position on 15 March 1784, at the end of a four-year period of ownership in which Carlo, Francesco, Pasquale and Ignazio Artaria held shares. The ledger discloses details of the firm's stock of 49 sets of music plates held in Vienna (pp. 66–7), amounting to 2070 plates altogether (of which 78 were blank), and a further listing of unsold copies mostly for the same editions (pp. 61–2). The list of plates is reproduced in Fig. 1, beginning with a sonata by Marianne Auenbrugger ('Auenbrug'), for which there were 18 plates. Each edition is valued in the right-hand column according to criteria that were apparently designed to reflect the age of each edition and the wear sustained by the surface of the plates.[19] Titlepages are valued separately at the end of this listing, together with the set of plates for Capuzzi's Op.2 string quartets, since these were engraved on copper (rather than pewter) plates, which would have been more suitable for engraving the often fine decorative titles on editions of this period.

Clearly the way in which the inventory was compiled and laid out reflects the imperative to come up with a total valuation, rather than any other function, such as an aid for locating and retrieving plates for a particular edition. Internal evidence, however, gives some reason for thinking that the inventory might also mirror the physical arrangement of the stock. Although presented broadly in alphabetical order by composer, more recent and forthcoming editions are grouped together at the end.[20] These include the second part of Haydn's collection of 24 *Lieder* (first advertised on 1 May 1784), three string quintets by Boccherini, Haydn's keyboard concerto in D major (24 August 1784), Johann Schröter's fantasy for piano *La battaille* (24 August 1784), and two keyboard concertos by Mozart (from a set of three, K.413–415, published separately in early 1785).[21] This suggests a physical separation between existing and new editions, perhaps because the newer works were in the process of being engraved or prepared for printing. The separate enumeration of title plates might also reflect the way in which the storeroom was organized, especially

*Rami di Musica in Magno*

| | | |
|---|---|---|
| 18. | Auenbrug Sonata | 7.30 |
| 35. | Benda Ariadne a Naxos | 18.— |
| 48. | Bocherini Concerto op. 34. | 36.— |
| 88. | Detto Quartetti — 33. | 85.— |
| 45. | Detto Detti — 32. | 40.— |
| 93. | Capuzzi Detti — 1. | 8.— |
| 97. | Haydn Quartetti — 33. | 50.— |
| 96. | Detto 6. Sinfonie 35. | 40.— |
| 108. | Detto Divertimenti 31. | 40.— |
| 57. | Detto Sonates — 30. | 50.— |
| 29. | Detto Cantata — | 6.— |
| 10. | Detto Sinfonia Laudon — | 5.— |
| 22. | Detto Lieder — | 25.— |
| 26. | Detto Aria — | 12.— |
| 26 | Clementi Sonates . 7. | 18.— |
| 23. | Detto Detti — 9. | 30.— |
| 78. | Hoffmeister Quartetti 7. | 30.— |
| 36. | Kozeluch 3. Sonate 1. | 12.— |
| 32. | Detto . 3. detti . 2. | 15.— |
| 49. | Detto . 3. detti — 3 | 30.— |
| 24. | Detto 1. d.a à 4. mani 4. | 10.— |
| 14. | Detto le Chase . 5. | 5.— |
| 56. | Detto 3. Sonate . 6. | 40.— |
| 37. | Detto Cantata . 7. | 12.— |
| 17. | Detto Aria — 8. | 15.— |
| 110. | Mozart 6. Sonate 2. | 66.— |
| 34. | Detto 2. 8.a à 4. mani . 3. | 18.— |
| 113. | Henkl 6. Sonate 17. | 100.— |
| 23. | Detto 12. pieces . — | 4.— |
| 71. | Fitz Quartetti — 1. | 15.— |
| 1519. | | Transporto 1842.30. |

*Fig. 1(a) & (b)* Artaria Inventory Ledger No. 3 (1784), pp. 66–67. Reproduced with the permission of the Wienbibliothek im Rathaus

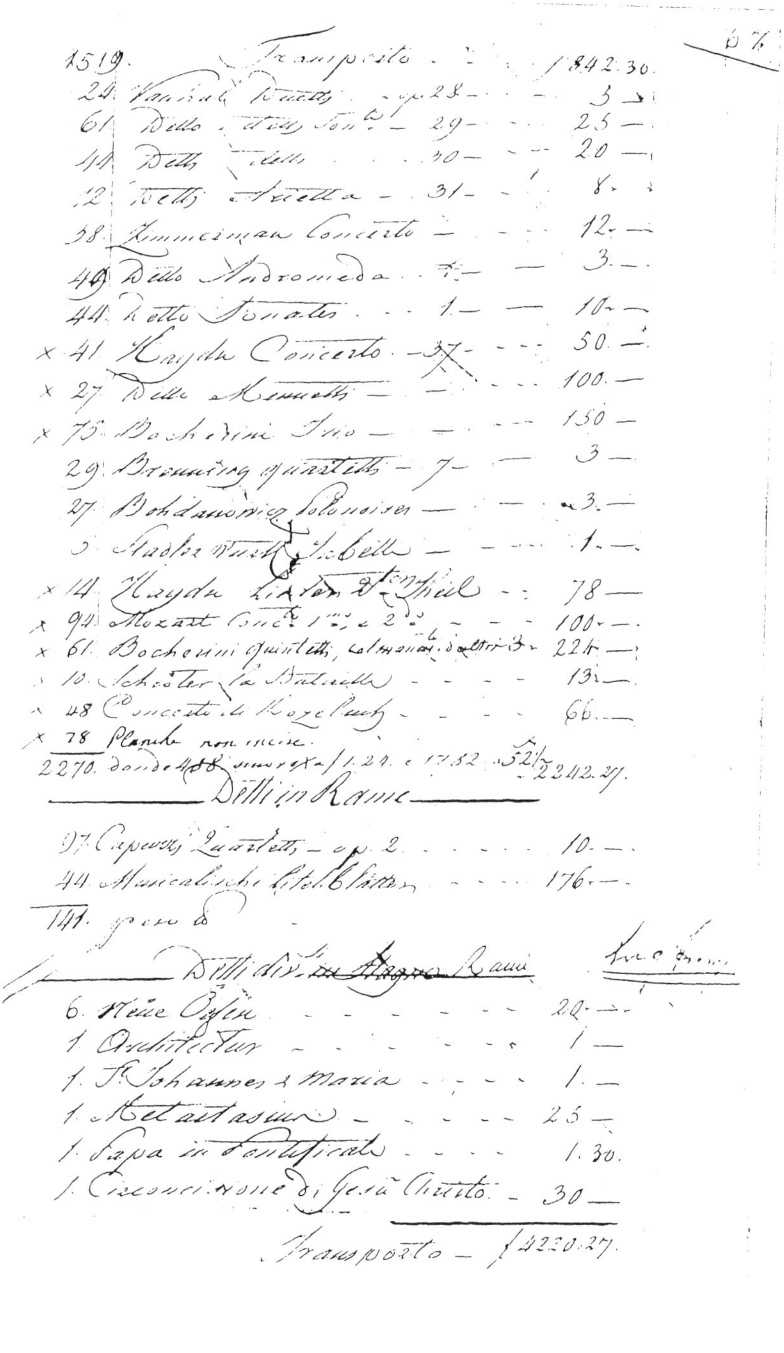

1519. Transporto ... f 1842.30.
24 Vanhal Duetti op. 28 — 3 —
61 Detto Detti Son.te 29 — 25 —
44 Detto Detti 30 — 20 —
12 Detto Ariette 31 — 8 —
38 Zimmerman Concerto — 12 —
49 Detto Andromeda — 3 —
44 Detto Sonates 1 — 10 —
× 41 Haydn Concerto 37 — 50 —
× 27 Detto Menuetti — 100 —
× 75 Bocherini Trio — 150 —
29 Brunning Quartetti 7 — 3 —
27 Bohdanowicz Polonoises — 3 —
3 Stadler Musik Tabelle — 1 —
× 14 Haydn Lieder 1ter & 2ter Theil — 78 —
× 94 Mozart Conc. 1mo e 2do — 100 —
× 61 Bocherini Quintetti, col mancanti d'altri 3 — 224 —
× 10 Schuster la Battaglia — 13 —
× 48 Concerto di Kozeluch — 66 —
× 78 Planche non incise
2270. donde 488 [illegible] f 1.24. 17.52 52½ 2242.27

Detti in Rame

97 Capuzzi Quartetti op. 2 — 10 —
44 Musicalische Titel Blätter — 176 —
141. pezzi

Detti di vari ~~[illegible]~~ Rami [illegible]

6. Neue Opfer — 20 —
1 Architectur — 1 —
1 St Johannes & Maria — 1 —
1 Metastasium — 25 —
1 Papa in Pontificale — 1.30
1 Circoncisione di Gesù Christo — 30 —
Transporto — f 4220.27

Fig. 1(b)

if some of the plates were designed to be used as passe-partout titlepages for more than one edition.

The lack of plate numbers in Ledger 3 points towards the conclusion that in March 1784 the numbering system did not yet form part of the firm's administrative procedures, or control the way in which the plates were stored. A significant difference in layout is to be found in Ledger 4, a bound volume of 76 folios paginated from fol. 3r to fol. 74v and dated 1 August 1787. The same partners as before retained shares during the period from March 1784 to 1 August 1787, although Pasquale Artaria died prematurely in 1785 and his shareholding was subsequently taken over by Domenico Artaria (1765–1823). The ledger contains three music-related listings, giving details of the firm's stocks of unsold copies divided between Mainz (pp. 18–20) and Vienna (pp. 76–9), and music plates held in Vienna (pp. 80–3). In place of the alphabetical sequence given in Ledger 3, the plates are now listed in number order, from 3 to 117, followed by a page of entries relating to the 'Raccolta d'arie' series. Figure 2 reproduces the first page in this listing, with entries for 38 editions from Conrad Breunig's violin duets Op.7 to Boccherini's string quintets Op.36. The fact that the first two numbers are missing from the list suggests that plates for the corresponding editions, of string trios by Paolo Bonaga, were absent when the inventory was compiled. As in Ledger 3, each edition is identified by a brief title and opus number, and the number of plates is recorded in a column headed 'Lastri'. This is followed by two columns of figures headed 'Impressioni' and 'Fogli' respectively, which report the number of printed impressions and the amount of paper required to produce a single copy of each edition. The final column on the right-hand side gives the value for each set of plates.

The introduction of plate numbers in Ledger 4, and their absence in Ledger 3, is potentially significant. If the ledger entries do bear a direct relationship to the physical arrangement of the stock, it would imply that a major reorganization of the storage area was carried out at some point between March 1784 and August 1787. The rationale for doing this might be explained in the following way. At first, the firm organized its stocks of plates and copies in an alphabetical sequence, as an aid to retrieving works by particular composers. New editions were inserted at the appropriate places and the existing stock was shifted around to make space. As the business expanded and the amount of material in storage increased, the need to introduce a more efficient system became more urgent. It was no longer practical to keep moving the stock in order to retain the alphabetical sequence. At this point, the firm decided to adopt plate numbers as a means to keep sets of plates together — if any went astray they could be

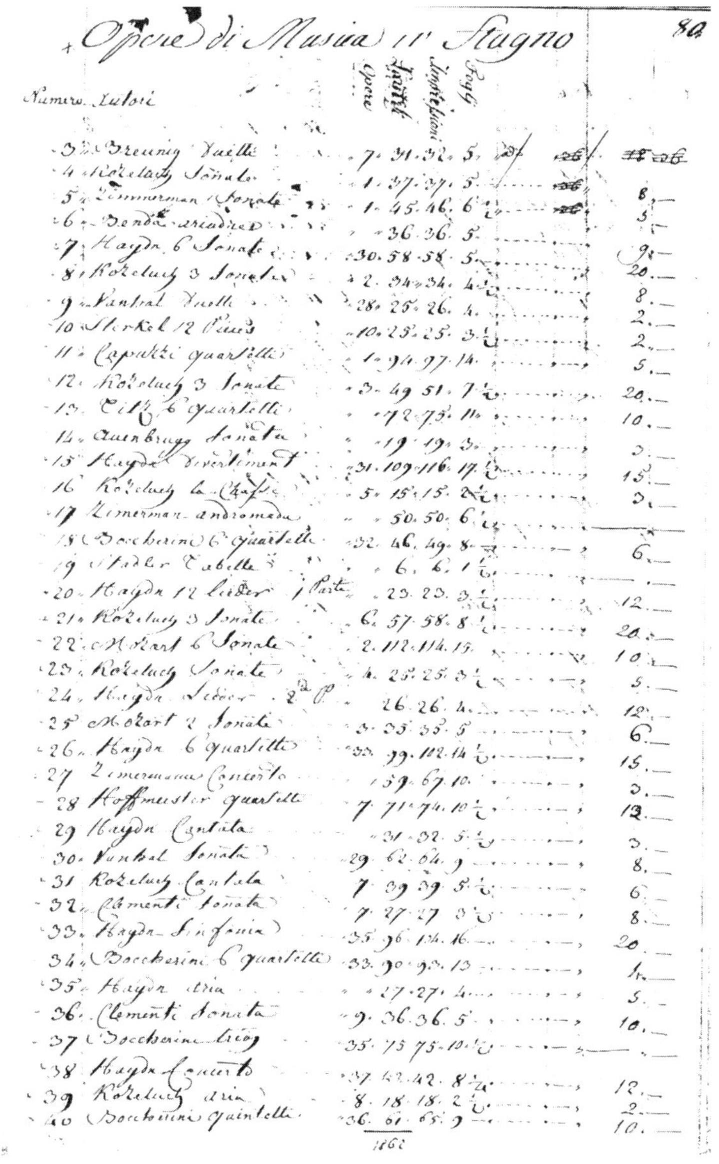

Opere di Musica N° Stagno — 80

| Numero | Autori | Opere | Lastre | Impressioni | Fogli | |
|---|---|---|---|---|---|---|
| 3 | Breunig Duetti | 7 | 31 | 32 | 5 | |
| 4 | Kozeluch Sonate | 1 | 37 | 37 | 5 | |
| 5 | Zimmerman Sonate | 1 | 45 | 46 | 6½ | 8 |
| 6 | Benda Ariadne | | 36 | 36 | 5 | 3 |
| 7 | Haydn 6 Sonate | 30 | 58 | 58 | 5 | 9 |
| 8 | Kozeluch 3 Sonate | 2 | 34 | 34 | 4½ | 20 |
| 9 | Vanhal Duetti | 28 | 25 | 26 | 4 | 8 |
| 10 | Sterkel 12 Pieces | 10 | 23 | 25 | 3½ | 2 |
| 11 | Capuzzi quartetti | 1 | 94 | 97 | 14 | 5 |
| 12 | Kozeluch 3 Sonate | 3 | 49 | 51 | 7½ | 20 |
| 13 | Cirri 6 quartetti | | 72 | 75 | 11 | 10 |
| 14 | Auenbrugg Sonata | | 19 | 19 | 3 | 3 |
| 15 | Haydn Divertiment | 31 | 109 | 116 | 17½ | 15 |
| 16 | Kozeluch la Chasse | 5 | 15 | 15 | 2½ | 3 |
| 17 | Zimerman andromeda | | 50 | 50 | 6½ | |
| 18 | Boccherini 6 quartetti | 32 | 46 | 49 | 8 | 6 |
| 19 | Stadler Tabelle | | 6 | 6 | 1½ | |
| 20 | Haydn 12 Lieder 1 Parte | | 23 | 23 | 3½ | 12 |
| 21 | Kozeluch 3 Sonate | 6 | 57 | 58 | 8½ | 20 |
| 22 | Mozart 6 Sonate | 2 | 112 | 114 | 19 | 10 |
| 23 | Kozeluch Sonate | 4 | 25 | 25 | 3½ | 5 |
| 24 | Haydn Lieder 2da P. | | 26 | 26 | 4 | 12 |
| 25 | Mozart 2 Sonate | 3 | 35 | 35 | 5 | 6 |
| 26 | Haydn 6 quartetti | 33 | 99 | 102 | 14½ | 15 |
| 27 | Zimmermann Concerto | 1 | 59 | 67 | 10 | 3 |
| 28 | Hoffmeister quartetti | 7 | 71 | 74 | 10½ | 12 |
| 29 | Haydn Cantata | | 31 | 32 | 5½ | 3 |
| 30 | Vanhal Sonata | 29 | 62 | 64 | 9 | 8 |
| 31 | Kozeluch Cantata | 7 | 39 | 39 | 5½ | 6 |
| 32 | Clementi Sonata | 7 | 27 | 27 | 3½ | 8 |
| 33 | Haydn Sinfonia | 35 | 96 | 104 | 16 | 20 |
| 34 | Boccherini 6 quartetti | 33 | 90 | 93 | 13 | 4 |
| 35 | Haydn aria | | 27 | 27 | 4 | 5 |
| 36 | Clementi Sonata | 9 | 36 | 36 | 5 | 10 |
| 37 | Boccherini trios | 35 | 75 | 75 | 10½ | |
| 38 | Haydn Concerto | 37 | 42 | 42 | 8½ | 12 |
| 39 | Kozeluch aria | 8 | 18 | 18 | 2½ | 2 |
| 40 | Boccherini quintetti | 36 | 61 | 65 | 9 | 10 |
| | | | 1862 | | | |

*Fig. 2.* Artaria Inventory Ledger No. 4 (1787), p. 80. Reproduced with the permission of the Wienbibliothek im Rathaus

readily identified from the number — and to allow it to store the plates chronologically, simply by adding each new set to the sequence as it was returned from the printer. This change would explain why a plate number was initially not included in the edition of Mozart's piano duet sonatas, but was later engraved on the plates when the stock was reorganized.[22]

A problem arises, however, when we consider the plate number sequence itself and its relationship to the schedule of press advertisements. This is illustrated in Table 1, which shows the chronology of Artaria's

*Table 1*. Artaria advertisement dates and the plate number sequence, 1778-85

| Advertisement date | Plate number |
| --- | --- |
| 12 Aug 1778 | 1, 2 |
| 10 March 1779 | 3, 5 |
| 20 Nov 1779 | 6 |
| 12 April 1780 | 7 |
| 20 May 1780 | 8 |
| 5 July 1780 | 9 |
| 13 Sept 1780 | 10, 11 |
| 31 Jan 1781 | 13 |
| 7 April 1781 | 15, 16 |
| 18 July 1781 | 17 |
| 6 Oct 1781 | 18, 21 |
| 8 Dec 1781 | 19, 22 |
| 29 Dec 1781 | 20, 26 |
| 10 July 1782 | 27, 28, 30 |
| 25 Sept 1782 | 32 |
| 24 May 1783 | 25 |
| 31 Dec 1783 | 39 |
| 31 Jan 1784 | 44 |
| 1 May 1784 | 24 |
| 25 Aug 1784 | 37, 38, 43 |
| 28 March 1785 | 41, 42 |
| 19 Jan 1785 | 45 |
| 25 Aug 1785 | 47 |
| No advertisement | 4, 12, 14, 23, 29, 31, 33–36, 40, 46, 48–53 |

advertisements and its relation to the plate number sequence given in Ledger 4. Thus numbers 1 to 20 were assigned sequentially to editions that were first advertised between 1778 and the last quarter of 1781. Thereafter the table reveals a number of significant departures from the chronology.

Editions numbered 21 and 22, for example, appear slightly 'out of sequence', having been advertised on 6 October 1781 and 8 December 1781, *before* plate number 20 was announced on 29 December. Numbers 24 and 25, by contrast, were first advertised much later, on 1 May 1784 and 24 May 1783 respectively. This evidence points to significant delays in the preparation of a collection of 24 *Lieder* by Joseph Haydn, which was published in two parts with plate numbers 20 and 24, and of Mozart's piano duet sonatas opus 3 (plate number 25). The delays associated with the Haydn editions can, at least in part, be explained with reference to passages in both Haydn's and Mozart's correspondence.

From an early stage Haydn and Artaria had planned two sets of twelve songs. The first set was despatched to the publisher on 20 July 1781, with the composer's promise of the second 'as soon as possible'.[23] Five days later, Mozart wrote to his father that he was having a collection of six violin sonatas (K.296, 276–80) engraved and had 'already discussed' the matter with Artaria.[24] Then, on 24 November 1781, Mozart informed his father that the sonatas had been published, fifteen days before the edition was first advertised as 'Opus 2'. This chronology is consistent with the notion that plate numbers were assigned by the firm as manuscripts were received, rather than at the point of engraving or publication. Thus Artaria would have taken receipt of the first set of Haydn *Lieder* shortly after 20 July and assigned it the number '20'. Discussions with Mozart about the publication of the opus 2 violin sonatas began shortly thereafter and the manuscripts of the sonatas cannot have reached Artaria before 25 July, at least a few days after the first set of Haydn *Lieder*. The Mozart edition was therefore assigned a later number, '22', even though it went on sale before the Haydn.

On 4 January 1782, a few days after the first set of 12 *Lieder* was advertised, Haydn wrote to Artaria with instructions to send complimentary copies to Anton Liebe von Kreutzner, the father of the set's dedicatee, and to his own brother-in-law, Joseph Keller. He added, 'you can subtract the sum from the second dozen.'[25] Then, on 20 January 1782, he wrote, 'I shall shortly send you a few Lieder.'[26] Nevertheless it took two more years for the second set to be published — mainly, it seems, because Haydn himself found various excuses to delay sending the remaining songs to complete the collection. On 31 December 1783 the edition was announced in the *Wiener Zeitung* in advance of its publication at carnival time ('Fasching'), and then on 1 May 1784 a further advertisement signalled its availability. The plate number assigned to the second set was '24', which would fit a publication dating from the early part of 1782 — not 1784. It therefore seems probable that the number '24' was assigned to the edition around the time that the first set was engraved, in August or September 1781, on the strength of Haydn's promise, even though the publication itself was not available until early 1784.[27] Similarly, to have been allotted the number '25' the edition of Mozart's duet sonatas Op.3 must have been planned as early as the summer of 1781, directly after the second set of Haydn *Lieder*, but was then delayed for nearly two years before it was advertised for the first time on 24 May 1783.[28] The delay is difficult to explain in the absence of any mention of it in Mozart's correspondence after August 1781. Both works had been written in the early 1770s, so Mozart merely needed to have copies produced to serve as the *Stichvorlage*. On 27 June 1781 Mozart had written to his father in Salzburg requesting a copy of the sonata in B flat major, K.358, and two concertos for two pianos 'as soon as possible', evidently to allow him to play the works with his pupil Josepha Aurnhammer (in the letter he describes the two pianos in his flat), but also to offer the sonata to Artaria for publication.[29] On 1 August he reports that he had 'just collected the sonata for 4 hands'.[30] In order to have been assigned plate number 25, the manuscript must have reached Artaria between 1 August and early November 1781, when Haydn is believed to have supplied manuscripts for the edition of his six string quartets Op.33, allotted plate number 26 in Artaria's sequence.[31] Haydn's quartets were prepared over the next two months, allowing Artaria to advertise them already on 29 December 1781. Weinmann treats this as the publication date, though in fact the text of the advert makes it clear that it was merely a pre-announcement for the scheduled publication 'in about 4 weeks'.[32] Issuing a pre-announcement in this way was an unusual tactic for Artaria and it underlines the importance the firm attached to this edition. In this context, and given the relative speed with which Artaria was aiming to release the quartets, the delay in advertising Mozart's sonatas appears all the more remarkable.

The publication history of these editions therefore shows that they were not numbered on publication, but were assigned numbers on receipt of the manuscript, or perhaps even when the work was commissioned from the composer. This evidence points to a degree of control over the publication of Artaria's music editions that may be best explained by the existence of a register in which details of forthcoming publications were recorded. Numbers were therefore allocated not by the music engraver but by one of the partners or an assistant in the firm. The register might also have been used to keep track of production costs, which would have included information about the physical dimensions of each edition, such as the number of printed impressions and the quantity of paper required. This may explain why Ledger 4 includes full details of each set of plates, in number order. The absence of this information in Ledger 3 may in turn point to a disjunction between the various administrative processes before 1784, which meant that the inventory had to be compiled directly from the stock, rather than copied from the register of editions. It also points to the conclusion that the numbering system was in use at this time, but had not yet been adopted as a means to identify, store and locate the plates themselves. This would explain why the number '25' was omitted from the plates of Mozart's Op.3 at first, before being added with reference to the register at a later stage. In that case, it follows that we would also expect the Mozart example not to be an isolated case, but that all editions published up to 1784 (and perhaps beyond) were first issued without plate numbers.

*Bibliographical evidence*
There are some obvious limitations to the bibliographical evidence that may be gleaned from Artaria's edition of Mozart's Op.3 sonatas. As noted above, surviving copies do not necessarily reflect every stage in the history of an edition and, in this particular case, the eleven extant copies can only represent a fraction of the total print run. Furthermore, it is not possible to date the printing of any particular copy with any degree of precision, either from internal bibliographical evidence or in relation to any known archival or documentary sources. The success of the edition, measured in terms of the frequency with which it was reprinted, is therefore impossible to gauge with any certainty. While it is clearly not possible to widen the net of internal evidence in respect of any particular edition unless more copies come to light, there is scope for deriving information about the firm's practices more generally by considering the Mozart edition in the context of Artaria's wider output in the early 1780s. These practices might include policy issues relating to the collation and physical make-up of editions in different formats, and various issues to do with what we might loosely describe as 'house style', ranging from the presentation of titlepages to the engraving of particular elements of notation.

In the course of preparing this article it has been possible to examine multiple copies of the 48 Artaria editions published between 1778 and the end of 1784 in ten major institutions in Europe and North America.[33] Two editions published in this period, a collection of *Oden und Lieder* by Franz Paul Riegler and a set of string quartets by 'Breuning' (presumably Conrad Breunig), are entirely lost.[34] Even though this is only a partial view, it is possible to identify three different states based on the presence of plate numbers. In Table 2 (see Appendix), the location of one exemplar of each state, where it can be identified, is given. Thus fifteen editions were initially printed without plate numbers (State 1). Of these, four editions were apparently never assigned a number, or at least no copies *with* numbered plates have yet been located. These are editions of Pietro Metastasio's *Canoni*, Crinazzi's *Sei Treni osia Cantata Lugubri in Morte di Maria Theresia* (advertised on 7 April 1781), Michael Kerzelli's six string quartets Op.1 (13 January 1779), and Kerzelli's six violin duets Op.2. All were published very early in Artaria's history, between 1779 and 1781, so it seems possible that the editions were discontinued and the plates either discarded or reused before the firm introduced plate numbers to its existing editions.[35] State 2 may be identified from copies of 33 editions, with numbers appearing on the music plates only; and finally State 3 is represented by copies of 28 editions. It is likely that further examples of each state will emerge in due course, with the investigation of additional repositories, but even this relatively small sample demonstrates that plate numbers were engraved in a phased approach to many of Artaria's early editions.

Knowledge of engraving practices in Vienna is very sketchy for the period around 1800. By the last quarter of the eighteenth century, music engravers in Vienna worked almost exclusively with sets of punches designed for each of the main constituents of music notation (dynamic markings, numbers, clefs, accidentals, and so on), and used the burin to engrave slurs freehand.[36] It is not clear where prospective music engravers would have acquired sets of punches, or who would have trained them, but it would be surprising to learn that music punches were manufactured in Vienna before 1800. From a technical point of view, questions remain over who determined how many plates would be required for a particular work, and whether the publisher laid down a guide for the number of staves to a page, or other details of layout. Nor do we know whether the engraver worked at the publisher's premises, at a workshop, or at home. An initial observation regarding music engraving is that punches belonging to different sets were often formed in different ways. The shape of the treble clef, for example, could vary considerably in different countries and traditions. Equally, two sets of punches produced by the same manufacturer can share similar characteristics, making it difficult to distinguish one from another. If engravers worked alongside one another at the same premises, it is also possible to imagine that sets of punches might become mixed up, or that individual punches might be shared between different engravers, or passed down to an apprentice. Making things more complicated, it is entirely possible that individual punches in a set may be replaced over a period of time. According to D. W. Krummel, there are also some examples of punches being distinctive to the publisher, in which case an individual engraver might use different sets of punches at different times, depending on which publisher he worked for.[37] A second fundamental observation concerns the way that a set of punches was used. One should make a distinction between the form of the punch, which remains constant, and the way in which the punch was applied to the plate to determine the positioning of the sign in the finished edition. An engraver's style would therefore be determined both by the shape of the punches and by a common set of characteristic ways in which those punches were used. More than one engraver might share these characteristics if there was a common approach or if one engraver was trained by another. One might even be able to describe a particular school of engraving styles.

All these factors should be taken into account when comparing different editions. There was a general division of labour, however, between engravers of titlepages or dedications and engravers of music in Vienna during the 1780s. This resulted from a desire on the part of some publishers to blur the commercial dividing line between sheet music and art engravings. Artaria sometimes adorned their music publications with ornamental titlepages, newly commissioned from notable Viennese art engravers such as Sebastian Mansfeld and Carl Schütz, thereby making the editions more attractive to the buyer. The name of the art engraver would normally appear somewhere on the titlepage as part of the illustration, as a statement of his artistic contribution to the publication. The music engraver's craft, by contrast, was not primarily artistic, even if laying out music in a clear and accurate way required a good degree of judgement and great skill, as well as a sense of the music's character (slow music being spaced differently from fast music) and the practicalities of performance (particularly with regard to page turns). Indeed, the clarity of the engraved image was occasionally cited at this time in publisher's advertisements and in music reviews as a desirable quality.

Perhaps because of the rather more utilitarian nature of their task, music engravers only rarely signed the editions they worked on and as a result only a few individuals may be identified.[38] Jiří Zahradníčzek, for example, worked as an engraver for Artaria in the late 1780s, while also being employed as a trumpeter at the Imperial court,[39] while Johann Schäfer can be identified from a signed edition of Joseph Eybler's three string quartets Op.1, published by Artaria in about 1795 (plate number 615).[40] The most important figure in the early formation of Artaria's music publishing activities was Anton Huberty, who moved to Vienna from Paris in 1776 and regularly signed the plates he engraved from 1778 until the late 1780s. Huberty's signature appears on 21 Artaria editions published between 1778 and 1784, as shown in Table 2.[41] In addition, fourteen editions published during this period may be ascribed to Huberty on the basis of the distinctive set of music punches that he used. These editions are identified as 'Huberty unsigned' in the final column in Table 2, while an example of an unsigned Huberty engraving — from the piano part of Mozart's violin sonatas Op.2 — is shown in Figure 3. Particularly notable punches in Huberty's set include a crotchet rest in the form of a reversed '7' that he typically engraved in a diagonal position, and a forte sign ('f') in which the horizontal beam extends to the right of the main stem, but not to the left. The clefs, braces, time signatures, and accidentals also share distinctive characteristics in Huberty editions. Of the firm's first 49 editions, therefore, Huberty prepared a total of 35.

The remaining fourteen editions were shared between three engravers, identified in Table 2 as 'Richter', 'Artaria 1' and 'Artaria 2'. Artaria's employment of additional engravers should be seen in the context of the steady expansion of its music operations in the early 1780s, with the attendant need to extend its capacity for producing editions within a reasonable time. Huberty undertook work not only for Artaria, but also for the rival firm of Christoph Torricella and others during the early 1780s, so he may sometimes have been unable to meet the increasing demands for

*Fig. 3.* Mozart, violin sonatas Op.2, K.296, 376–80 (Vienna: Artaria, 1781), p. 22.
Reproduced with the permission of the British Library Board

*Fig. 4.* Mozart, piano duet sonatas Op.3, K.381 and 358 (Vienna: Artaria, 1783), p. 5.
Reproduced with the permission of the British Library Board

his services.[42] Richter's name has been found on eleven editions, of music
by C. P. E. Bach, Haydn, Michael Kerzelli and Leopold Kozeluch,
variously published by Artaria and Kozeluch in the 1780s. In Michael
Kerzelli's violin duets, for example, the statement 'Graves [*sic*] par Richter'
appears on the titlepage directly below the imprint.[43] The punches used in
the Kerzelli duets match with the edition of Bohdanowicz's polonaises for
piano (plate number 53), bringing Richter's tally for Artaria to two editions before the end of 1784. Artaria 2 was responsible only for the
Capuzzi string quartets Op.2, which were very unusually engraved in
copper and valued separately in Ledger 3 (see Fig. 1). More important to
the firm was Artaria 1, who engraved eleven editions published between
1782 and 1784. It is probably no coincidence that his first two assign-
ments were editions of sonatas for piano duet by Kozeluch (Op.4) and
Mozart (Op.3) respectively, music that required a similar approach to
issues of layout and notation, with the two parts engraved on facing pages
(the first page of the primo part of the Mozart sonatas is reproduced in
Figure 4). These were the first editions of music in the duet genre to
appear under Artaria's imprint, so it is not surprising to find that the firm

subsequently entrusted Johann Baptist Vanhal's two duet sonatas Op.32 to the same engraver. Characteristic features of his engraving notably include a sharp sign in the shape of the letter 'x' with double lines and the tall thin treble clef.

*Fig. 5*

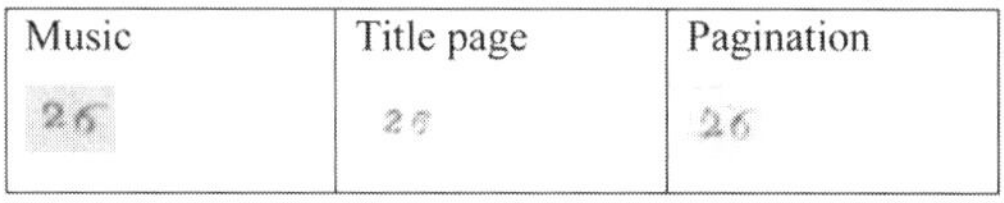

| Music | Title page | Pagination |
|-------|-----------|------------|
| 26 | 26 | 26 |

As a general rule, two different sets of number punches are to be found in Huberty editions published during the period under investigation. A single set was normally employed on music plates for plate numbers and page numbers, suggesting that these elements were both engraved by one person, most likely Huberty himself.[44] The putative first 'numberless' state shown in Table 2 therefore does not apply to editions engraved by Huberty, with the exception of three special cases where a number was almost certainly never assigned (Crinazzi's *Sei Treni*, Kerzelli's Op.1 string quartets, and Metastasio's *Canoni*). A different set was used on titlepages, reflecting the fact that the title plate was usually engraved separately. This also reinforces the notion that title plates were stored separately from music plates in Artaria's stock-room, mirroring the layout of the inventory in Ledger 3. The edition of Haydn's six string quartets Op.33, published in parts with plate number 26, is a good example (see Fig. 5). The punches used to engrave the digits '2' and '6' on the music plates are identical, characterized by an especially long and open arc on the upper part of '6'. On the titlepage, the figure '6' is presented in a more closed formation, with a lower and shorter arc. The same distinctive punches are found in the edition of Leopold Kozeluch's *La Chasse* for piano, plate number 16, which was also engraved by Huberty.

*Fig. 6*

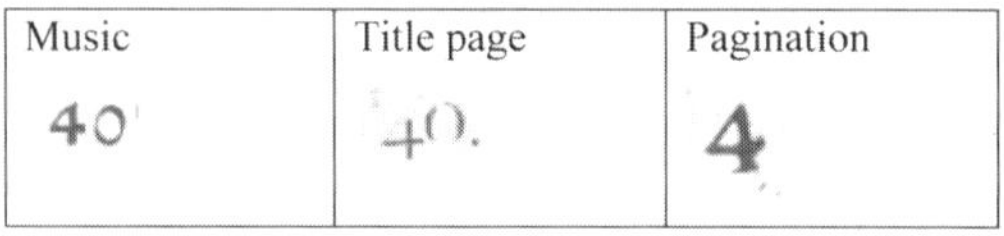

| Music | Title page | Pagination |
|-------|-----------|------------|
| 40 | 40. | 4 |

In the case of editions engraved by Artaria 1, it is possible to identify up to three different sets of number punches. Figure 6 provides an illustration from the edition of Boccherini's three string quintets, Op.36, which was allotted plate number 40. Here, the shape of the figure '4' is most distinctive: the punch used to engrave the number on music plates is open at the top, with the upper beam extending upwards towards the right, beyond the vertical stem. The page number '4' may be distinguished by the horizontal beam at the base and by the upward curve of the beam protruding to the right of the stem. The punch used to engrave the plate number on music plates, by contrast, lacks the horizontal 'foot' at the base of the digit and the diagonal beam is slightly curved. In this case, we may infer that the plate number was added in two stages, first to the music plates and then to the title. It is therefore quite possible that the edition was sent to the press before the plate number was added either to the music or title plates, and that copies matching the putative first and second states may be identified in due course.

*Fig. 7*

| Music | Title page | Pagination |
|---|---|---|
| 3 7 | 3 7 | 3  17 |
| 2 5 | 2 5 | 5 |

More often, editions engraved by Artaria 1 exhibit two different sets of number punches, including one for the pagination, which means that plate numbers were engraved throughout using the same set. The examples shown in Figure 7 are taken from Boccherini's six string trios Op.35 (plate number 37) and Mozart's piano duets sonatas Op.3. This evidence points towards the conclusion that the plate number was typically engraved after Artaria 1 had finished the music, by a different engraver using a distinct set of number punches, or in two steps if the titlepage was dealt with separately. Unlike Huberty, Artaria 1 was either not aware of the plate number or had not been instructed to add it to the plates. It is also possible that the relatively large size of the number punches that Artaria 1 used would not have been deemed suitable for the plate number, which was meant to appear unobtrusively at the bottom of the page. Copies of the initial unnumbered state have therefore been identified for four editions engraved by Artaria 1: Boccherini's cello concerto, Kozeluch's piano duet sonata Op.4, Mozart's piano duet sonatas Op.3, and Vanhal's piano sonatas Op.30. We might go further and posit the original existence of 'numberless' states for every edition engraved by Artaria 1, including six editions where no copies have yet been located: notably Haydn's piano concerto Op.37 and his *Raccolta di Menuetti Ballabili*.

*Conclusion*

The absence of plate numbers in the first issue of Artaria's edition of Mozart's Op.3 sonatas may be explained with reference to the wider context of the firm's administrative and engraving practices in the early 1780s. In general, the plate number sequence falls quite neatly into line with the chronology of publication between 1778 and 1784, as far as it may be determined from Artaria's advertisements in the Viennese press. The system was therefore introduced at an early stage, even if it was not at first embedded into the firm's storage or stocktaking procedures, as shown by the absence of plate numbers in Artaria's inventory of stock compiled in 1784 (Ledger 3). Numbers were allotted at the time a manuscript was received, rather than at the point of publication, which means that Artaria must have maintained a logbook or register of editions from at least 1781 onwards to maintain administrative control over the production process. This explains why the number 25 was allocated to the Mozart edition, soon after the composer received a copy of the B flat major sonata from his father in August 1781, and was retained throughout the lengthy publication process until the edition finally appeared in May 1783. Bibliographical evidence suggests that the application of numbers to an edition often took place in two steps, depending on who engraved the music. Anton Huberty was aware of the system, having previously made use of it himself in Paris, and usually engraved the plate number at the same time as preparing the music. Perhaps through a lack of communication, Artaria 1 was either unaware of the requirement to engrave plate numbers or was not in a position to do so. The absence of a plate number was therefore not exceptional, but was instead associated with the work of a particular engraver.

The reason for Mozart's frustration with Viennese music publishing, expressed in his letter to Sieber in April 1783, therefore cannot be aligned with an irregularity associated with the initial lack of a plate number. The possibility that the employment of Artaria 1 related in some way to dissatisfaction with Huberty's work cannot be discounted, especially given the reference in Mozart's letter to the Op.2 violin sonatas, an edition prepared by Huberty. Indeed, preliminary research suggests that Artaria's Mozart editions published in 1785 and 1786, including the piano concertos K.413–415 and the six string quartets dedicated to Joseph Haydn, were entrusted not to Huberty, but to Artaria 1. A more plausible explanation for Mozart's comment arises from the lengthy delay of between 18 and 20 months from the point at which the edition was agreed to the appearance of an advertisement in the *Wiener Zeitung* on 24 May 1783. Seen in the context of the firm's publication schedule in 1782 and early 1783 the delay was unusually protracted. Artaria's swift announcement in December 1781 of the imminent publication of Haydn's string quartets Op.33, for example, suggests a degree of urgency attached to that edition not replicated in Mozart's case, which may even have had an impact on the schedule for producing other forthcoming publications. The employment of Artaria 1 might also be seen as an attempt to increase capacity at a time when Huberty's work was being stretched not only by demands on his time, but also by the internal pressure to expedite publication of certain editions. Any frustration at the delay is understandable when one considers that, by April 1783, Mozart had been resident in Vienna for over two years and yet only one edition — the violin sonatas Op.2 — had so far appeared from Artaria's press. This might well have been one of the factors that prompted Mozart to write to Sieber to offer his works for publication in Paris in the first place.

Whatever the true reason for the delay in publishing Mozart's Op.3 sonatas, for the employment of Artaria 1 rather than Anton Huberty to engrave them, and for the priority given to Haydn's edition, the circumstances that surround their publication provide a good illustration of how a newly established music publisher began to take control of its administration and tackled the problem of storing, valuing and controlling information about its editions in the 1780s. Archival evidence points to greater integration of the various administrative processes after 1784. In Ledger 3, the inventory of music plates was most likely compiled with reference to the physical contents of Artaria's storeroom, rather than from the music register. By 1787, however, the number of editions in stock had increased from about 50 in March 1784 to well over 120, leading to a change in the way that Ledger 4 was compiled. Now the firm maintained more detailed information covering the size and content of each edition, management information that was required in order to calculate both the cost of replenishing stocks of older editions and of printing new editions alike. The inventory of music plates could be collated from a separate record that was updated and maintained, rather than being assembled from scratch. Thus the inventory of plates in Ledger 4 is presented in plate number order, with details not only of the number of plates in stock, but also the number of printed impressions and quantity of paper required to print each copy. With this degree of control over the publication process and with more sophisticated information relating to the cost of printing and reprinting its editions, the firm was able to continue to grow and expand its operations throughout the late 1780s and 1790s, becoming the most important early publisher of Mozart's music during the composer's lifetime and beyond.

## References

Research towards this essay was made possible with generous support from the Music Libraries Trust (2007) and the Bibliographical Society (2006).

1. Gertraut Haberkamp, *Die Erstdrucke der Werke von Wolfgang Amadeus Mozart* (Tutzing: Schneider, 1986).

2. Ian Willison, 'The History of the Book as a Field of Study within the Humanities', http://sas-space.sas.ac.uk/dspace/bitstream/10065/8/3/July.pdf, p. 17.

3. Exemplars of this state of the edition are to be found in the Öffentliche Bibliothek der Universität Basel, the Royal Library, Copenhagen, the British Library, and the Bibliothèque nationale de France. See Haberkamp, *Die Erstdrucke*, p. 176.

4. Letter, Mozart to J. G. Sieber, 26 April 1783. Wilhelm Bauer, Otto Erich Deutsch and Joseph Heinz Eibl (eds.), *Mozart: Briefe und Aufzeichnungen*, 7 vols (Kassel: Bärenreiter, 1962–1975), vol. 3, p. 266 (no. 741, lines 5–10): 'sie werden vermuthlich wissen von meinen Sonaten auf Pianoforte mit begleitung einer violin, welche ich hier bey Artaria und Compagnie habe stechen lassen; — da ich aber mit dem hiesigen Stiche nicht allzusehr zufrieden bin, und wenn ich es auch wäre, Meinen LandsManne in Paris auch einmal wieder möchte etwas zukommen lassen.' Translated with reference to Emily Anderson (ed.), *The Letters of Mozart and his* Family, 3 vols (London, Macmillan, 1938), vol. 3, p. 1261 (no. 487). Anderson understands the phrase 'mit dem hiesigen Stiche' as a reference to engraving standards, but Mozart tended to use the word 'Stich' rather more loosely to denote publishing in general.

5. Ibid. (lines 12–13): 'Artaria will sie Stechen. allein sie, mein freund, haben den vorzug.'

6. Samuel F. Pogue and Rudolf A. Rasch, 'Roger, Estienne', in *The New Grove Dictionary of Music and Musicians*, ed. Stanley Sadie and John Tyrrell (London: Macmillan, 2001), vol. 21, p. 512–13.

7. On Walsh, see William C. Smith, *A bibliography of the musical works published by John Walsh during the years 1695–1720* (London: Bibliographical Society, 1948), p. xxiii. On Huberty, see Anik Devriès and François Lesure, *Dictionnaire des éditeurs de musique française*, 2 vols. (Geneva: Minkoff, 1979–88), vol. 1: *des origines à environ 1820*, p. 82.

8. It should be noted that some of these editions may have been reprints taken over from other publishers, with the original plate number unchanged.

9. *Wiener Zeitung*, no. 85 (24 October 1781), Anhang (unpaginated).

10. O. W. Neighbour and Alan Tyson, *English Music Publishers' Plate Numbers in the first half of the Nineteenth Century* (London: Faber and Faber, 1965), p. 11: 'It would be highly desirable if an exact correlation between a particular series of numbers and a particular year … could be established for each publisher. But that is never possible. Irregularities occur to a greater or lesser extent in every list.'

11. Kathi Meyer and Inger M. Christensen, 'Artaria Plate Numbers', *Notes for the Music Library Association*, 15 (1942), pp. 1–22.

12. Meyer and Christensen's work anticipated that of Otto Erich Deutsch, whose *Musik Verlags Nummern: eine Auswahl von 40 datierten Listen* (Berlin: Verlag Merseburger, 1961) includes plate number listings for selected music publishers in Austria, Germany,

the Netherlands, Switzerland and the UK, and remains an essential reference tool in many cases. See also Otto Erich Deutsch, *Music Publishers' numbers: a selection of 40 dated lists 1710–1900* (London: Aslib, 1946), reprinted from the *Journal of Documentation*, vol. 1, no. 4 (March 1946) and vol. 2, no. 2 (September 1946) with some alterations.

13. These sources were supplemented by the editor of the journal with reference to copies in the Sibley Music Library, Eastman School of Music, Rochester, New York.

14. Meyer and Christensen, 'Artaria Plate Numbers', p. 1.

15. Alexander Weinmann, *Artaria & Comp.: Vollständiges Verlagsverzeichnis*, 'Beiträge des Alt-Wiener Musikverlages Reihe 2, Folge 2' (Vienna: Krenn, 1952; 2nd edn 1978); the list of 'Raccolta d'arie' publications is further supplemented in Rosemary Hilmar's general history, *Der Musikverlag Artaria & Comp.: Geschichte und Probleme der Druckproduktion* (Tutzing: Schneider, 1977).

16. Wienbibliothek im Rathaus, Handschriftensammlung: 859 Jc and 86904 C.

17. *Wienerisches Diarium*, no. 64 (Wednesday, 12 August 1778), Nachtrag, repeated in *Wienerisches Diarium*, no. 65 (Saturday, 15 August 1778), Nachtrag: 'Um die Zahl der Exemplare für hier und fremde Länder genauer bestimmen zu können, wie auch den Käufern die Kosten zu verringern, hat man den Weg der Pränumeration gewählt.'

18. A large part of Weinmann's collection is now held by Duke University Library.

19. Austrian currency is used for the plate listing, with values given in the standard denominations of gulden and kreuzer, whereby 60 kreuzer was equivalent to 1 gulden. The valuation method employed here is described in Rupert Ridgewell, 'Music Publishing and Economics', in *Music publishing in Europe 1600–1900: concepts and issues, bibliography*, ed. Rudolf Rasch (Berlin: Berliner Wissenschafts-Verlag, 2005), pp. 89–133.

20. An inexplicable departure from the alphabetical sequence in this listing, where Haydn is placed above Clementi (see Fig. 1), is not mirrored in the corresponding list of unsold copies.

21. Artaria's editions of all three Mozart concertos were advertised in the *Wiener Realzeitung* on 28 March 1785. An earlier advertisement that was supposedly printed in a supplement to the *Wiener Zeitung* of 12 January 1785 has not been located. See Otto Erich Deutsch, *Mozart: Die Dokumente seines Lebens* (Kassel: Bärenreiter, 1961), pp. 207, 211.

22. An example from a later period is provided by the London-based publisher Augener, which is known to have retained printer's copies and the proofs for each of their publications. According to Oliver Neighbour, who examined the firm's archive in 1968, 'these were arranged in the order of the publisher's numbers, and tied up in sequence in large bundles.'

23. Joseph Haydn, *Gesammelte Briefe*, ed. Denés Bartha, Kassel, 1965, p. 100, letter 35: 'Übersende hiermit die ersten 12 Lieder, und werde trachten sobald möglich das 2. Duzend Euer Hochedlen zu uberschücken.'

24. Mozart had originally planned to distribute written copies of the sonatas on a subscription basis, having written to his father on 19 May 1781 that 'the subscription of 6 sonatas is in progress and for that I will receive money'. See *Mozart: Briefe*, vol. 3, p. 118 (letter 598, lines 37–8): 'Nun ist die Suscription auf 6 Sonaten im Gang, und da bekomme ich geld.'

25. *Joseph Haydn: Gesammelte Briefe*, p. 109, letter 41: 'Sie können sich am zweiten Duzend davon zahlhaft machen.' Translated in H. C. Robbins Landon, *The Collected*

*Correspondence and London Notebooks of Joseph Haydn* (London: Barrie and Rockliff, 1959), p. 34.

26. *Joseph Haydn: Gesammelte Briefe*, p. 111, letter 42: 'ich werde Ihnen mit nächsten einige lieder übermachen.'

27. *Wiener Zeitung*, no. 104 (Wednesday, 31 December 1783), Anhang: 'Der 2te Theil Lieder des Herrn Kapellmeisters Joseph Haydn wird diesen Fasching auch zuverläßig erscheinen.' *Wiener Zeitung*, no. 35 (Saturday, 1 May 1784), Nachtrag: 'In der Kunst-handlung Artaria Comp. auf dem Kohlmarkt der Michaelerkirche gegenüber ist nun zu haben: Von Herrn Kapellmeister Joseph Haydn, 2ter Theil, der deutschen Lieder beym Klavier zu singen, enthaltend 12 Stück wie im ersten, 1 fl. 30 kr.'

28. *Wiener Zeitung*, no. 42 (Saturday, 24 May 1783), Anhang (unpaginated): 'Bey Artaria Kompagnie, Kupferstich, Landkarten, und Musikalienhändlern in Wien sind zu haben […] W. A. Mozart, 2 Sonaten für vier Hände auf einem Klavier, Opera III. 2 fl.'

29. *Mozart: Briefe*, vol. 3, p. 135 (letter 608, lines 37–9): 'lassen sie mir doch die Sonate à 4 mains ex B und die 2 Concerte auf 2 Clavier abschreiben — und schicken sie mir sie so bald möglich'.

30. *Mozart: Briefe*, vol. 3, p. 143 (letter 615, line 5): 'die Sonate auf 4 hände habe ich gleich abgeholt'.

31. Haydn mentions the quartets in his letter to Artaria of 18 October 1781, stating his intention to complete them within three weeks. See *Joseph Haydn: Gesammelte Briefe*, p. 104, letter 38a: '… die dermahlige bearbeitung 6 neuer quartetten so in 3 wochen fertig seyn werden'.

32. *Wiener Zeitung*, no. 104. Anhang (unpaginated): 'Auch sind die 6 ganz neue Quart-etten dieses grossen Mannes [i.e. Haydn] in größter Beschäftigung der Auflage, und hoffen es in ungefähr 4 Wochen herausgeben zu können.' This announcement incurred Haydn's wrath, as he made clear in a letter of 4 January 1782, since he was in the process of distributing subscription copies and claimed he would stand to lose 50 ducats in lost subscriptions.

33. According to the *Répertoire Internationale des Sources Musicales* (RISM) Series A/1 there are *c.*800 extant copies of these editions preserved in libraries in Europe and North America. My research has encompassed collections held by the British Library, the Library of Congress, the Österreichische Nationalbibliothek, the Wienbibliothek im Rathaus, the archive of the Gesellschaft der Musikfreunde in Wien, the Sächsische Landesbibliothek Dresden, the Bayerische Staatsbibliothek, the Bodleian Library Oxford, the Bischöfliche Zentralbibliothek, Regensburg, and the Bibliothèque nationale de France.

34. Both editions are listed in Ledger 3. The Riegler is thought to have been published in 1782 and is described as lost in Louis Munkachy, 'Rigler, Franz Paul', *Grove Music Online*, ed. L. Macy (accessed 31 March 2008), http://www.grovemusic.com.

35. None of these editions is listed in the inventory of music plates in Ledger 3 or 4.

36. Examples of Viennese music engraving dating from before 1778 indicate that all the elements of the engraved image were produced freehand with the burin, the standard tool of the art engraver. See Hannelore Gericke, *Der Wiener Musikalienhandel von 1700 bis 1778*, 'Wiener musikwissenschaftliche Beiträge, Bd. 5' (Wien, Köln, 1960). In much of central Europe until the 1770s, however, music printing was mostly the preserve of book publishers who issued sporadic typeset editions for a limited market.

37. D. W. Krummel (compiler), *Guide for Dating Early Published Music: A Manual of Bibliographical Practises* (Hackensack, NJ: Joseph Boonin; Kassel: Bärenreiter, 1974), p. 96.

38. If the music engraver did engrave his or her 'signature' on an edition, it would most commonly appear at the bottom right-hand corner of the first page of music, or sometimes at the very end of the edition.

39. Jiří Zahradníčzek (1748–1828) was a trumpeter for the Hungarian Life Guard and a member, in 1790, of the masonic lodge 'Zur neugekrönten Hoffnung'. See Heinz Schuler, *Mozart und die Freimaurerei* (Wilhelmshaven: Florian Noetzel Verlag, 1992), p. 52.

40. I am grateful to David Wyn Jones for bringing this edition to my attention. A copy of the edition held by the Musiksammlung of the Wienbibliothek im Rathaus (shelfmark M.833) is signed at the end of the violoncello part with the words 'Gestochen von Johann Schäfer in Wienn. 1794'. According to Weinmann, this edition was originally published by Hoffmeister, but the signature date is consistent with the notion that it was first published by Artaria in 1795. See *Weinmann, Artaria & Comp.*, p. 42.

41. Artaria later reissued several Torricella editions that had also been engraved by Huberty.

42. Huberty initially attempted to establish his own business in opposition to Artaria, but soon settled for working for various publishers, including Artaria, Christoph Torricella and Rudolf Gräffer. See Alexander Weinmann, *Kataloge Anton Huberty (Wien) und Christoph Torricella*, 'Beiträge des Alt-Wiener Musikverlages Reihe 2, Folge 8' (Vienna, 1962).

43. See RISM Series A/1: B114, H2744–47, K483, K1378, K1386, K1423 (in which he is identified as Philipp Richter), K1435, K1728.

44. In a few cases, Huberty evidently forgot to add the plate number to individual pages in an edition.

*Appendix*

Table 2. *Copies of Artaria editions issued before 1785*

| Plate No. | Composer/title | RISM | State 1 Copies lacking plate no. | State 2 Plate no. on music only | State 3 Plate no. added to titlepage | Engraver |
|---|---|---|---|---|---|---|
| 14 | *Marianne von Auenbrugger* Keyboard sonata | A2851 | | A Wgm: VII 48738 | A Wst: M.13891/c | Huberty (unsigned) |
| None | *C. P. E. Bach* Klapstocks Morgengesang am Schöpfungs Feste | B114 | GB Lbl: Hirsch.III.614 | | | Richter |
| 18 | *Luigi Boccherini* String quartets G.201-206 | B3138 | | D Mbs: 2 Mus.pr.1784/3 | A Wn: M.S.41622 | Huberty |
| 37 | 6 string trios G.101-106 | B3089 | | A Wgm: IX.31801 | GB Lbl: h.42.c.(1.) | Artaria 1 |
| 40 | 3 string quintets Op.36, G.295-297 | B3179 | | | GB Lbl: R.M.17.b.3.(4.) | Artaria 1 |
| 52 | Cello concerto G.483 | B3215 | GB Lbl: Hirsch.III.127 | | A Wgm: IX.7461 | Artaria 1 |
| 53 | *Basilius Bobdanowicz* 12 polonaises for piano | B3304 | GB Lbl: e.283.k. | D Dl: Mus.3940-T-1 | | Richter (unsigned) |

| Plate No. | Composer/title | RISM | State 1 Copies lacking plate no. | State 2 Plate no. on music only | State 3 Plate no. added to titlepage | Engraver |
|---|---|---|---|---|---|---|
| | *Paolo Bonaga* | | | | | |
| 1 | 6 string trios Op.1, part 1 | B3442 | | I Nc | | Huberty (unsigned) |
| 2 | 6 string trios Op.1, part 2 | B3442 | | I Nc | | Huberty (unsigned) |
| | *Georg Benda* | | | | | |
| 6 | *Ariadne auf Naxos* | B1870 | | A Wn: M.S.11205 | D Mbs: 4 Mus.pr.29941 | Huberty |
| | *Conrad Breunig* | | | | | |
| 3 | 6 duets for violin and viola Op.2 | B4349 | | A Wn: M.S.31047 | | Huberty |
| | *G. Antonio Capuzzi* | | | | | |
| 10 | 6 string quartets Op.2 | C962 | A Wgm: IX.2040 | | A Wst | Artaria 2 |
| 11 | 6 string quartets Op.1 | C964 | | A Wgm: IX.23280 | | Huberty |
| | *Muzio Clementi* | | | | | |
| 32 | 3 piano sonatas Op.7 | C2779 | | F Pc: Ac.p.2385 | GB Lbl: e.282.c.(3.) | Huberty (unsigned) |
| 36 | 3 piano sonatas Op.9 | C2780 | | | F Pn: Vm7 5381 | Artaria 1 |
| | *Crinazi* | | | | | |
| None | *Sei Treni osia Cantata Lugubri in Morte di Maria Theresia* | C4413 | A Wgm: III 7005 | | | Huberty |

| Plate No. | Composer/title | RISM | State 1 Copies lacking plate no. | State 2 Plate no. on music only | State 3 Plate no. added to titlepage | Engraver |
|---|---|---|---|---|---|---|
| | *Joseph Haydn* | | | | | |
| 7 | 6 keyboard sonatas Op.30 | H3886 | | GB Lbl: f.186v | | Huberry |
| 15 | 6 divertimenti concertanti Op.31 | H3345 | | A Wst: M.12137/c | | Huberry (unsigned) |
| 20 | *Lieder*, part 1 | H2617 | | GB Lbl: Hirsch III.802 | GB Lbl: E.409.p | Huberry (unsigned) |
| 24 | *Lieder*, part 2 | H2618 | | | GB Lbl: E.409.p | Huberry |
| 26 | 6 string quartets Op.33 | H3414 H3415 | | A Wgm: IX.965 | A Wn: M.S.50151 | Huberry |
| 29 | Aria *Ah come il core mi palpita* | H2558 | | A M: IV.65 | A Wst: M.12140/c | Huberry |
| 33 | 6 Sinfonie Op.35 | H3288 | | A M: IV.65 | GB Lbl: h.2872.h | Huberry (unsigned) |
| 38 | Keyboard concerto Op.37 | H3311 | | A Wn: SH Haydn.898 | GB Lbl: h.655.p. | Artaria 1 |
| 44 | *Raccolta di Menuetti Ballabili* | H4011 | | GB Lbl: h.2872.o. | D Mbs: 2 Mus.pr.1511 | Artaria 1 |
| | *Franz Anton Hoffmeister* | | | | | |
| 28 | 6 string quartets Op.7 | H5947 | | D Mbs: 4 Mus.pr.14559 | GB Lbl: h.77.a. | Huberry (unsigned) |
| | *Michael Kerzelli* | | | | | |
| None | 6 quartets Op.1 | K482 | A Wgm: IX 23381 | | | Huberry |
| None | 6 duos for 2 violins Op.2 | K483 | A Wgm: IX 7442 | | | Richter |
| | *Leopold Kozeluch* | | | | | |
| 4 | 3 piano sonatas Op.1 | K1716 | | D Dl: Mus.3540-T-1 | GB Lbl: e.5.m.(7.) | Huberry (unsigned) |

| Plate No. | Composer/title | RISM | State 1 Copies lacking plate no. | State 2 Plate no. on music only | State 3 Plate no. added to titlepage | Engraver |
|---|---|---|---|---|---|---|
| 8 | 3 piano sonatas Op.2 | K1719 | | GB Lbl: e.284.a.(8*) | GB Lbl: Hirsch IV.1626 | Huberty |
| 12 | 3 piano trios Op.3 | K1469 | | A Wn: M.S.27258 | A Wst: M.12251/c | Huberty |
| 14 | *Denis Klage auf den Todt Marien Theresian* | K1375 | | A Wgm: II.12544 | | Huberty |
| 16 | La Chasse for piano Op.5 | K1771 | | A Wgm: VII29413 | A Wn: M.S.27268 | Huberty |
| 21 | 3 piano trios Op.6 | K1478 | | A Wn: M.S.27259 | D Mbs: 2 Mus.pr.5122 | Huberty |
| 23 | Piano duet sonata Op.4 | K1641 | GB Lbl: E.1050.gg. | A Wst: M.52336/c | A Wn: M.S.9959 | Artaria 1 |
| 31 | Cantata *Quanto e mai tormentosa* | K1376 | | A Wn: M.S.27058 | A Wgm: VI.15177 | Huberty (unsigned) |
| | *Pietro A.D.B. Metastasio* | | | | | |
| None | Canoni | M2460 | GB Lbl: A288 | | | Huberty |
| | *W.A. Mozart* | | | | | |
| 22 | 6 violin sonatas Op.2 | M6678 | | GB Lbl: e.490.1 | GB Lbl: Hirsch IV.23a | Huberty (unsigned) |
| 25 | 2 piano sonatas (4 hands) Op.3 | M6678 | GB Lbl: Tyson P.M.143 | | GB Lbl: e.57.q.(3.) | Artaria 1 |
| 47 | 3 piano sonatas Op.6 | M6780 | | F Pc: Ac.p.2836 | GB Lbl Tyson P.M. 142 | Artaria 1 |
| | *J.F.X. Sterkel* | | | | | |
| 10 | 12 pieces for piano Op.10 | S5997 | | GB Lbl: e.284.c.(10.) | | Huberty |
| 51 | 6 piano trios Op.17 | S5918 | D Dl: Mus.3569.Q.6 GB Lbl: f.246.c.(1.) (piano only) | | GB Lbl: Hirsch.III.528 | Huberty (unsigned) |
| | *Anton Ferdinand Titz* | | | | | |
| 13 | 6 string quartets Op.1 | T779 | | A Wgm: IX.23487 | | Huberty |

| Plate No. | Composer/title | RISM | State 1 Copies lacking plate no. | State 2 Plate no. on music only | State 3 Plate no. added to titlepage | Engraver |
|---|---|---|---|---|---|---|
| | *Johann Vanhal* | | | | | |
| 9 | 6 violin duets Op.28 | V571 | | A Wn: M.S.41918 | | Huberty (unsigned) |
| 30 | 2 piano trios and 1 piano quartet Op.29 | V410 | | GB Lbl: e.792.a | A Wgm: XI 10864 | Huberty |
| 46 | 2 piano duet sonatas | V673 | | | GB Lbl: e.792.c.(1.) | Artaria 1 |
| 49 | 3 keyboard sonatas Op.30 | V674 | GB Lbl: e.5.c.(9.) | | US NH: Mc20 W13x op.30 | Artaria 1 |
| | *Anton Zimmerman* | | | | | |
| 5 | 3 violin sonatas Op.1 | Z222 | | D Dl: Mus.3484-R-1 | | Huberty |
| 17 | Andromeda und Perseus | Z215 | | GB Lbl: Hirsch IV.1309 | | Huberty |
| 27 | Piano concerto Op.3 | Z219 | | D Rp: BH.8507 | F Pn: Vmg 7589 | Huberty (unsigned) |

A Wgm: Archiv der Gesellschaft der Musikfreunde in Wien
A Wn: Österreichische Nationalbibliothek
A Wst: Wienbibliothek im Rathaus
D Dl: Sächsische Landesbibliothek, Dresden
D Mbs: Bayerische Staatsbibliothek
D Rp: Regensburg, Bischöfliche Zentralbibliothek
F Pc: Bibliothèque du conservatoire (held by F Pn)
F Pn: Bibliothèque nationale de France
GB Lbl: British Library
I Nc: Biblioteca del Conservatorio di musica S. Pietro a Majella, Naples
US NH: Yale University, Music Library (New Haven, Conn.)

# Mahler and Music Publishing in Vienna, 1878–1903

PAUL BANKS

MUSIC PUBLISHING ACTIVITY in Vienna in the eighteenth and early nineteenth century has been relatively well documented, not least thanks to the herculean labours of Alexander Weinmann (1901–87).[1] But the Viennese music publishing industry of the second half of the nineteenth century has been generally less thoroughly explored, despite the fact that by 1900 there was a growing perception that Viennese publishing generally, and the music publishing sector in particular, was in something of a crisis.[2] This paper will use a brief account of Gustav Mahler's early engagement with Viennese publishers to explore tentatively some of the issues and the key personalities involved.

Mahler (1860–1911), like a number of other individuals who will appear later, was born and educated in the Czech Lands, but moved to Vienna, in his case, to study piano and later composition at the Vienna Conservatoire (1875–8). By this time the high-art end of musical life in the Habsburg capital was already rather conservative, but among living composers the dominant figures were Brahms (normally deemed to be a representative of tradition) and Wagner (the challenging representative of innovation), with Wagner's Viennese admirer, Anton Bruckner (1824–96), occupying an as yet minor role in the city's musical life. Mahler soon became a fervent admirer of Wagner (whose music dramas were central to Mahler's repertoire as a conductor) and got to know Bruckner, and it was through the latter association that Mahler had his initial dealings with a Viennese publisher.

On 16 December 1877 Bruckner conducted the first performance of his most overtly Wagner-inspired symphony, the Third, at a concert of the Gesellschaft der Musikfreunde. It was a success with neither the public (many of whom walked out before the end) nor the critics, but a small group of admirers remained, including Mahler and an aspiring publisher, Theodor Rättig.[3] As a member of the Singverein Rättig had attended the rehearsals of the Symphony and, despite the evident antipathy (to put it no stronger) of the orchestral musicians, had been so impressed by the work that after the performance he offered to publish it at his own expense (about 3000 fl.).[4] Rättig was as good as his word, and the Symphony did eventually appear, though the date and circumstances of its publication remain somewhat unclear: nevertheless even the currently incomplete account of its history offered below brings into focus some notable features of the state of music publishing in Vienna.

Theodor Rättig was born in Gumbingen, East Prussia, in 1841 and trained as an administrator. By 1870 he was living in Vienna, and while he worked as a bank official, the music trade seems to have been a hobby, though the details of his business connections and roles are not wholly clear. One clue is provided by the titlepage of what appears to be the earliest copy of the score he published of Bruckner's Third Symphony:

*Symphonie / in / (D moll) / für grosses Orchester / componirt / von Anton Bruckner / Partitur* [blank] */ Stimmen* [blank] */ Clavier-Auszug Vierhändig* [blank] */ Eigenthum der Verleger für alle Länder. Eingetragen ins Vereins-Archiv. / Den Verträgen gemäss deponirt. / Verlag von / A. BÖSENDORFER'S Musikalienhandlung / (Büssjäger & Rättig.) / WIEN I. Herrengasse 6.*[5]

The nature of the relationship between Bussjäger & Rättig and the music dealer and publisher Adolf Bösendorfer is not certain: one secondary source reports that the latter had been acquired by Rättig,[6] but if so it was continuing to publish under its own imprint until at least 1890. Whatever the connection, it seems to have been severed by the time of the production of what appears to be a later copy of the score: the upper portion of the titlepage, including the decorative elements and some of the text remains identical to that of the Bösendorfer issue, but the lower portion shows some significant differences:[7]

*Partitur Pr.* $\frac{Fl. 18.-}{Mk. 30.-}$ */ Stimmen Pr.* $\frac{Fl. 22.50.}{Mk. 40.-}$ */ Clavier-Auszug Vierhändig Pr.* $\frac{Fl. 7.20.}{Mk. 12.-}$ *Eigenthum der Verleger für alle Länder. Eingetragen ins Vereins-Archiv. / Den Verträgen gemäss deponirt. / Verlag von /* [blank, but overprinted using a ?rubber stamp:] *TH. RÄTTIG / MUSIK-VERLAG & SORTIMENT / WIEN, I., MAYREDERSTRASSE, 3 /* [second rubber stamp:] *TH. RÄTTIG / MUSIK-VERLAG & SORTIMENT / WIEN / I. Bellariastrasse 10.*

So it would seem that Rättig had not only severed connections with Bösendorfer, but also parted company with his associate Rudolf Bussjäger, who in fact continued to publish with Bösendorfer[8] while also issuing music under his own name into the 1890s.[9]

On the other hand, the titlepage of the arrangement of the Symphony for piano duet, while using the same basic design, gives some significant additional information, not least the dedication (which was very important to Bruckner) and the name of the arranger:[10]

*Meister RICHRD WAGNER in tiefster / Ehrfurcht gewidmet / Symphonie / in / (D moll) / für grosses Orchester / componirt / von Anton Bruckner / Partitur Pr.* $\frac{Fl.\ 18.-}{Mk.\ 30.-}$ */ Stimmen Pr.* $\frac{Fl.\ 22.50.}{Mk.\ 40.-}$ */ Clavier-Auszug VierhändigPr.* $\frac{Fl.\ 7.20.}{Mk.\ 12.-}$ */ (Arr. v. Gustav Mahler) / [rule] / [printed in curve over next line:] Eigenthum der Verleger für alle Länder. Eingetragen ins Vereins-Archiv. / Den Verträgen gemäss deponirt. / [rule] Verlag von [rule] / A. BÖSENDORFER'S Musikalienhandlung / (Büssjäger & Rättig.) / WIEN I. Herrengasse 6. / Jos. Eberle & Co.*

How Mahler came to be involved in the preparation of the arrangement is not clear, and according to Göllerich-Auer, the work on the transcription was actually shared between Mahler and his fellow conservatoire student and Bruckner admirer, Rudolf Krzyzanowski (1862–1911), with Mahler's piano teacher at the Conservatoire, Julius Epstein (1832–1926), acting as supervising editor.[11] The extent of Krzyzanowski's unattributed contribution is not unambiguously documented, but there is some evidence that it was confined to the last movement of the Symphony. Göllerich-Auer also seems to be the main source for the frequently repeated assertion that the score, parts and duet arrangement were published in 1878, but this has to be treated with some caution. To begin with, in a letter to Wilhelm Tappert (1830–1907) dated 9 October 1878,[12] Bruckner discussed his Symphonies 2–4 and reported that

Herr Rättig certainly wants to have the piano arrangements of the above-mentioned symphonies, in order to publish them.[13]

So, the Mahler arrangement of the Third cannot have been in print at that time. No early reviews of the publication (which might suggest a publication date) have been located, but one valuable source now available in electronic format offers a powerful research tool in the study of late nineteenth-century Viennese publishing.

In 1829 the music publisher, Friedrich Hofmeister of Leipzig established the *Musikalisch-literarischer Monatsbericht neuer Musikalien, musikalischer Schriften und Abbildungen* which his family firm continued to issue throughout the nineteenth century and beyond. Music publishers were invited to send notification of new publications to Hofmeister for inclusion in one of the monthly issues of what was both a contribution to music bibliography and a trade periodical. Although the *Monatsberichte* need to be used with due caution (see below), their potential value as a tool for dating printed music has been long recognized.[14] However the use of the *Monatsberichte* was hampered by the fact that no complete run for the nineteenth century survived in any public collection (these were ephemeral trade publications that tended to be thrown away by their chief users, suppliers of music) and that for most years the internal organization was classified, making a search for a particular composer rather tedious.

The possibility of applying ICT to the problem, in order to produce a searchable version of the nineteenth-century issues was explored over a number of years by a working group of IAML (International Association of Music Libraries, Archives and Documentation Centres), thus laying the foundations for a successful funding bid to the AHRB (the Arts and Humanities Research Board as it then was, now the Arts and Humanities Research Council) which established a three-year project based at Royal Holloway College London, headed by Professor Nicolas Cooke and managed by Liz Robinson. By great good fortune the Austrian National Library was at the same time pursuing a project to produce an online digital facsimile of the complete run of *Monatsberichte*, and thanks to the collaboration between the two projects, users now have access to powerful searching capabilities and (through automatically generated links) facsimiles of the original entries.[15]

When using the *Monatsberichte* for bibliographical research two major limitations need to be borne in mind. Firstly, coverage was by no means universal. Until 1933 the scope was international, and the volumes contained entries from a large number of European countries,[16] but even within German-speaking territories, which almost inevitably provided the overwhelming bulk of references, coverage was determined entirely by the submission policies of the contributing publishers themselves; and the coverage of other countries was rather more limited. By cross-checking the holdings for various Viennese publishers of the Music Collection of the Austrian National Library (*A-Wn*) against the Hofmeister database, it emerges that (as one might have suspected) publishers were being selective about which new publications they reported to Hofmeister: the process was not cost-free in terms of staff time and decisions about which titles to advertise were no doubt also moulded by perceptions of likely markets. Secondly, it is clear that the date of entry in the *Monatsberichte* is not always a reliable guide to the date of publication: Neil Ratliff points out that Hofmeister entries are often retrospective, but that in some cases publications were pre-announced in its pages.[17] Despite these features, the *Monatsberichte* can offer useful information.

In the case of the first publication of Bruckner's Third Symphony the most immediate question is date and here the *Monatsberichte* provide more and less information than one might expect or want, with *four* entries:[18]

March 1880, p. 74

**Bruckner, Anton,** *Symphonie (Dm.)* f. gr. Orch. Part. Mk 30. St. Mk 40. Wien, Rättig. [No plate number]

April 1881, p. 83

**Bruckner, Anton,** *Scherzo aus der Symphonie (Dm.)* f. Pfte zum Concertvortrage einger. v. Josef Schalk. Wien, Rättig Mk 2. [Plate number T.R. 187]

February 1885, pp. 26, 34

**Bruckner, Anton,** *Symphonie (Dm.) f. gr. Orch.* Part. Mk 30. St. Mk 40. Wien, Rättig. [No plate number]

**Bruckner, Anton,** *Symphonie (Dm.) f. Orch., arr. f. Pfte zu 4 Hdn.* Wien, Rättig Mk 12. [Plate number B. & R. 165]

So the score and parts of the Symphony were listed twice, in March 1880 and February 1885: perhaps the second announcement was bound up with the fact that Rättig was by then in business on his own, had retained some (at least) of the works he had published earlier with Bussjäger, and was about to publish a further group of works by Bruckner, starting with the *Te deum* (announced in the December 1885 *Monatsbericht*). Rather more curious is the fact that it was only in 1885 that the duet arrangement was announced, but there is other evidence that suggests that it was indeed published rather earlier. Although no comprehensive listing of datable Bussjäger and Rättig and Rättig plate numbers is available (and there is some evidence that the assignment of numbers may not always have been in strict chronological order), there is a short sequence that can be reconstructed:[19]

*Table 1*

| Title | Hofmeister date | Plate number |
|---|---|---|
| Montenuovo, Fürst v., Jubelfest-Marsch f. Pfte | June 1879 | 152 |
| Kremser, Ed., Schul-Hymne: „*Völkerjubel aller Orte*" | June 1879 | 156 |
| Gernerth, Franz, *Rose u. Eiche f. 1 Singst. m. Pfte* | June 1879 | 157 |
| Dubez, Josef, *Kompositionen f. Pfte.* | June 1879 | 158 |
| Strauss, Ed., Op. 183. „*Un petit rien*", *f. Pfte* | March 1880 | 177 |
| Pick, Gustav, „*Wie's juckt, wie's zuckt*" | April 1881 | 184 |
| Bruckner, Anton, *Scherzo aus der Symphonie (Dm.)* f. Pfte zum Concertvortrage einger. v. Josef Schalk | April 1881 | 187 |

This suggests that the piano duet arrangement (plate number 165) was probably issued for the first time in late 1879 or early 1880.

The contents of Table 1 are striking for another reason because, unlike the Bruckner items, the other publications are of works in small-scale genres, and a search of the Hofmeister and *A-Wn* databases confirms that

that is overwhelmingly the case for all three publishers in some way associated with Bruckner's symphony: it stands out as being an exceptional example of large-scale, high-art music, surrounded in their lists by small-scale works in popular instrumental, vocal and dance forms. This raises a more general issue: were there any Viennese publishers engaged in publishing large-scale art-music at the time and how did the Viennese industry's involvement with the genre compare with that of Germany? The *Monatsberichte* again provide some food for thought if we compare the numbers of entries by Viennese publishers with those of one of the major publishing centres in Germany.

*Table 2*

| Date | Leipzig Total Listings | Symphonies | % of total | Vienna Total Listings | Symphonies | % of total |
|------|------|------|------|------|------|------|
| 1870–79 | 11,011 | 151 | 1.3 | 4201 | 16 | 0.4 |
| 1880–89 | 14,587 | 176 | 1.2 | 4030 | 13 | 0.3 |
| 1890–99 | 26,189 | 245 | 1.0 | 5075 | 20 | 0.4 |

Even allowing for the fact that one might expect that Viennese publishers were less active in submitting notifications to Hofmeister (who was, after all, in Leipzig) the disparity between the levels of music publishing activity in the two cities is quite striking, particularly in view of the similar population sizes of the new German Reich (40.8 million) and the Austro-Hungarian Monarchy (35.8 million) at the start of this period. One factor in this discrepancy was presumably that the market in Austria-Hungary was much more fragmented than that in Germany (unified in 1870): the German-speaking population of the Dual Monarchy was less than 50% of the total (though this would have been a more significant factor in book publishing), and the disparity in economic and social development between the western and eastern parts of the Monarchy was notable. If we turn to the proportion of publishing activity in the two centres devoted to distributing the symphonic repertoire, the disparity is clear: in Vienna between 25–50% less than in Leipzig. However, for the young symphonic composer there was one positive aspect of the situation: in Leipzig during this period, about 70 (12.25%) of the listings were for new (or revised versions of) works by living composers, compared with twelve new works (24.5%) in Vienna. Those works were:

*Table 3*

| Composer | Work | Publisher | Date |
|----------|------|-----------|------|
| Herbeck | Symphony op. 20 | Spina | Feb. 1878 |
| Bruckner | Symphony No. 3, ver. 2 | Rättig | Mar. 1880 |
| Cowen | Scandinavian Symphony | Gutmann | May 1882 |
| Olsen | Symphony No. 1 | Gutmann | Oct. 1883 |
| Bruckner | Symphony No. 7 | Gutmann | Dec. 1885 |
| Bruckner | Symphony No. 4 | Gutmann | Sep. 1889 |
| Bruckner | Symphony No. 3, ver. 3 | Rättig | Mar. 1890 |
| Bruckner | Symphony No. 8 | Haslinger | Mar. 1892 |
| Bruckner | Symphony No. 2 | Doblinger | Nov. 1893 |
| Bruckner | Symphony No. 1 | Doblinger | Nov. 1893 |
| Bruckner | Symphony No. 5 | Doblinger | Apr. 1896 |
| Bruckner | Symphony No. 6 | Doblinger | Apr. 1899 |

In itself, this list is most notable for what it does not include and the misleading information it offers. At first sight it might appear impressive that all of the completed and acknowledged symphonies by one of the Austrian capital's most challenging and controversial composers should find Viennese publishers. In fact Bruckner's involvement with local firms may well have contributed to the relative slowness with which his music became well known outside Austria because, with the partial exception of Albert Gutmann,[20] Bruckner's publishers were chiefly involved in the publication of Viennese popular music, particularly dance and operetta: their marketing and distribution activities were not focused on the market for serious and demanding concert works. Why, one might be inclined to ask, were they interested in publishing Bruckner at all? The answer was that they were not — except at a price. The publication of each of his symphonies was subsidized to a greater or lesser extent (see Table 4).

The chief source of information about the negotiations in 1892 between Bruckner and Joseph Eberle's printing company is the Göllerich-Auer biography of the composer. Although no sources are cited, the anecdotes it relates suggest strongly that the account was founded at least in part on details provided by one of the main participants, Josef Stritzko:

After the great success of recent years Bruckner's reputation as a composer, even in Vienna, was so secure, that a local company, the printing establishment Josef Eberle & Co. (which later turned into Universal Edition A.G.)[21] announced its interest in printing the Master's as yet unpublished works.

The negotiations with the publisher Josef Eberle were led by the latter's Director of Publication and son-in-law, Josef Stritzko, who had been a student of Bruckner at the Conservatoire and who subsequently made a name for himself as a composer of operettas and choruses.

At the outset major industrialists were to be persuaded to cover the printing costs, but they all withdrew. So Eberle resolved to print the works at his own cost — which amounted to 36,000 Gulden. When Stritzko reported this to the Master, he was overjoyed....[22]

*Table 4*

| Work | Publisher | Date | Subsidy |
|------|-----------|------|---------|
| Symphony No. 3, ver. 2 | Rättig | Mar. 1880 | Rättig |
| Symphony No. 7 | Gutmann | Dec. 1885 | Herman Levi[23] |
| Symphony No. 4 | Gutmann | Sep. 1889 | Herman Levi[24] |
| Symphony No. 3, ver. 3 | Rättig | Mar. 1890 | Franz Josef[25] |
| Symphony No. 8 | Haslinger | Mar 1892 | Franz Josef[26] |
| Symphony No. 2 | Doblinger | Nov. 1893 | Josef Eberle |
| Symphony No. 1 | Doblinger | Nov. 1893 | Josef Eberle |
| Symphony No. 5 | Doblinger | Apr. 1896 | Josef Eberle |
| Symphony No. 6 | Doblinger | Apr. 1899 | Josef Eberle |

Josef Eberle (1845–1921) had established his printing company in Vienna in 1873, and was also active, in a minor way, as a music publisher.[27] The first reference to the firm in Hofmeister's *Monatsbericht* — an edition of Carl Czerny's Op.139 (probably not the first Eberle title) — appears in the February 1888 issue, but after a series of entries up to July 1889 there is a hiatus until July 1899, probably reflecting a lack of interest in obtaining listings in the *Monatsbericht* rather than a lack of publishing activity. The two batches of entries, though, are quite distinct in repertoire, suggesting a shift in publishing (or at least international marketing) strategy. The earlier series is made up of Czerny technical exercises and editions of classic repertoire: Beethoven Piano Sonatas 'nach G. Nottebohm's Aufzeichnungen revid. v. Eusebius Mandyczewski', Schubert *Lieder* 'nach den ältesten Ausg. revid. v. Jos. Stritzko' and a complete edition of Josef Lanner's dance music edited by Eduard Kremser. The later (and much larger) series consists of entries for relatively small-scale and popular genres and it is this repertoire that constitutes the majority of the copies surviving in *A-Wn* (over 350) — songs, dance music, marches, works from operettas — alongside the staple teaching material. Large-scale works by Bruckner would certainly have looked out of place in such a catalogue, but this can hardly have been a factor lying behind Eberle's policy of licensing the rights to Doblinger, whose speciality was that of operetta. Perhaps the deciding factor was that Doblinger had a better developed international distribution network.

In the meantime, Mahler had left Vienna and had been rapidly developing a career as a conductor of opera, starting at small provincial theatres and at the age of just 28 moving on to the directorship of the Royal Opera House in Budapest in 1889, and then to the position of first conductor at the Hamburg Stadttheater in 1891. While in Leipzig in 1887–9 he completed an unfinished comic opera by Weber, *Die drei Pintos*, which proved something of a success and was enthusiastically published by C. F. Kahnt in Leipzig. This not only provided Mahler with a degree of financial security[28] but also fanned the flames of his own creativity, and between 1888 and 1896 he completed a number of songs and his first three symphonies. Finding a publisher for them was more difficult: in 1892 Schott in Mainz issued a collection of songs, the *Lieder und Gesänge*, but rejected the symphonic works. It was only through the financial support of two wealthy Hamburg admirers that the Second Symphony was eventually printed *In Commissionsverlag* by Friedrich Hofmeister in Leipzig in 1895–7.[29]

Early in 1897 Mahler finally achieved his greatest ambition as a conductor, and was appointed Kapellmeister at the Court Opera in Vienna (and became Director later that year). Within a few months he was signing a contract for the publication of an important orchestral song cycle, his *Lieder eines fahrenden Gesellen*, with a new and rapidly expanding music publisher in Vienna, Joseph Weinberger, and the work was published at the end of the year.[30]

Weinberger (1855–1928) was born in Lipto St Miklos in Moravia, but moved to Vienna with his family in the mid-1860s. They formed part of the enormous wave of immigration into Vienna that followed the demolition of the city walls, and the improved civil rights for Jews living in the Habsburg lands after 1860. Josef's father was a goldsmith who ensured that his son had a commercial training, but Weinberger had a keen interest in music, being a capable pianist and singer. In 1885 he joined forces with Carl Hofbauer to form 'Josef Weinberger and Carl Hofbauer' art and music dealers, at 34 Kärntnerstrasse, Vienna. Their first entries in the *Monatsbericht* appeared in the March-April issue of 1886 and included Franz Roth's *Das tanzende Wien* (Walzer f. Pfte.) Op. 336; over the next four years 84 titles were listed, the last appearing in April 1890. By that date the two partners had split up. As early as 1889 Weinberger had established a separate firm of his own, based in Leipzig. The main impetus behind this move was probably a desire to secure improved international copyright protection: at the time Austro-Hungary was not a signatory to the Berne Convention, but Germany was. This meant that whereas new music published in Austro-Hungary only received copyright protection in those foreign states with which the Dual Monarchy had negotiated bilateral copyright treaties (and by 1890 it had concluded such agreements with only France (1866) and Italy (1890)[31]), such music published in Germany in 1890 received reciprocal copyright protection in the nine states that were co-signatories to the convention.[32] Weinberger's strategy seems to have been adopted in the 1890s by other Viennese music publishers, including Robitschek (c.1894) and Hofbauer (c.1895). The first of Weinberger's Leipzig publications to be listed in the *Monatsbericht* appeared in October 1889, and on 1 January 1890 he opened his own premises at 8–10 Kohlmarkt in Vienna and it was from there that Weinberger managed the company.

How Mahler came into contact with the publisher is not clear. Weinberger's office was only a few steps away from the opera house, but a development that reflected a shift in the focus of Weinberger's business may have been more significant. In 1895 he acquired over 1,500 works from the Kratz catalogue of theatrical works. This included a number of works with international performing rights, which encouraged Weinberger to open a Parisian branch in 1896, but it also reflected a shift in Weinberger's publishing interests towards theatrical music generally. Another major step in that direction was taken in 1897, when the entire theatrical catalogue of Gustav Lewy — which included the stage works of Johann Strauss the younger and Millöcker — were taken over, with the Strauss performing rights following in 1899. The significance is that Lewy, as well as being a publisher, was one of the major artists' agents in Vienna, and he had been Mahler's representative for many years.

At about this time Weinberger was also playing a leading role in developments that were to have a major impact on Austrian music publishing, and also directly on Mahler. The new Austrian copyright law of 26 December 1895 (the first since 1846[33]) established for the first time performing rights for non-theatrical musical works, thus enabling publishers and composers to demand performance fees for concert works. Weinberger played a leading role in the formation of the Gesellschaft der Autoren, Komponisten und Musikverleger in Wien (AKM) established in 1897 in response to this legislation; he was elected its first President and in 1910 became an honorary member. The Gesellschaft acted as a collecting agency for performance fees, and it seems likely that it was Weinberger (who was Mahler's publisher for the *Lieder eines fahrenden Gesellen*) who persuaded the composer to join in the year of its foundation.[34]

In November 1898 Weinberger issued a publicity flyer announcing that Mahler's First and Second Symphonies would be available from his publishing house:[35] an apparently unambiguous statement, which actually masked the complex underlying publishing arrangements. For one thing all but the orchestral and chorus parts of Mahler's Second Symphony had already been published by Hofmeister in Leipzig (see above p. 187): the plates were almost certainly transferred from the original printer of the Hofmeister editions, C. G. Röder, to Vienna,[36] and it seems likely that part or all of the unsold stock of the first issue was probably passed on to Weinberger as well. More significantly the announcement skated over the fact that Mahler's contract for these two works, and all the others subsequently published in Vienna up to 1906, was not with Weinberger (or Doblinger, who appears as 'publisher' of the Fourth Symphony), but with Josef Eberle & Co. As with the publication of some of Bruckner's symphonies, this is connected with the fact that no Viennese publisher would take on such a costly and potentially loss-making project without a subsidy, though in this case the subsidy was coming not from Eberle, but from a cultural association in Bohemia.

The key player in the necessary negotiations, which must have begun in 1897, was Guido Adler, a childhood friend of Mahler, who in later years was a key figure in the early development of musicology as a distinct academic discipline.[37] In 1885 he was appointed Professor of Musicology in Prague and remained there until 1898 when he took up a similar position at the University of Vienna. In 1891 the Gesellschaft zur Föderung deutscher Wissenschaft, Kunst und Literatur in Böhmen was founded by a group of leading German-speaking tertiary-level teachers in Prague, most of them, including Adler, professors at the Deutsche Karl-Ferdinands-Universität. The initial impetus was provided by the creation the previous year, of the Böhmischen Kaiser Franz Joseph-Akademie der Wissenschaften, Künste und Literatur in Prag, at a time of growing cultural tensions within the Czech Lands, and the function of the Gesellschaft was embodied in its title: the promotion of German scholarship, art and literature in Bohemia.[38] It was almost certainly Adler who came up with the plan to request financial support for the publication of the First and Third symphonies (full scores, parts and piano duet arrangements) and the Second Symphony (parts) from the Gesellschaft. Apart from the publications themselves — some issues of which acknowledge the financial support — relatively few documents have been located that trace this process. Of greatest significance are the two reports that Adler submitted to the Gesellschaft, dated 23 and 24 January 1898, drafts of which are now in the Guido Adler papers at the University of Georgia.[39] The second of these drafts includes details of the costs involved, and Adler's specific proposals for payment and acknowledgement:

The expense of printing the score, vocal score and parts of the First and Third Symphonies and the orchestral parts of the Second will amount to about 12,000 fl., according to the calculations of Eberle & Co. in Vienna one of the best-equipped printers, who publish among other things the symphonies of Bruckner. On the recommendation of the under-signed as adviser they have agreed to take on Mahler's works too, on the understanding, and with the wish, that part of the costs can be raised in the form of a subsidy.... Therefore: to accomplish on the one hand the great task which it is our duty here to fulfil, and on the other hand to pay due respect to the apportionment of our finances, the proposal should be put that we vote 3,000 Fl. for the publication and propagation of the works of Gustav Mahler, payable in two instalments, the first payment at once, the second instalment in January 1899. We attach one condition to this grant, namely that the following note should appear on the orchestral and vocal scores of the First and Third symphonies and on the cover of the orchestral parts or perhaps on the violin part, of the Second: 'with the support of the Society for the Advancement of German Science, Art and Literature in Bohemia'.[40]

To put the production costs into some sort of perspective, the total was worth about $5,784,[41] or more pertinently, it was exactly Mahler's starting annual salary as Director of the Vienna Court Opera.[42]

Clearly there must have been substantive discussions between Adler and Eberle some time prior to his drafting of the references, and there would have been ample opportunity for him to raise the matter with the company since it was responsible for the production of the *Denkmäler der Tonkunst in Österreich*, being published by C. A. Artaria under his editorship. The negotiations in 1897–8 for the grant application and associated publishing plans must also have involved exchanges between Adler and Mahler. A brief note from the composer to his friend and lawyer, Emil Freund, probably refers to the preparation of Adler's references:[43] 'Adler has just written to say that if he does not receive my *curriculum vitae* within the next two days, the [whole undertaking] will have to be put off until the autumn.' Nevertheless there must have been some assurances given even before Adler's references were submitted, since Mahler's confidante Natalie Bauer-Lechner recorded that by New Year's Eve, 1897, the composer was celebrating the prospect of the publication of the works:

Mahler told me the happy news that, thanks to the efforts of Guido Adler, the scores of both his still unpublished symphonies (the First and the Third) as well as

the piano reductions and the orchestral parts [to all three], are to be printed by
Eberle in Vienna. As a result, he is at last freed from anxiety as to the storing and
preservation of these works. Furthermore, there is the prospect of their becoming
known and performed, where before — quite apart from anything else militating
against their acceptance — Mahler possessed only two copies ([the] original and
one copy) which he did not dare let out of his hands simultaneously. Having spent
years in the most arduous efforts to bring this about, and having [gained] nothing
but bitter experiences and disillusionments, his desire is now being realized almost
without his having to raise a finger.

'It's always like that,' said Mahler. 'To him that hath, shall be given; and from
him that hath not shall be taken away even that which he hath.'[44]

The reference to 'Klavierauszüge' seems to relate to the piano duet arrangements of all three symphonies that were indeed issued, but which were not
referred to in Adler's reference. The first editions of the arrangements of
the first two symphonies carry appropriate acknowledgments, but none
appears on that of the Third — perhaps an oversight.

Although we know quite a lot about the terms of the subsidy, Mahler's
contract with Eberle has not come to light. It seems clear that Mahler understood that it gave Eberle and Co. some sort of option on subsequent works,
and when Peters Editionsverlag expressed some interest in the Fifth Symphony in 1903, Mahler turned to his lawyer Emil Freund for advice:

Please give me a tip how to tackle this.
1. To do as well as possible for myself.
2. To avoid acting contrary to my obligations towards Stritzko.
N.B. I should like at least 10,000 florins for my work. — Would it not be best for
me to approach Stritzko first, asking whether he will pay me that amount —
perhaps letting him understand that otherwise I should like to accept some other
publisher's offer?[45]

Whatever the contractual details, the situation resolved amicably, as
Mahler was able to report to his young colleague, the conductor Bruno
Walter:

Luckily I have just reached an amicable settlement with my previous publisher so
that from now on I can now dispose my works freely! I shall therefore be happy to
negotiate with P[eters] if he can offer really decent terms.[46]

Further insight can be gleaned from a letter written by Mahler to an
unidentified publisher (almost certainly the Berlin firm of Lauterbach and
Kuhn) which apparently dates from the summer of 1908, and in which he
offers them the Seventh and Eighth Symphonies:

Herr Fried, who is here at Toblach, has mentioned your publishing house to me
and I should be very glad to enter into relations with you. Assuming that it is not

your principle to acquire an author's work outright (in which case I must ask you to state your terms), I would suggest an arrangement I adopted with the publisher of my first four symphonies and my songs. According to this, you would print the Eighth Symphony and undertake its entire publication, and pay me half the receipts. At the same time you would undertake to pay me a suitable advance on receipt of the manuscript. An account to be presented at the end of the business year.[47]

Of course Mahler is being disingenuous. Some of the early Eberle publications had been supported by financial subsidy, and Alma Mahler remembered another element in the arrangement with Eberle:

When I returned to Toblach that summer [1910] Mahler told me that Hertzka of Universal Edition had been to see him. He had taken over Mahler's first four symphonies from Waldheim & Eberle. The terms of publication were that the symphonies were to earn 50,000 crowns (10,000 dollars) before yielding Mahler any royalty. They were now within 2,500 crowns of doing so, and Mahler was therefore just about to profit from them.[48]

If Alma Mahler's memory was correct, Eberle had sought to recoup costs for the four symphonies (but it may have also included the songs and *Das klagende Lied* as well, as these were also Eberle publications taken over by Universal Edition in 1910), the equivalent of 25,000 Fl., compared with the 12,000 Fl. Adler had quoted for the production costs of the First and Third Symphonies and the parts for the Second. This provision is broadly similar to one in Bruckner's contract with Eberle, though the subsidy that was forthcoming for Mahler was well below the 50% of production costs mentioned there, so if Mahler really was credited with 50% of the receipts, he had negotiated a rather better deal.

It would appear that the details of the contract were not yet quite finalized when, in mid-January 1898, Mahler wrote to his Hamburg friend and patron Hermann Behn: it was Behn, and the Hamburg businessman Wilhelm Berkhan who had paid for the publication of the full score of the Second Symphony in 1897, so reporting the news about the grant from Prague that would subsidize the publication of the parts of the work was of considerable import. Mahler commented:

The firm of Eberle only engraves; they are printers in the style of Röder, with plenty of capital (a corporation) and were created to promote Austrian works; they also secure the most suitable publisher: my work will probably go to Doblinger. Advertising and distribution will be on a large scale.[49]

Apparently Stritzko's first thought was to license the works to Doblinger, but for some reason that firm's involvement in the publication of Mahler was postponed until the Fourth Symphony (1902), after — and it is not clear whether this is significant — the publication of the last major work in their Bruckner portfolio (the Sixth Symphony: see above, p. 185). Perhaps in 1897 the firm concluded that for the moment it had enough large-scale symphonic works in its publishing schedule. On the other hand, another Viennese publisher of some importance, Weinberger, had accepted Mahler's *Lieder eines fahrenden Gesellen* for publication, so two or three symphonies by the same composer would not look so out of place in his catalogue. With the appearance of the full score of the First Symphony in December 1898, Eberle's Mahler series began to take shape: it eventually included all of the works by the composer published between 1899 and 1903, all bearing plate numbers in a single sequence (see Table 6 on p. 195).

There are some anomalies early in the sequence, at least in part the result of the fact that it was incorporating the three printed formats of the Second that had been published by Friedrich Hofmeister on commission in 1895–7:

*Table 5*

| Title | Format | Pl. no. | Date |
|---|---|---|---|
| Symphony No. 2 | Full score | 1 | 1897 |
| Symphony No. 2 | Arrangement for two pianos | 3 | 1895 |
| Symphony No. 2, 4th movement | Vocal score | 4 | 1895 |

Hofmeister seems not to have issued any material for the work with a plate number '2', though this may have been notionally assigned to the orchestral and chorus parts. It would appear that Eberle decided simply to retain the original plate numbers for new printings of the other Hofmeister items, though a *Titelauflage* or new edition of the arrangement for two pianos was never issued — presumably because sales of the original edition were not encouraging.

Otherwise, Eberle assigned plate numbers for the publications associated with each symphony in a relatively systematic way, score, parts and arrangements in that order: the arrangement Hofmeister had probably planned for the Second Symphony. It is therefore particularly curious that Eberle did not use the vacant '2' for the orchestral and choral parts of that work, but instead used the '4' already assigned to the vocal score of *Urlicht* (though there is a logic in this: all three publications could be conceived as 'performance material' for the Symphony). Eberle also commissioned and published an arrangement of the Second Symphony for piano duet and, logically, assigned it the next number in the sequence, '5'.

The parts and duet arrangement of the First Symphony carry the numbers '7' and '8' respectively, but inexplicably the number '1' was used on the plates for the full score — so there were now two Mahler publications with this number in the Weinberger catalogue. The error was eventually corrected in 1906 when Universal Edition was licensed to issue smaller-format study scores of the first four symphonies: all were photolithographically reduced from revised states of the full score plates. Symphonies 2, 3 and 4 retained the plate numbers of the full scores; for the study score of the First Symphony the 'correct' plate number '6' was adopted. It may be that a simple error also accounts for the final anomaly. It would seem that the plate number for the parts for the Fourth Symphony should have been '32', but they were actually assigned a number in the Doblinger sequence (D. 2720).

All in all, the Eberle series reflected a serious and sustained commitment to the publication of a highly controversial composer on the Viennese musical scene, but the commercial arrangements that underpinned it reflect the difficulty the local music publishing industry had in supporting Viennese composers producing new, large-scale concert works aimed at the high-art end of the market. By the end of 1903 Mahler had achieved some influential international successes. Performances of the Second Symphony in Liege in 1898 and 1899, and in Basel in 1903, had established the work, and the triumphant première of the Third Symphony in Krefeld in 1902 aroused enormous interest: by the end of 1911 the piece had received a further 28 performances. In this context Mahler found that he no longer had to make do with subsidized publications by Viennese publishers of relatively modest international importance: one of the largest German publishers, Peters Edition, was willing to pay an enormous sum for his Fifth Symphony in 1903.[50] Meanwhile some of the publishers he had worked with in Vienna had in 1901 undertaken a venture that would transform the status of Vienna as a publishing centre (overtly challenging the dominance of the Leipzig-based Peters Edition) and eventually provide modern music with a publishing outlet: the founding of Universal Edition. By the end of 1910 the new company had an exclusive contract with Mahler and had taken over all Eberle's rights, thus becoming Mahler's main publisher: the narrative of that phase of Mahler's career sheds light on one of the most fascinating periods in the history of music publishing in the Habsburg capital.

*Table 6*

| Title | Format | Pl. no. | Date | Publisher |
|---|---|---|---|---|
| Symphony No. 1 | Full score | 1 | 1899 | Weinberger |
| Symphony No. 2 | Full score, second issue | 1 | 1899 | Weinberger |
| Symphony No. 2: 4th movement | Vocal score, second edition | 4 | 1899 | Weinberger |
| Symphony No. 2 | Orchestral parts, first edition | 4 | 1903? | Weinberger |
| Symphony No. 2 | Vocal parts, first edition | 4 | 1903? | Weinberger |
| Symphony No. 2 | Piano duet arrangement | 5 | 1899 | Weinberger |
| Symphony No. 1 | Orchestral parts | 7 | 1899 | Weinberger |
| Symphony No. 1 | Piano duet arrangement | 8 | 1899 | Weinberger |
| Symphony No. 3 | Full score | 9 | 1902 | Weinberger |
| Symphony No. 3 | Orchestral parts | 10 | 1902 | Weinberger |
| Symphony No. 3 | Piano duet arrangement | 11 | 1902 | Weinberger |
| *Lieder aus Des Knaben Wunderhorn* (*DKW*) 1–12 (3 vols) | Piano and voice version | 12a–c | 1900 | Weinberger |
| *DKW* No. 1 | Full score and parts | 13/13a | 1900? | Weinberger |
| *DKW* No. 2 | Full score and parts | 14/14a | 1900? | Weinberger |
| *DKW* No. 3 | Full score and parts | 15/15a | 1900? | Weinberger |
| *DKW* No. 4 | Full score and parts | 16/16a | 1900? | Weinberger |
| *DKW* No. 5 | Full score and parts | 17/17a | 1900? | Weinberger |
| *DKW* No. 6 | Full score and parts | 18/18a | 1900? | Weinberger |
| *DKW* No. 7 | Full score and parts | 19/19a | 1900? | Weinberger |
| *DKW* No. 8 | Full score and parts | 20/20a | 1900? | Weinberger |
| *DKW* No. 9 | Full score and parts | 21/21a | 1900? | Weinberger |
| *DKW* No. 10 | Full score and parts | 22/22a | 1900? | Weinberger |
| *DKW* No. 12 | Full score and parts | 24/24a | 1900? | Weinberger |
| *Das klagende Lied* | Vocal score | 25 | 1902 | Weinberger |
| *Das klagende Lied* | Full score | 26 | 1902? | Weinberger |
| *Das klagende Lied* | Orchestral parts | ? | ? | Weinberger |
| *Das klagende Lied* | Chorus parts | ? | ? | Weinberger |
| Symphony No. 3, 4th movement | Vocal score | 27 | 1902 | Weinberger |
| Symphony No. 3 | Chorus parts | 30 | 1902? | Weinberger |
| Symphony No. 4 | Full score | 31 | 1902 | Doblinger |
| Symphony No. 4 | Piano duet arrangement | 33 | 1902 | Doblinger |
| Symphony No. 4, 4th movement | Vocal score | 34 | 1902 | Doblinger |
| Symphony No. 3 | Chorus score (Particell) | 35 | 1902? | Weinberger |

*References*

1.  For a biography and a comprehensive list of writings, see *The New Grove Dictionary of Music and Musicians*, ed. Stanley Sadie, 2nd edn (London: Macmillan, 2001), vol. 27, 242–3. Weinmann studied musicology under Mahler's childhood friend, Guido Adler, whose name will figure later in this narrative.

2.  See Murray G. Hall, *Österreichische Verlagsgeschichte 1918–1938* (Vienna, Graz, Cologne: Hermann Böhlaus Nachf., 1985) and Carl. Junker, *Zum Buchwesen in Österreich: gesammelte Schriften (1896–1927)*, ed. Murray G. Hall (Vienna: Edition Praesens, 2001).

3.  August Göllerich, *Anton Bruckner: ein Lebens- und Schaffensbild*, completed and ed. Max Auer (Regensburg: Gustav Bosse, 1922–37), IV/1, 474–82.

4.  Ibid., IV/1, 478.

5.  See the facsimile in Renate Grasberger, *Werkverzeichnis Anton Bruckner* (Tutzing: Schneider, 1977), 226.

6.  Leopold Nowak, *Anton Bruckner: Musik und Leben* (Linz: Trauner, 1973), 321.

7.  See the facsimile in Grasberger, 227.

8.  E.g. Paul Caro, String Quartet no. 2 in B minor (Vienna: Bösendorfer/Rudolf Bussjäger, 1886).

9.  E.g. Raoul Mader, *Nur rrrasch: „Alles kommt zu seiner Zeit". Schnellpolka für Männerchor mit Pianoforte op.123* (Vienna, Bussjäger, 1894).

10. Donald Mitchell, *The Wunderhorn Years: Chronicles and Commentaries* (Woodbridge: Boydell Press, 2005), 65. In what is presumably a latter issue, the printed publisher's details are omitted and the area blank, but overprinted with a ?rubber stamp: *TH. RÄTTIG / MUSIK-VERLAG & SORTIMENT / WIEN / I. Bellariastrasse 10* (see the facsimile in Franz Grasberger, *Anton Bruckner: Zum 150. Geburtstag* (exhibition catalogue) (Vienna: Österreichische Nationalbibliothek, 1974), 86.

11. Ibid., IV/1, 481.

12. Reprinted in *Anton Bruckner, Gesammlte Briefe: Neue Folge*, ed. Max Auer (Regensburg: Gustav Bosse Verlag, 1924), 148.

13. Despite his interest, Rättig did not publish either of the other two symphonies.

14. See *Guide for the Dating of Early Published Music: A Manual of Bibliographical Practices*, compiled by D. W. Krummel (Hackensack: J. Boonin, 1974), 193–5, which includes an invaluable summary of the history of all three music bibliographical series published by Hofmeister.

15. See http://www.hofmeister.rhul.ac.uk/cocoon/hofmeister/index.html (accessed 07.01.2008), and http://www.onb.ac.at/sammlungen/musik/hofmeister1.htm (accessed 07.01.2008).

16. See http://www.hofmeister.rhul.ac.uk/cocoon/hofmeister/pubPlaces_maps.html (accessed 07.01.2008).

17. See Krummel, *Dating*, 194.

18. The plate numbers in square brackets are derived from Renate Grasberger, *Werkverzeichnis*, and the online music catalogue of the Austrian National Library (links from http://www.onb.ac.at/sammlungen/musik/ index.htm ).

19. Prepared by collating the *Monatsberichte* listings for the two publishers, and the relevant online catalogue records from *A-Wn*.

20. Albert J. Gutmann (1851–1915) opened an art and music shop with associated music publishing business in 1873; in addition he was one of the most important artists' agents in Vienna, with offices in London, Paris and Berlin. (See *Oesterreichisches Musik-*

*lexikon*, ed. Rudolf Flotzinger (Vienna: Österreichischen Akademie der Wissenschaften, 2002– ); online version: http://www.musiklexikon.ac.at.

21. This is not quite correct — but Josef Eberle & Co. was part of the original consortium that established Universal-Edition.

22. Göllerich/Auer, IV/3, 256; all translations are my own unless otherwise stated.

23. Levi collected 1000 fl. from various admirers; see Franz Scheder, *Anton Bruckner Chronologie* (Tutzing: Schneider, 1996), I, 444.

24. Levi again collected 1000 fl. from various admirers, and some funds may have been forthcoming from Franz Josef; see Hans-Hubert Schönzeler, *Bruckner* (London, Calder and Boyars, 1970), 91, and Scheder, I, 519.

25. Schönzeler, 93 and Leopold Nowak, 'Vortwort', in *Anton Bruckner, III. Symphonie D-moll: Fassung von 1889*, Sämtliche Werke, III/3 (Vienna Musikwissenschaftlicher Verlag, 1959), v.

26. Leopold Nowak, 'Vortwort' in *Anton Bruckner, VIII. Symphonie C-moll: Fassung von 1890*, Sämtliche Werke, VIII/2, 2nd edn (Vienna Musikwissenschaflicher Verlag, 1955), vi.

27. For further information see http://www.cph.rcm.ac.uk/MahlerCat/pages/Publishers/Eberle.htm.

28. The publishers' advance was 10,000 marks, approximately equivalent to something over €50,000; see Helmut Bremmer, 'Gustav Mahler Finanzen und das Bank- und Währungswesen um 1900', in Gustav Mahler, *Liebste Justi!: Briefe an die Familie*, ed. Stephen McClatchie and Helmut Brenner (S.l., Weidle Verlag, n.d.), 551–62. Unfortunately this useful essay is not included in the English edition published by Oxford University Press.

29. For details of the Hofmeister publications, see the relevant pages in my catalogue of Mahler's music (www.rcm.ac.uk/Mahlercat).

30. For a facsimile of the contract see Mitchell, *Wunderhorn Years* , 91.

31. Online scans of both treaties are available at http://alex.onb.ac.at.

32. For a list of contracting parties and the dates of their signing up, see http://www.wipo.int/treaties/en/ip/berne/. Austria finally signed in 1920.

33. For scans of both, see at http://alex.onb.ac.at.

34. See *Gustav Mahler — Richard Strauss, Correspondence 1888–1911*, ed. Herta Blaukopf, trans. Edmund Jephcott (London: Faber and Faber, 1984), 152.

35. See http://www.cph.rcm.ac.uk/MahlerCat/pages/Symph1/Symph1announcement.htm.

36. See the unpublished letter, dated 13 January 1898, Mahler wrote to an unnamed recipient (probably Hermann Behn) in connection with the transfer of the plates (sold at Sotheby's in May 1989, lot 176).

37. For an account of Adler's relationship with Mahler, see Edward R. Reilly, *Gustav Mahler and Guido Adler: Record of a Friendship* (Cambridge: Cambridge University Press, 1982).

38. For one account of its history, see M. Neumüller, 'Gesellschaft zur Föderung deutscher Wissenschaft, Kunst und Literatur in Böhmen — Deutsche Akademie der Wissenschaften in Prag: Rekonstruction des Mitgliederstammes und Untersuchungen zu seiner Struktur (1891–1945)', *Germanoslavica: Zeitschrift für germano-slawische Studien*, II (VII) (1995), 49–64; for an overview of the changing fortunes of the German-speaking minority in Prague (and the Czech lands generally), see G. B. Cohen, *The Politics of Ethnic Survival: Germans in Prague 1861–1914*, 2nd edn (West Lafayette: Purdue

University Press, 2006). A more detailed account by the present author of Mahler's connection with the Gesellschaft is in preparation.

39.  See http://www.libs.uga.edu/hargrett/manuscrip/guidoadler.html for details.

40.  Kurt Blaukopf, *Mahler: A Documentary Study* (London: Thames & Hudson, 1976), 216.

41.  Reilly, *Mahler*, 139, n. 37.

42.  Henry-Louis de la Grange, *Gustav Mahler.Vienna: The Years of Challenge (1897–1904)* (Oxford: OUP, 1995), 53.

43.  *Selected Letters of Gustav Mahler*, ed. Knud Martner, trans. Eithne Wilkins & Ernst Kaiser and Bill Hopkins (London: Faber and Faber, 1979), 226. This note was undated, but the editors suggest spring 1897. The latter seems unlikely: sometime rather later that year or even early January 1898 seems more probable.

44.  Natalie Bauer-Lechner, *Recollections of Gustav Mahler*, trans. Dika Newlin, ed. Peter Franklin (London: Faber Music, 1980), 109–10.

45.  *Selected Letters of Gustav Mahler*, 270.

46.  Ibid., 270–1.

47.  Alma Mahler, *Gustav Mahler: Memories and Letters*, ed. D. Mitchell, trans. B. Creighton (London: John Murray, 1973), 307–8.

48.  Ibid., 176.

49.  Henry-Louis de la Grange, *Mahler* (New York: Doubleday & Company, 1973), 466; the otherwise unpublished letter is at the Mediathèque Musicale Mahler, Paris.

50.  For an exceptionally detailed account of the publication of this work by Peters, see Eberhardt Klemm, 'Zur geschichte der Fünften Sinfonie von Gustav Mahler. Der Briefwechsel zwischen Mahler und dem Verlag C. F. Peters und andere Dokumente', *Jahrbuch Peters* 2 (1979), 9–116.

*Appendix*

# The Gerald Coke Handel Collection at the Foundling Museum

KATHARINE HOGG

*Handel and the Foundling Hospital*

The Foundling Hospital was established by Royal Charter in 1739, after a long struggle by Captain Thomas Coram, a successful shipwright and sailor who had retired to England after a life's work in the New World of America. Coram had been appalled by the discarded and dying children in the streets of London, and his scheme for a 'Hospital for the Maintenance and Education of Exposed and Deserted Young Children', to provide a refuge for foundlings, was the first of its kind in England, although other countries were already further advanced. Nevertheless Coram encountered much prejudice from those who thought it would encourage irresponsible behaviour on the part of the mothers, and it was only when he enlisted the ladies of the nobility to support his request to Parliament that he was successful in obtaining the necessary Royal Charter. The site for the Hospital, originally 56 acres in the country just north of London, was acquired from the Earl of Salisbury in 1740, and money was raised by public donations. In 1745 children were moved into the new buildings, designed by Theodore Jacobsen, who was also a Governor of the Hospital.

From the start, artistic influence on the Hospital was firmly established, led by the painter William Hogarth. He was a founding Governor of the Hospital and recognized the opportunity for artists to display their work whilst supporting the charity, by donating works to decorate the fine rooms in the building — chiefly the Governors' offices, where polite society and potential donors could be received. There were no art galleries in England at this time and Hogarth's designs were no less groundbreaking for artists than Coram's were for abandoned children. Patronage was unreliable and there were few opportunities to display artists' work in public. A generous donation of works of art to the Foundling Hospital could bring many rewards, raise the artist's profile and attract future commissions.

The first endowment — Hogarth's portrait of Thomas Coram, given to the Hospital in 1740 — served as an example to Hogarth's peers of the benefits of philanthropy. These intentions were well realized as both artists and collectors donated pieces for the ornamentation of the hospital, as gestures of goodwill which would receive wide attention. Other artists of the time contributed to what is still one of the most impressive eighteenth-century interiors in London, the Hospital's Court Room, which was formally opened in 1747. It includes paintings by Hogarth, Francis Hayman, James Wills and Joseph Highmore, all featuring children or foundlings from Biblical stories — Moses was represented as one of the first foundlings. The room contains an ornate plasterwork ceiling, chimney-piece, with Rysbrack's bas-relief over the fireplace, plaster busts and a series of roundels all donated by the artists and craftsmen; the roundels have landscapes and views of eight London hospitals, including Greenwich, Christ's and Charterhouse, painted by artists including Gainsborough, Samuel Wale, Edward Haytley and Richard Wilson.

The unique environment of the Foundling Hospital, which had been designed from the outset not only as a children's home, but as a place of polite assembly, meant that it quickly became one of the most fashionable places to visit during the reign of George II, and a hub of philanthropic activity, where artists, children and patrons were able to benefit mutually from the contemporary culture of 'enlightened self-interest'. The inclusion of a Picture Gallery added to the attraction for polite society, and another fund-raising initiative, the Ladies' Breakfasts, became so popular that in 1747 it is recorded that the windows had to be nailed shut to prevent uninvited guests from climbing in.

The governing artists benefited from the Hospital not only as an exhibition space, but also as a place to meet and discuss their activities, as an alternative to the St Martin's Lane Academy. The annual Foundling Hospital dinner, attended by the Governors and London's leading artists, provided an opportunity for lively discussion. At this occasion in 1759, Francis Hayman proposed the idea of founding 'a great museum all our own', and this museum — the Royal Academy of Arts — was finally established in 1768. However, artists and patrons continued to donate works to the Hospital, including, for example, the Roubiliac bust of Handel presented in 1844 by Sir Frederick Pollock, but only recognized as Roubiliac's work after restoration in 1966.

Alongside Coram and Hogarth, the other major benefactor was George Frideric Handel. The composer had already supported the 'Fund for Decay'd Musicians', established in 1738, and this charitable society was to benefit from a bequest in his will. Handel's first appearance in the

Committee minutes of the Foundling Hospital, on 4 May 1749, records that he attended to offer a fund-raising performance to benefit the building of the chapel:

Mr Handel being present and having generously and charitably offered a performance of vocal and instrumental music to be held at this Hospital, and that the money arising therefrom should be applied to the finishing the chapel of the Hospital Resolved — That the thanks of this Committee be returned to Mr Handel for this his generous and charitable offer.[1]

Donald Burrows has suggested that Handel's interest may have come about through his music publisher John Walsh, who had been elected a Governor in 1748 and would have known of the financial difficulties encountered by the Hospital.[2] Most Governors of the Hospital attended only one meeting, to pay their donation. The title of Governor seems to have been only nominal, as few took any active part in the Hospital governance, other than attendance, at their own expense, at the annual Foundling Hospital dinner.

Handel's name was put forward to be a Governor after his offer of a concert in 1749, but he declined the invitation; the Minutes report that

the Secretary acquainted the Committee that Mr. Handel called upon him last Saturday, and returned his thanks to the Committee for the Honour intended him of being a Governor of this Hospital; But he desired to be excused therefrom that he should serve the Charity with more Pleasure in his way, than being a member of the Corporation.[3]

The 1749 concert took place three weeks after Handel's offer to the Committee, and was a great success. It was attended by the Prince and Princess of Wales, attracted a full house and raised over £350. The final work in the concert was the Foundling Hospital anthem, which Handel created largely from existing material (including the 'Hallelujah chorus' which he borrowed from his then little-known *Messiah*) with words from the Scriptures. The composer's conducting score of this work is now on display in the Foundling Museum.

Handel continued to serve the charity 'in his way'; the concert in 1749 was so successful that the Governors asked him to put on another concert the following year, and he chose to perform *Messiah*. The oratorio had been composed eight years earlier but had not yet been well received by London audiences; its few performances had been overshadowed by a debate over whether it was appropriate to perform a work with so sacred a subject in a theatre, which was commonly associated with more worldly interests. The performance of *Messiah* in 1750 was oversubscribed, and the Hospital minutes note that the High Constable and his assistants were to be asked to attend to keep gate-crashers out. There were double-bookings for the first performance in May, when tickets were sold at the door as well as in advance, and Handel attended a further meeting at the Hospital, when a second performance was hastily arranged to accommodate the ticket-holders who had been turned away. The performance in the Foundling Hospital Chapel, for the benefit of such a worthy cause, made the oratorio acceptable to London audiences, and Handel then gave an annual benefit performance of *Messiah* in the chapel, a practice which continued after his death, and which also established *Messiah* in the concert repertoire. *Messiah* became very closely associated with the Foundling Hospital, and in his will the composer directed that a score and parts of the oratorio be given to the Hospital, so that benefit performances could continue.

In the 1770s a proposal was made to the Court of Governors to form a public music school made up of children from the Foundling Hospital. Charles Burney's motive in making the proposal, according to his daughter, was 'to supply artists of a high standard to benefit the national economy, so that Britain did not have to seek a constant supply of genius and merit from foreign shores' and his inspiration came from the conservatoires established in Naples and Vienna.[4] However, there were those who disapproved, suggesting that it might give the children ideas above their station, and the plan was set aside, being outside the scope of the Act of Parliament which had enabled the Hospital's foundation. Nevertheless, the children's education must have been enlightened for its time, as they were trained in choral singing, and those with the best voices sang in the Chapel choir. Ensuring a high standard of music was important, as it became fashionable to go to the Chapel to hear the children sing, and large congregations meant bigger contributions to the collections, which were a significant source of income for the Hospital. In 1847 a boys' band was established and, as one of the main destinations for foundling boys was the army, this provided a regular supply of musicians for military bands for 100 years.

In addition to its collections of works of art, the Foundling Hospital has a poignant assortment of items relating to its social function. Despite its name, the children were usually not strictly foundlings, abandoned to their fate, but were brought to the Hospital by mothers who could not support them. The archives include many tokens which mothers left with their children so that they might identify them again one day if they were in a position to reclaim them. These include tags, buttons and pieces of jewellery, poems or scraps of paper with a name and perhaps a date of birth. All children were given a new name on admission; at first they were frequently named after benefactors and Governors, until suspicions about paternity were raised and this practice was discontinued. The Hospital applied various selection criteria over the years, most famously the ballot, when a mother picked a coloured ball out of a bag and, depending on the colour drawn, her child would or would not be admitted.

The Foundling Hospital moved out of London in 1926, by which time the building was no longer in healthy country air, as London had expanded rapidly. The original Hospital buildings were demolished, but the Court Room was taken down in sections, including the plasterwork ceiling, and reassembled in a room built to the same dimensions for that purpose in the new administrative building which is now the Foundling Museum. The Hospital ceased to be a foundling institution in 1953, and is now the childcare charity Coram, in premises adjoining the Foundling Museum. The original gates and walls of the front of the Hospital can still be seen; they now form the entrance to a children's park and playground which adults can enter only if accompanied by a child. The Foundling Museum opened in 2004 and received the Gerald Coke Handel Collection, allocated by the State in lieu of inheritance tax.

*The Gerald Coke Handel Collection*
Gerald Coke (pronounced 'Cook') was a businessman who described himself as 'a willing victim of the collecting bug'. In his case this led to the creation of two main collections at his home, Jenkyn Place in Hampshire: one devoted to eighteenth-century English porcelain decorated in the studio of James Giles, now in the Porcelain Museum in Worcester; the other concerned with the life and work of the composer George Frideric Handel. Coke himself was a banker, who combined a successful career in the City of London with contributions to music and gardening. He was a founder of the Glyndebourne Arts Trust, a Governor of the BBC and a Director of the Royal Opera House, Covent Garden, and of the Royal Academy of Music. His home also had extensive gardens which were opened to the public on occasion.

Coke started to collect Handel material in the 1930s, combining his love of music and fine books. He chose Handel after a brief period collecting Mozart (which proved too expensive) because, as he said, 'virtually the whole of Handel's output was first published in England, and was still obtainable at a reasonable price'. The collection was developed over the next half-century to include books, documents and objects important to the understanding of the life and work of Handel.

Coke himself always acknowledged the help of a network of friends in music libraries and publishing, and among booksellers, in building up his collection: in particular the book dealer Percy Muir, of Elkin Mathews Ltd, and William Smith, then head of the Music Department at the British

Museum. He also consulted and befriended the Handel scholars of the day, seeking their advice and opinion on items to be acquired and those in the collection, and allowing generous access and hospitality to those who wished to study items in his home.

His collection grew rapidly to include such significant items as one of the two original copies of Handel's will, autograph letters, rare first editions and contemporary portraits. In later years he also acquired the manuscripts of the Earl of Shaftesbury, and William Smith's Handel collection, including 39 boxes of his working papers relating to both his published and his unpublished books.

The Coke collection now comprises several thousand items, chiefly manuscripts, books and music by or relating to Handel and his contemporaries. However, with the freedom of the private collector, Coke also acquired paintings, prints, ceramics and other works of art, and a large collection of programmes, libretti and ephemera, which now form one of the major Handel research collections in the world. Coke also extended the scope of his collection to include such objects as medals, ceramics, admission tickets and tokens, press cuttings, sale catalogues, photographs and other material, even a nineteenth-century Swiss musical box, covering a continuous period from the composer's lifetime to the present day.

Gerald Coke was an avid and knowledgeable collector, in particular of eighteenth-century material, and every reprint was considered — quite rightly — a separate item, however slight the change. This makes his collection valuable for students of music printing and publishing history, where, for example, odd pages of re-engraved music can be identified within various printings of the same item; it also requires very detailed cataloguing, now in progress. Although not a music scholar, he clearly gained a great deal of knowledge about his chosen subject, but would call on the relevant expert when advice was needed on particular items: the collection now includes numerous boxes of his correspondence with the Handel scholars of the twentieth century. His central place in Handel research is confirmed by the large number of books and journal articles in the collection inscribed to Coke by their authors, as well as several gifts from music dealers.

The large collection of manuscripts includes another private collection, assembled by the Earl of Shaftesbury, which passed through his family until acquired by Gerald Coke in 1987. In this instance Coke was able to reunite with the rest of the collection a volume from the Shaftesbury collection — Handel's oratorio *Joshua* — which had gone missing in 1757, and which Coke had purchased before 1939. Contemporary manuscripts in the collection, copied as soon as a work was composed, can be studied alongside a range of contemporary published editions of the music. Other manuscripts offer alternative versions of particular arias, for example, composed for different performers in early performances; many manuscripts note the names of the first performers at the head of the songs. This is also true of the printed music and programmes, and these sources provide a wealth of information about the early performers and their repertoire.

Coke was both fortunate and astute in the choices he made, assembling a rich collection for comparatively little financial investment in today's terms. His collection includes, for example, unique copies of the first printed edition of the *Messiah* libretto, purchased for a few pounds. Coke's posthumously published account of his own collecting recalls various triumphs and disappointments.[5] As a collector rather than scholar, Coke delighted in buying items in their original wrappers or bindings, even where he already had another copy of the publication in a later binding; the satisfaction he gained from acquiring items 'as issued' makes the Coke collection particularly rich in this area, and many items are in pristine condition. Performers who visit the collection take particular pleasure in seeing items in the state in which they would have been at their first performance, with the individual instrumental and voice parts in their distinctive blue-grey paper wrappers.

The non-book items in the Coke collection are also carefully chosen and of particular interest to those studying Handel. The collection of hand-painted busts from the workshop of Ralph and Enoch Wood reflect the continued popularity of Handel after his lifetime. Handel was the first composer to have a collected edition of his works published, the first composer to have a statue erected to him in his lifetime, and the first European composer to have an extensive biography published, in this case within a year of his death. The numerous commemorative medallions in the collection also illustrate the continued interest throughout the nineteenth century, along with the extensive runs of programmes from London and the provinces, providing rich source materials for those researching individual performers, local history, and amateur music-making in England.

What Coke described as 'a minor triumph' was the purchase of one of Roubiliac's models for the monument to Handel in Westminster Abbey. Coke bought it unseen after it was found in an antique shop in Bristol, and the terracotta model, which differs from the monument in the Abbey, is now in the collection. Ironically Coke was particularly pleased to have beaten the Victoria & Albert Museum to this particular acquisition, as he wanted 'to prevent this terracotta from passing into the dead hands of a museum' — we hope he would not be disappointed in its present home.

Gerald Coke died in 1990, and his widow Patricia died in 1995. The Handel collection was left to the nation in lieu of death duties, with the request that it be allocated to the Thomas Coram Foundation (now Coram). Gerald Coke was particularly anxious that the collection be kept together, which influenced his choice of a final home for it. Coram, as a childcare charity, was already considering how to look after its valuable collection of eighteenth-century paintings and artefacts which had been given to the Foundling Hospital over the years and now required care beyond the scope of the charity. In 2004 a new charity was formed — the Foundling Museum — which now holds the Foundling Hospital's major collection of eighteenth-century art, an exhibition on the social history of the Hospital, and the Gerald Coke Handel Collection. An endowment from the Coke estate is administered by the Gerald Coke Handel Foundation, and funds the collection's continued development and running costs.

Coke's choice of the charity to benefit from his collection was carefully made, not least because Handel had been a Governor of the Foundling Hospital and had offered support as a major fund-raiser for many years through annual benefit concerts. One particularly happy reunion has been made by the bringing together of the Hospital's archives and Gerald Coke's collection. Handel's will survives in two copies — one at the National Archives and the other in Coke's collection — and it made a specific bequest to the Foundling Hospital of a copy of the score and parts of *Messiah*. This enabled the benefit concerts to continue, as there were no printed orchestral parts at that time. The music was duly copied and given to the Hospital, where it has been preserved and now sits alongside the will from the Coke collection in the Handel exhibition gallery.

As a private collector Coke did not acquire all of the scholarly articles in learned journals, especially those from overseas, so there are gaps in the collection which are now being filled. Similarly he did not have the bibliographical resources required to create a detailed catalogue, but there is still a remarkable collection of material to support current research. The Gerald Coke Handel Foundation continues to buy new publications, fill gaps in the collection by purchase or donation, acquire programmes and ephemeral material, and, where money allows, to purchase antiquarian material from dealers or at auction. The breadth of the collection provides many opportunities for exhibitions, and items are also loaned to other institutions. The study facilities serve a range of scholars — primarily performers, editors and musicologists, but also historians and students of art and architecture, local studies researchers, creative writers and historians of book and music printing and publishing. The range of material in terms of artefact and content reflects every aspect of Handel and his contemporaries and offers a multi-faceted approach to the composer and his music.

## References

1. Foundling Hospital General Committee minutes, Thursday 4 May 1749. The archives of the Foundling Hospital are now held at the London Metropolitan Archive.
2. Donald Burrows, 'Handel and the Foundling Hospital', *Music and Letters,* vol. 58, no. 3 (1977), pp. 269–84.
3. Foundling Hospital General Committee minutes, Wednesday 10 May 1749.
4. R. H. Nichols and F. A. Wray, *The history of the Foundling Hospital* (Oxford, 1935).
5. Gerald Coke, 'Collecting Handel', *Handel collections and their history*, ed. Terence Best (Oxford, 1993), pp. 1–9.

# Index

References to illustrations in *italic*